BIRTHING WITH TRAUMA AND FEAR
A GUIDE TO AN EMPOWERING BIRTH EXPERIENCE

Moran Liviani

Birthing with Trauma and Fear
© Moran Liviani 2025

All rights reserved. No part of this publication may be reproduced, stored in a retrieval system, or transmitted in any form or by any means, electronic, mechanical, photocopying, recording or otherwise, without the prior written permission of the author.

Disclaimer
The information contained in this book is based on personal experience and research and is intended for educational purposes only. It is not intended as medical advice or as a substitute for professional healthcare consultation. Readers are encouraged to seek appropriate medical advice from qualified healthcare professionals.

External References
Certain quotes and references are the property of their respective authors.

Trademark Acknowledgment
Hypnobirthing® is a registered trademark of Marie Mongan and the HypnoBirthing Institute.

Fair Use Statement
All quotes are used under fair use for educational and commentary purposes. Every effort has been made to credit the original sources.

ISBN: 978-1-923512-42-9

 A catalogue record for this work is available from the National Library of Australia

Cover Image: Além D'Olhar Fotografia
Cover Design: Moran Liviani and Clark & Mackay
Format and Typeset: Clark & Mackay
Published in Australia by Moran Liviani.
Editorial, design, and production support by Clark & Mackay

Proudly printed in Australia by Clark & Mackay

CONTENTS

Author's Note 5
Dedication 7
Endorsements for 9
Foreword 15
Introduction 19

CHAPTER 1
My Story – The Journey That Shaped Me 23

CHAPTER 2
Postpartum – Navigating the Fourth Trimester 37

CHAPTER 3
My Trauma – The Shadows I Carried 43

CHAPTER 4
Understanding Trauma – Unveiling the Impact 53

CHAPTER 5
Birth Trauma – When Birth Leaves Scars 61

CHAPTER 6
Fear – Holding It Without Letting It Hold You 73

CHAPTER 7
The Essential 10 – Foundations for an Empowering Birth 81

CHAPTER 8
Safety – Redefining Safety in Childbirth..................................... 91

CHAPTER 9
Intuition – Listening to Your Inner Guide............................... 105

CHAPTER 10
Oxytocin – The Love Hormone in Action 123

CHAPTER 11
Continuity of Care – The Foundation of Trust 145

CHAPTER 12
Doula Support – A Steady Hand Through the Journey........................ 181

CHAPTER 13
Mind–Body Connection – Aligning Mind and Body for Birth..............201

CHAPTER 14
Therapeutic Healing – Finding Strength Through Healing Practices 231

CHAPTER 15
Community – The Village That Lifts Us Up 251

CHAPTER 16
Birth Plan – Your Vision, Your Voice, Your Birth 261

CHAPTER 17
Resilience – Bending Without Breaking 287

CHAPTER 18
Birth After Trauma & Fear – My Rebirth in Birth............................. 301

Afterword 311
Resources for Further Support & Exploration........................313
References & Sources..319

AUTHOR'S NOTE

This is a memoir based on personal memories and reflections. Some names, locations, and identifying details have been changed or omitted to protect privacy. Some events are interpreted through the lens of lived experience and may differ from others' recollections.

DEDICATION

To my husband, Carlo —
Thank you for standing beside me through every
storm and triumph, for believing in me fiercely,
even when I couldn't see it for myself.
To my daughters, Bella, Portia, and Talia—
My shining lights. My greatest teachers.
To Bella, my firstborn—who stirred something deep within me,
lit the fire that led me here, and gave me the reason to keep
going.
To Portia, whose birth brought healing and reminded me of my
strength.
To Talia, whose birth unveiled my calling—
and the path I now walk to support others.
To my mother—
Your love is the thread I carry in everything I
do. I feel your pride with me, always.
To my sister—
My lifelong rock and constant presence. Thank
you for always being there—for showing up,
holding steady, and loving me through it all.
With all my love—this book is for you.

ENDORSEMENTS FOR

BIRTHING WITH TRAUMA AND FEAR

The following endorsements are shared with deep gratitude for the voices who see and support the purpose of this book.

Review of
Birthing with Trauma and Fear
Jane Hardwicke Collings
Agent of the Goddess; Founder, School of Shamanic Womancraft

This book Birthing with Trauma and Fear comes at the perfect time, when people everywhere, women and birth practitioners alike, are awakening to the mind-body connection and how we hold trauma in our bodies, and how this affects how we give birth.

Trauma-aware care, trauma-informed care for pregnancy, birth, and postpartum is so necessary, especially at a time when there is so much intervention at birth.

This precious book, a treatise to the potential and possibility for healing in childbirth, through childbirth, and after childbirth, is such a gift to everybody.

Moran shares deeply and intimately her own story and many other women's stories to highlight the connection between our past — our generational and inherited trauma, our own childhood and everything that has gone before the time we become pregnant and give birth. Everything that happened before influences what happens next, including and especially giving birth.

Moran explains how the body works and how re-triggering can happen in childbirth and what to do about it. She has developed what she calls the "Essential 10", the basic foundations required for a woman to create the best environment for her to feel safe and therefore give birth to her potential, whatever that is.

It is also a workbook, very helpful, with questions to help understand past experiences and prepare for the next. There are real stories and examples that women reading can relate to.

As Moran says, it's not about going with the flow and hoping for the best, but rather about making conscious, deliberate choices to prepare holistically for birth.

Thank you, Moran, for creating this wonderful guide and resource for the world — at a time when there is more traumatic birth than ever before.

Review of
Birthing with Trauma and Fear
Billie Harrigan
Traditional Birth Companion

My heart sank when I saw the title of Moran Liviani's book: Birthing with Trauma and Fear. How did we get to this point? Why are such books needed? The shocking reality is that this book is needed. And desperately so.

Having just survived years of targeted attacks on our very humanity through the global nonsensical response to a declared pandemic, we are a society that is generally not ok. Many women's experiences of birth prior to this time were already shockingly awful. Rife with talk of risk, dead babies, coercion, loss of autonomy and lack on consent, there was already a true global pandemic of birth related trauma stemming largely from obstetrical violence, institutional policy, and lack of individualised care. Today, we are seeing the after-effects of more trauma where more survivors are trying to put back the pieces.

Indeed, trauma can rear its ugly head through the childbearing experience, but it doesn't have to. We have tools and strategies that can lessen its impact, build resilience, and promote healing.

This is where Moran's Birthing with Trauma and Fear comes as a light in a dark space. Written with profound compassion, Moran offers her personal experiences as a birthing mother, a doula, and a survivor along with encouraging stories from other women who worked alongside their own fear and trauma to write a new story for themselves and their children. Using Moran's practical 10 Essentials, readers are invited to create a working template where "trauma and fear don't cancel out beauty or strength. They sit alongside it."

I wish this book didn't have to be written. But it does, and Moran has provided us with an exceptional guide for reclaiming birth and more importantly, for reclaiming our humanity.

Review of
Birthing with Trauma and Fear
Sammy Griffin
Birth & Postpartum Doula

What an honour it is to be asked to contribute to Moran's book in any way. The way Moran demonstrates both micro and macro acts of birth activism — from sharing real stories online to creating this powerful body of work — is deeply inspiring. Her work is reshaping the way women perceive their role in birth. No longer passive participants, women are stepping forward as active agents, reclaiming their power. And at the forefront of this movement is Moran Liviani.

The statistics Moran presents around birth trauma are not just numbers. They represent real women. They represent me. I saw my own story reflected back — unhealed trauma that shaped my first birth and left me broken. But my second birth — a VBAC — was the most empowering day of my life. I unknowingly applied what Moran calls "The Essential 10," but only because I'd been a doula for years.

We can't expect women to train as doulas just to access this kind of support. That's why this book matters. Moran has birthed a resource that arms women with real tools — ones they can carry into their first births or hold close for the next. This time, they're not walking blindly. They are supported, informed, and empowered.

Thanks to Moran's work, that journey just became a little clearer — and a lot more powerful.

Review of
Birthing with Trauma and Fear
Jo Henderson
Clinical Psychologist

As a clinical psychologist, I've seen firsthand how trauma can profoundly reshape a person's emotional world, sense of safety, and connection to their body.

This book offers a compassionate, clear-eyed exploration on how unresolved trauma can influence nervous system responses and the mind-body connection—particularly in the context of pregnancy, birth, and postpartum recovery.

Moran weaves together psychological insight, trauma-informed care principles, and practical, evidence-based strategies with warmth and wisdom. Through real-life stories and grounded guidance, she empowers readers to navigate the birthing journey with agency, confidence, and support.

This is an essential resource for anyone preparing for birth after trauma. It offers not only information, but true emotional scaffolding—helping readers reclaim a sense of safety, power, and healing in one of life's most vulnerable moments.

Review of
Birthing with Trauma and Fear
Philippa Scott
Trauma Therapist and Founder of The Family Architect Studio and The Mother Awakening™

Birthing with Trauma and Fear cracked something open in me. It is raw, necessary, and beautifully unrelenting in its truth. Moran Liviani gives voice to what so many women have never dared to say out loud—the grief of a birth that betrayed them, the silent rage beneath compliance, the aching disconnection from their own power.

Her story is not just her own—it is ours.

This book is a hand in the dark. A steady voice saying: you are not too much, and you are not alone. It is a lifeline for mothers who have been told to be grateful, even as they quietly break.

Moran's words embody the spirit of The Mother Awakening™—inviting women to come home to themselves, to rewrite the story, and to reclaim the sacred act of birth as one of power and truth.

This is more than a memoir. It's a mirror, a reckoning, and a revolution. Read it. Let it stir you. Let it change you.

FOREWORD

by Stuart J. Fischbein, MD

I have been honored by author, doula and mother, Moran Liviani, to write the foreword to this book. First, let me start with honesty and just state the obvious out loud. Conceiving, growing, and birthing a baby is simply the normal workings of the miraculous human female body. We are designed for this to play out to be nearly perfect and happen without thinking. In fact, because the human mind is so complex, thinking actually impedes nature's design. So then, one should ask, how did we reach such a point in our history where fear and trauma are so pervasive in birth? Why should we even need this book to exist? But sadly, we are at a point where these issues are front and centre. "The system has taken something sacred and made it clinical." Much research and empirical observation tells us that far too many women are traumatized emotionally and physically. The modern culture propagates fear in childbirth. Obstetricians are trained to fear birth, to see pregnancy as a high-risk condition and inevitably project it onward to the women and families who trust them for their care.

> *"What is fear but voices airy? Whispering harm where harm is not...."*
> *William Wordsworth*

The language surrounding birth has become coercive and destructive. Everything is labeled high risk. Interventions such as ultrasound, fetal monitoring, induction, and cesarean section are rising. After all this a woman is still told her labour stalled, she failed to progress, her body is broken, it is her fault. Whatever intent has led to the medicalization of birth does not matter. What matters is, are we a healthier society? Have our outcomes improved? Sadly, the truthful answer is no and that is why this book,

Birthing with Trauma and Fear could not be more necessary.

Until the past few years the term "Trauma-Informed Care" did not exist in the world of pregnancy to my knowledge. Yet now we hear it all the time. Through her own personal journey and the insightful use of storytelling Moran weaves a path forward for women and families that have lived through abuse and for others to avoid it. She describes ten essential tools to help guide the pregnant woman towards a more joyous and secure pregnancy. Acknowledging the importance of feeling safe and the value of a supportive partner and community. Offering helpful ways to express your feelings and not bury them. Learning to trust your instincts and awakening to the reality that how you give birth matters in every respect.

I am often quoted as saying, "All that matters in the medical birth model is a live baby in the bassinet. And how that baby gets there and what happens to that baby, the mother and the mother's future babies does not matter!" The birthing process is not one size fits all. Hospital policies are not laws. And good and nurturing care is not an algorithm and cannot be regulated. As a mother, Moran experienced a traumatic first birth. As a doula herself, Moran knows the importance of individualizing care on improving outcomes. This book highlights ways to navigate your pregnancy and labour and in the final chapter we get to understand her own journey to find rebirth in birth. There are a lot of wonderful books on birthing to be found out there. I would add *Birthing with Trauma and Fear* to the list. Reading Moran's book made even me feel validated and reassured.

BIRTHING WITH TRAUMA AND FEAR

In shadows of the past, I used to stay, Where hurt and pain would cloud my way. But in the moment my child came through, I found my strength, my life felt new.
With courage born from fear and pain, I faced the past, broke every chain.
Through labour's trials, I found my voice,
And in the storm, I made my choice.
Each surge, each cry, brought something more, A piece of me I'd lost before.
With every push, a healing light,
I claimed my power, my sacred right.
The past still whispered, tried to bind, But deep within, my strength did shine.
In this birth, I found my worth, A love that healed, a new rebirth.
Through tears and effort, I stood tall, A phoenix rising from it all.
And in my arms, this life so new, A promise kept, a dream come true.
So let this story softly say,
In pain, we rise, we find our way.
Through birth's dance, we bloom, we grow,
And in love's light, our spirits glow.

INTRODUCTION

Why This Book Matters

Women often go into birth believing that fear is normal, that trauma is just something to endure. But birth should not be about survival, it should be about transformation. This book is for the woman who feels afraid, who carries wounds she may or may not even recognise yet, and who longs for an empowering birth experience. Through my own story and the stories of others, I will help you uncover the impact of trauma and fear on birth and, more importantly, how to reclaim your power.

Birth is more than a medical event. It is an emotional, spiritual, and psychological transformation. Yet for too many women, birth is clouded by fear, unresolved trauma from their past and uncertainty. We also live in a society that teaches us to be afraid of birth, to hand over our power to others, and to believe that previous traumatic life events have no influence on our future birth experiences or that birth trauma is just something we have to accept. But it doesn't have to be this way.

We are told to trust the experts, to listen to the system, and to silence our intuition. But what if birth wasn't meant to be something that happens to us? What if we could step into birth fully aware, fully prepared, and fully in control of how we experience it?

This book is not about rejecting medical support — rather, it's about ensuring that support is grounded in respect, consent, and individual needs. It is about equipping you with knowledge, awareness, and confidence so that you remain at the centre of your own birth experience. Because birth should never be something you simply endure. It should be something you emerge from feeling strong, empowered, and whole.

What You Will Find in This Book

> An honest and raw look at how trauma and fear affect birth and postpartum

> Tools to help you navigate fear and reclaim your voice in birth

> Stories of healing, resilience, and empowerment from real women

> Guidance to help you rewrite the narrative of birth as a space of power, not fear

This book is for the mother who carries unseen scars, for the woman who has been told she is "too anxious" or "too sensitive" about birth. It is for the survivor who feels the weight of her past but doesn't yet see how it connects to the present. It is for the first-time mother who fears the unknown and for the mother who still feels unhealed from births that left her feeling powerless.

My journey into birth was shaped by my own trauma, and for years, I didn't understand the impact that my past had on my birth experience. I didn't see how my history was shaping my body's response to labour, how unresolved fears were surfacing when I was most vulnerable. Like so many women, I assumed birth was something I had to endure rather than something I could shape.

But I now know that birth is not just a moment in time, it is a reflection of our deepest beliefs about ourselves, our bodies, and our power. When I finally understood this, I was able to reclaim my birth experience. I found healing where I once felt fear. I found strength where I once felt helpless.

Birth has the power to break us, but it also has the power to heal. My hope is that through this book, you will discover that your story is not over. It is just beginning.

CHAPTER 1

My Story -
The Journey That Shaped Me

"Study the past, if you would divine the future."
— Confucius

I didn't scream. I didn't roar.

I froze—trapped somewhere between the woman I was and the mother I wasn't ready to be.

And in that stillness, something inside me gave way.

That was the beginning of a story I didn't know I was about to write.

If you're reading this, you may be preparing for birth with questions, fear, uncertainty, or the quiet weight of past experiences. Maybe you've experienced trauma, or maybe you simply want to feel informed and supported as you approach one of the most transformative experiences of your life. I wrote this book for you—to guide you, and to remind you that you are capable and never alone.

I know, because I've stood where you stand now—searching for answers, wanting reassurance, and not knowing where to begin.

My moment came out of nowhere, long before I ever imagined I'd become a doula or write this book. I remember standing in the bathroom of my in-laws' house, where my husband and I were living at the time, holding that positive pregnancy test in my shaking hand, thinking: *What the hell am I going to do?* My heart raced. My mind spiralled. I was 23, barely prepared for my own life, let alone someone else's. I had my husband, but I was living in a country that didn't quite feel like home yet, with no family nearby for support. I didn't feel completely alone, but I still felt unsure and overwhelmed by what lay ahead.

I had no idea that moment—scared, pregnant, and unsure of everything—would set me on a path that changed my life in such a profound way and how I show up for women today.

And I could never have imagined how my experience would eventually lead me here, to writing this book.

When I first thought about writing this book, I thought I'd write a very different book. I wanted to stay less vulnerable, hold back my personal story, and just share what had worked for so many of the women I've had the privilege of supporting over the past 13 years in the birthing space. But as I sat with the idea, I knew that wasn't enough. If I wanted to be truly authentic, I had to let my story unfold alongside theirs—so you can see that this is viscerally real, and that I am living proof of what's possible.

This book is a culmination of my experiences as a girl, a woman, a mother, and a birth doula. It's the book I know I needed when I was preparing for birth and motherhood. It's filled with my thoughts, from someone who has been in the thick of it and come out the other side—so other women don't feel alone.

I knew there were already tons of books out there on pregnancy, birth, and postpartum—but none of them gave me what I was really looking for: something practical and personal. Something real. That's what I've tried to create here. Through sharing my own journey and everything I've learned from years of supporting women, I started to see certain patterns—things that consistently helped women shift from fear or trauma into strength. Those insights eventually became what I call The Essential 10. You'll get to know them soon.

These women, like me, were the ones who did the work. They prepared for their birth in a conscious, mindful way to create the positive experience they wanted for themselves and their babies. I've pulled all of that together so you can use it as a guide on your own path. Take what speaks to you, use what feels right, and leave the rest.

Every journey has a beginning. For me, it all started with the moment that changed everything. A sliding doors moment: the birth of my firstborn, Isabella—or as we instantly fell in love with calling her, Bella. Her birth is what brought me to where I am today, and for that, I will always be eternally grateful.

Her birth wasn't the positive experience I had hoped for, especially as a first-time mother. But with time, reflection, and a lot of healing, I've come to see it differently. I needed that experience to begin my own rebirth. From that darkness, I created light. No one did it for me—I did it for myself. And I'm proud to say that. Proud of the strength it took, and the wisdom I've gained to understand just how far I've come.

When they say that birth changes you, I deeply thought it was something people exaggerated about. Something passed down from one generation to the next, maybe just a scare tactic to stop teenagers from getting too excited about sex. Or a dramatic badge of honour women wore to terrify each other at baby showers. But going through my first pregnancy, I was definitely naive—maybe I can blame it on my age, since I was so young when I was pregnant with Bella. Maybe there was a lot more to it. I didn't know what I didn't know and nor was I seeking that information.

Bella was a surprise baby. When I found out I was pregnant, I think I went into a bit of shock. I hadn't expected to have a baby so early in life, but I was genuinely excited. We weren't in the most stable place financially, but our heads were on straight—and the news was a wake-up call to get our shit together. Nothing does that quite like finding out you're having a baby.

At the time, I was living with my Italian in-laws. I was close to them, but I kept a bit of distance. Think *Everybody Loves Raymond*—but with more unsolicited advice and no laugh track. I'd learned from my childhood that people can hurt you without warning, so I'd built a habit of shielding myself, just in case.

I also wasn't close to my own mother. We hadn't spoken in years, and I had no intention of telling her she was going to be a grandmother. I knew it would have brought her joy, but I wasn't ready to let her in. Back then, I didn't realise how much that absence would later shape my experience of birth and motherhood. At the time, I just kept going the only way I knew how: head down, get through it, pretend I had it all under control.

With my mother out of the picture, I thought I'd at least have my father to lean on. I was so wrong. Throughout my pregnancy with Bella, my relationship with my dad was toxic—strained, distant, and centred around his own selfish perspective. We barely spoke, and when we did, it was tense. He didn't really see me or what I was going through.

And then came the plot twist—straight out of a trashy *Jerry Springer* episode. My dad's girlfriend was also pregnant. Our due dates? Two days apart. So, my daughter and her uncle would be the same age. I wish I was joking. It made my skin crawl. What should have been a sacred, personal experience suddenly felt hijacked, and I was left feeling resentful and angry.

The only relief was that my dad lived in another country. Long-distance dysfunction has its perks. Still, he found ways to inject his opinions—criticising my life, my choices—and that added a heavy weight I didn't need.

But despite all that chaos around me, my actual pregnancy was physically good. I felt like my normal self in every way, other than some first-trimester tiredness and a bout of anaemia that made me faint once. I knew how to manage that with what I ate and by taking it easier on some days. I worked throughout my whole pregnancy, which I think was a godsend. It kept my mind busy and my body moving—probably exactly what I needed to burn off the adrenaline from the limited, but stressful, contact I had with my dad.

I was only a few weeks pregnant, still trying to wrap my head around it all.

Those early days felt like a blur of disbelief. But once the fog lifted, I followed my instinct, leaning into what felt natural—or at least, what I *thought* was natural at the time. What I didn't expect was how much work it actually takes to make "natural" happen.

Looking back, I realise that mindset shaped everything that came next. I took a "go with the flow" approach—not exactly the smartest move when you're preparing for one of the biggest moments of your life. But honestly, I just didn't know any better yet. That same carefree mindset carried right into my first big decision: choosing who would actually "deliver" my baby—a word I've never liked. It always made it sound like I was waiting for someone to drop something off, not give birth.

Early in my pregnancy I went to my local general practitioner who then just asked one question and that is, 'do you have private health' I was like 'I indeed do' and so I got a list of obstetricians in my area and my own selection process was to pick the first Jewish name you can identify off the list. Yep. Not exactly the most thoughtful strategy for choosing the person who'd be front and centre during one of the most intense experiences of my life. But naive me did just that. I was raised with the mentality that you always pick a Jewish Doctor, Jewish Lawyer and Jewish Accountant and so I did. Just shows you how inbuilt belief systems are just so ingrained and automatic that you don't even question them when it's really important.

At the time, I thought I was making a simple, practical choice. I didn't realise I was already starting to hand over control.

Looking back now, I can see what was really happening underneath my choice.

This was my first initiation into the mainstream tribe of women unknowingly giving their power away. Because really—how could we possibly know how to birth a baby without hiring an expert on our own bodies? Yes, that's sarcasm—but in all seriousness, that's exactly what I did. I considered myself pretty clued in when it came to most areas of my life—or so I thought. But when it came to pregnancy and birth, I didn't feel that inner knowing, and I had no idea how to even access it.

I was young. I wasn't seeking more information. And in hindsight, I can see that some of the things that happened during my birth were just standard practice—part of how the modern maternity system works. But for me, those moments chipped away at my power, and no one on my support team stepped in to say otherwise.

And so off to the Jewish obstetrician I went and at every appointment I sat in his waiting room for longer than I actually saw the guy, but I thought that's just what you do and look how important this guy is by how many people are sitting in the room waiting for him. Little did I know at the time that we were all robots of our subconscious upbringing, as all of us in one way or another are sitting there because we don't know any better and we've been fed the same mantra of doctor knows best.

When I reflect back and think what did this doctor do with me that was so worth waiting for, the answer would be – not much. Literally I think any general practitioner could've done the same. He did weigh me at each appointment, just to make sure I wasn't gaining too much weight, which only made me more self-conscious about what I was eating. If the number stayed within his range, he'd slap a sticker on a palm card like I was some kind of obedient student. And of course, my inner 'good girl' wanted that damn sticker—even though deep down, I knew how messed up it all was. But I accepted it for what it is as I'm sure so did all the women that were waiting to see him.

As I neared towards the end of my pregnancy, I had an appointment with him, and he said to me that he wouldn't like my pregnancy going any further than my due date. I thought that was a bit odd, but I didn't question it. I did ask though what would happen if it did, and he just said he's already booked me in for an induction on my due date so not to worry.

I left his office that day feeling my first pangs of anxiety. I felt scared and deeply worried.

My husband, who was with me for every appointment and was so supportive throughout the pregnancy, just had no clue about what to do and how to navigate what the doctor said, and he didn't really question it. He sort of took the attitude of we'll cross that bridge when we get there. I on the other hand had deep rooted and an instinctual response of think ahead, this can't be so. I didn't clearly understand what an induction entailed but I knew the medical route was never my preferred choice with anything, especially getting my baby out. I felt lost.

I wasn't particularly spiritual back then, but whenever I felt overwhelmed or out of my depth, I'd talk to my grandfather—in my head, like a quiet prayer to someone I hoped was still listening. He had this incredibly calm energy—like just being near him made you breathe easier. The kind of person who didn't need to say much to make you feel safe. My last memory of him is of him hugging my sister and me, crying as he apologised for what we'd gone through as kids. (Don't worry—we'll get to that backstory later.)

A week later, he passed away. I've always felt like his heart just couldn't carry the weight anymore.

Even after he was gone, he never really left. When I was younger, he used to visit me in dreams—always when I needed him most. I'd wake up and just know he'd been there. He doesn't show up as often now, but I can still see his face so clearly in my mind, like he's just waiting in the wings, keeping an eye on me. Over the years, I've noticed little signs and signals—moments that made me feel like he was near. So during the later stages of my pregnancy, when I felt scared and alone, I found myself reaching out to him again—longing to feel close to family, even if it was just in spirit.

I went into labour two days before my due date, and I can't help but feel my grandfather had something mystical to do with it. There was no warning, no dramatic moment—just a quiet shift, like the air around me had changed. My body knew before my mind did. Something was beginning, and there was no stopping it.

As I felt the buildup in early labour, like a pressure cooker building to a boil, dread took over every part of me. I wanted to hit rewind, find a way out, but there wasn't one. Why didn't I think this through more? What was I thinking? How could I have been so naive to believe I could handle this? There was no pause button. No escape. I was in it, and all I could do was survive. The pressure gave way to panic. Suddenly, it felt like I was strapped into a ride I couldn't get off. In that moment, it felt like my mind started to spin out of control—each thought crashing into the next, building tension second by second, breath by breath, like something big was coming but I couldn't quite see it yet.

Then, without warning, the drop hit. Panic surged through me like the coaster flying downhill, no brakes, no control—just a blur of noise and speed. Everything in my head went from steady to chaos in a heartbeat. Thoughts collided, spiralled, crashed. There was no guiding it anymore—just holding on and hoping it would end.

You'd think I was recalling something horrifying, something earth-shattering. But this was just what was happening inside my mind as the first wave of a contraction hit my body. It wasn't even that intense but, in my mind, I felt the ripple effect tear at the very core of my being.

I wanted to run. Not physically—but from everything happening inside my body. Part of me just wanted to wrap myself up in a blanket and comfort the younger version of me who felt terrified and overwhelmed. I wanted to tell her, "It's okay. You don't have to do this. You don't have to carry all this if it's too much."

What scared me most wasn't just the pain or how my body was opening—it was the unknown waiting on the other side of it.

I had to care for a baby that I intensely didn't feel ready for. I was still just a kid. I never really got to be young. No one showed me the way—there was no mum to lean on, no carefree teen years, no space to just be. I felt like I was 12 going on 23 and about to have a baby. What was I doing? How was this even real? And deep down, I kept wondering—how do I make this stop?

But of course, I couldn't. The only option was to face it, and for that, I needed help. The people I chose to guide me in this birth were my husband and my sister.

My husband, though supportive, was as uneducated as I was about birth and everything that comes with it. He came from a family of five siblings and a mother who never questioned medical advice. My Italian mother-in-law was the type who had a pill for everything—ten prescriptions, each with ten side effects, and a filing cabinet full of medical records to match. Her body had been through more surgeries than I could count, most of them probably unnecessary. So no, she wasn't exactly my go-to for natural or alternative birth advice. I think my husband at the time felt intimidated to question medical authority, and you go in with the mentality of 'isn't that why we hired a medical professional for?'

My sister, by contrast, had always been my right hand. Growing up, we both carried the weight of our shared upbringing and the loss of a mother figure. Being a few years older than me, she stepped into that role for me as best she could. When she found out I was pregnant, her reaction was intense. She mourned what she saw as the loss of my youth and was devastated by what she felt was the biggest mistake of my life.

I now understand her own trauma shaped that emotional response, but back then, it only deepened my anxiety. I believe it's part of why she ultimately chose not to have children herself. She tried her very best to support me through labour, but she was still carrying her own pain and uncertainty. Her fears unintentionally transmitted to me, and I absorbed them like a mirror, reflecting back what she couldn't contain. Strangely, I welcomed it. I had no other choice. It was all I knew at the time: take it on, push through, and survive.

My husband and sister did their best, but they couldn't give me the kind of support I truly needed. Even with the best intentions, they struggled to offer the emotional and physical comfort I was hoping for—the kind of protective care I desperately needed. It wasn't that they weren't capable, but they didn't fully understand what I was looking for. Their own beliefs, experiences, and personal history came with them into my birth space. And like I always tell my doula clients: your support team needs to leave their shit at the door.

They weren't fully equipped to guide me—and honestly, neither was I.

As part of my birth preparation, I did what you typically do if you're planning a highly managed experience—I thought, "The doctors have got this," and figured I had a pretty good pain tolerance, so I left it all to fate and chance… and did nothing. I did absolutely nothing.

The only book I read during my pregnancy was *What to Expect When You're Expecting*, which seemed more focused on telling me my baby was the size of an avocado and less focused on how to stay sane when your emotions are a hormonal cocktail of fear, fatigue, and 'how do I get this baby out of me without losing my mind?'

I had no friends having babies, no mother to turn to, and no real guidance. I was flying blind into one of the biggest experiences of my life.

And that's where the deeper truth begins.

Because while I was blaming my lack of preparation or support system, what I hadn't yet understood was that something much older—and much deeper—was about to surface.

My childhood trauma. The patterns, the pain, the coping mechanisms I built so young—they were all there, tucked away, waiting.

These days, the word trauma gets thrown around so much it's almost lost its meaning. When I had Bella, more than 21 years ago, I didn't even know trauma could show up in birth. I just thought, shit happens, and you deal with it. I never imagined how much it would grip me quietly but tightly, or how it would stop me in my tracks without warning. I especially didn't realise how deeply it would affect my birth, my recovery, and my ability to function as a mother in a whole, healthy way.

The realisation of my childhood trauma remained hidden—until the first uterine contraction surged through my body. The physical pain of the contraction was overshadowed by a flood of adrenaline that pulsed relentlessly through every fibre of my being, compelling me to want to run away, literally to escape my own body. Confronted with my inability to escape, fear gripped me, rendering me paralysed by my own emotions, with no rescuer in sight. I was literally experiencing fight or flight in every sense, but my body couldn't fight as hard as it tried, and my body couldn't flee so it froze in fear of what was to come.

Still at home during the early stages of labour, I turned to my husband desperately seeking relief. The thought of a Caesarean section was a tempting escape from the pain, the pain in my mind. My husband called the hospital where I was supposed to give birth and requested a Caesarean on my behalf. Sadly, their response was not what I had hoped for: "We do not offer Caesareans as a method of pain management." I can recall that moment as clearly as if it were yesterday—I felt hopeless and helpless. Despite this disappointment, we eventually made our way to the hospital without a clear reason why. I was counting on someone to rescue me but instead found myself confined in a hospital where the staff struggled to understand my needs and the maternity system seemed intent on medicating me into submission.

I remember this pivotal point in my labour. We were given a birthing suite room; my husband and sister were tired from supporting me at home and they welcomed the midwife's suggestion to maybe start with a Panadol to try and get some sleep. I remember taking the Panadol, lying down and then I felt this huge surge go through my body and then my waters broke. It felt like something was breaking me, I looked up at my husband who looked tired and helpless. I looked at my sister and all I saw was fear as she didn't recognise me in this state. I knew she felt like she wanted to save me but couldn't. And so, I gave up. I felt like I was hitting a wall I couldn't break through—completely petrified, in every sense of the word.

The temptation of an epidural became too strong, silencing my fear more easily than facing the path of pain. And with every intervention that followed—Syntocinon infusions to speed up contractions, continuous monitoring, and IV fluids—it felt like I was being prodded and poked from all sides. This was far from the vision I had nurtured of bringing new life into the world.

After 48 hours that felt like a spectator sport, my doctor—who at the time I viewed as my 'rescuer'—intervened, elevating my legs into stirrups without a whisper of consent. "Let's get this baby out," he asserted, and I felt relief that someone—anyone—was here to save me, even though that's not what he was really doing. Then, without warning or permission, he grabbed the forceps and used surgical scissors to perform an episiotomy before pulling my baby from me with a detachment that matched the cold, unrelenting pressure of the moment.

The end result of that was a numbness I don't think I could ever fully describe. Was this birth??? It didn't feel like it. There was no surge of joy, no cinematic moment of triumph—just silence inside me. I didn't feel power or love. I didn't feel anything. If I'm honest, the only thing I did feel was relief—that it was over. That the struggle had ended. But even that relief came with guilt, like I'd missed something important, something I was supposed to feel but didn't. I'd crossed a threshold that was meant to be sacred, and instead I felt hollow, like I'd been a spectator to my own experience.

So, this was it, I just experienced birthing my first baby. How do women have multiple children? I didn't get it. I felt like my body was bruised and battered but my mind just wanted to cry.

I wanted to be held, to be seen for the experience I had just gone through—but there was no time for that. I was a mother now, apparently, and the job had already started. So, I put on the brave face and got on with it.

Within minutes of giving birth—still covered in blood, still in complete shock—my husband, who came from a big Italian family, decided it was the perfect time to call in the in-laws to my birth suite. Yes, *minutes*. In walked his mother, a woman who, by nature and life experience, was one of the toughest women I've ever met. Crying in front of her? Not an option. This is the same woman who didn't shed a tear through multiple natural births *and* two C-sections where she wasn't fully numbed and *felt* them cutting her. So no, I wasn't about to show any weakness—not with her watching.

My husband was young and still deeply influenced by his family back then. But let's just say… he's learned his lesson. By the time we had our next babies, I made it crystal clear: no visitors, no early drop-ins, no in-laws in the birth suite. The new rule? Family could meet the baby after I had showered, slept, and reclaimed some sense of self. So, they saw us a few weeks later. And guess what? Everyone survived. Including him.

But in that raw, shell-shocked moment after Bella's birth, I wasn't thinking about future babies. I confided to my husband that this would mark the definite end of biological motherhood for me—a declaration made so that I would never, ever do this again. How could I? How could anyone? Why would I put myself through such an experience ever again?

Amidst all these questions, I looked inside myself, thinking about why I felt weak compared to other women who faced similar challenges. Was I just not as tough? I wrestled with that doubt, like a heavy blanket stitched together from all the hard moments of my life. Memories of my childhood, which I hadn't fully dealt with, mixed with the overwhelming helplessness of my birth experience. Those feelings didn't just disappear; they stuck with me, refusing to let go.

I was moving forward, whether I felt ready or not. And as the reality of motherhood settled in, one question echoed louder than the rest: *What comes next for me?*

CHAPTER 2

Postpartum - Navigating the Fourth Trimester

"The moment a child is born, the mother is also born. She never existed before. The woman existed, but the mother, never. A mother is something absolutely new." — Osho

Motherhood begins with a moment—breathtaking, disorienting, and unlike anything you imagined. I remember staring at my baby thinking, "How is this real? How am I responsible for this tiny human?"

As the weeks unfold, the postpartum period reveals itself as something more layered and complex. It's a time of profound transition, where the physical, emotional, and mental demands of caring for a newborn intertwine with your own healing and self-discovery. It's beautiful and raw. And no two journeys are the same. For some women, there's a safety net: family who stay and nurture; partners who understand what true support looks like and step up in ways that truly matter. Some have friends or neighbours organising meal trains, delivering food and kindness when it's needed most. For others, it looks very different: isolation, exhaustion, or feeling invisible in the middle of the most vulnerable time of their life. My own experience? Let's just say it looked nothing like the first one.

I was reflecting on my first postpartum experience recently, not just for this chapter, but also during an impromptu episode of Doulas Uncensored with my cohost, Sammy. We were talking about our own early days of motherhood, and she described her postpartum period as a "baptism by fire"—which, fittingly, became the title of that episode. I completely understood why she chose those words; her experience was its own kind of chaos and intensity, and she's walked through her own version of hell her first time around.

That said, when I heard the phrase, I remember thinking, *baptism by fire?* That would've been generous for what I went through. Mine felt more like a full-blown wildfire—unpredictable, out of control, and burning through everything in its path. It was a blur, a haze, a total unravelling. I look back on that time with so much compassion for the woman I was—exhausted, isolated, and just trying to survive.

But there's also pride there. Because somehow, even without any real support, I got through it. Me and this tiny baby girl, doing the best we could with what we had.

Looking back, I can see now that those hard-won lessons became the quiet preparation for my future work.

Years later and two years into my doula practice, I started seeing other mothers face the same emotional undercurrents I had once buried. I remember early in my doula career, about 11 years ago, working with a client who struggled with severe anxiety throughout her pregnancy. She couldn't shake the intrusive thoughts and found it hard to fully embrace the experience. At the time, I was guiding her through HypnoBirthing®, a practice I was relatively new to myself. Each couple I worked with responded differently to the HypnoBirthing® scripts that were part of the program, but there was always a shared desire to release control and absorb the calming, affirming words designed to connect the body and mind.

However, with this particular mother, I sensed something deeper was at play. She hinted at a troubled childhood but never shared the details. During one of our sessions focused on fear release, she settled in, intending to let go of her worries. But just five or ten minutes into the hypnosis, she sat up abruptly and said, "I can't do this." When I asked why, she explained that her mind wouldn't allow her to let go, it was too overwhelming. We ended up discussing her fears about the birth, trying to find ways to ease their grip on her, but it was clear that much remained unsaid. I felt uneasy for her, sensing from my limited experience at the time that her birth might be more difficult, driven by subconscious fears acting as a defence mechanism. Unfortunately, that's exactly what happened. She went into labour with intense, fast contractions that felt unbearable. She behaved as though she were in transition, though she wasn't, and all her fears seemed to manifest physically. In an attempt to regain control, she chose to get an epidural. After a long labour, she eventually gave birth, but the challenges didn't end there. As I had feared, her postpartum period was even more difficult. She called me many times just to talk, struggling with breastfeeding, postnatal depression, and anxiety. Her husband was left caring for both her and the baby, as she couldn't cope.

Over the years, I've seen this pattern show up time and time again—mothers who bury their feelings during pregnancy, hoping they'll just disappear, or believing they don't have the time or space to deal with them. I get it. It's easier to focus on the nursery or the hospital bag than to sit with the messy, unspoken stuff that lives deeper down. But I've learned that emotional work during pregnancy matters. It's like there's a threshold you have to cross to come through the birth and postpartum experience truly whole. And when that work is left undone, it doesn't just vanish. It waits. And often, it shows up in labour… or later, when you're already knee-deep in sleepless nights and trying to hold it all together.

I know this because I had to cross that threshold myself. But at the time, I didn't even know it existed.

The year that followed the birth of my first daughter unfolded like a slow unravelling. It started with panic attacks that came out of nowhere, often in the stillness of the night. A sudden warmth would surge through me, like my blood was boiling over, followed by this unbearable need to escape my own skin. My hands would tremble. I'd get lightheaded and disconnected, like I was floating outside of myself. I couldn't explain it—not to myself, not to anyone else. It felt like the threads of my sanity were slipping through my fingers. And it scared me so deeply that I kept it hidden, convinced that if I said the words out loud, someone might take my baby away.

I eventually mustered the courage to talk to my husband about how I was feeling. He tried to be supportive, but it was hard for him to fully grasp what I was going through—it was new to him too, and we were both just trying to find our footing. Outside of him, I didn't share what was happening with anyone else. My "inner circle" at the time was basically just he and my sister.

Thankfully, my sister had flown in especially for the birth and was staying with us for about a month. I dreaded the day she'd leave. The thought of being on my own sent me into tears almost daily. I was in no emotional or mental state to face that kind of separation so soon after giving birth. And while she didn't really understand what I was going through—she was still young herself, with no real grasp of what postpartum looked or felt like—just having her there brought a kind of comfort. She couldn't offer the support I really needed, but her presence made the loneliness a little less sharp.

In those early weeks, the panic would come and go. But then it began to settle in, like an unwanted houseguest who refused to leave. I became anxious about everything—especially my physical health, every hour my husband was away, every little unknown. That constant undercurrent of fear slowly gave way to something heavier. It was like I was sliding, without brakes, into something I couldn't name.

Sometimes, I'd beg my husband not to go to work because I couldn't bear the thought of being alone with those feelings. What started as intense anxiety eventually spiralled into agoraphobia. I was too scared to leave the house. I didn't recognise the woman I was becoming. The nights were the worst. The quiet made my anxious thoughts louder in my head. I'd lie awake dreading morning, knowing my husband would leave for work and I'd be left alone again—with my baby, yes, but also with a mind I couldn't trust.

I didn't know who to turn to or what I needed to do to get better. Most days, I'd feel a little better for a moment, only to have a panic attack pull me right back into it. What I longed for most was comfort. Some sign that I could get through this. I never found the sign I was hoping for, but I did find something else—my baby girl. She became my anchor, the one thing pulling me back to the present when my thoughts tried to drag me somewhere darker. She didn't know it, of course, but just by being there, she gave me something to hold onto. Even when I felt like I was barely holding it together, she kept me grounded.

With a lot of stubborn determination (and the occasional whispered pep talk to myself in the mirror), I did my best to get through each day. I wasn't thriving—but I was surviving. And at the time, that was more than enough. What I didn't fully grasp back then was how connected everything is. Major life events don't exist in neat, separate boxes. They bleed into each other, shape each other, echo into the future in ways we can't always see at the time. What happened to me in those early days of motherhood didn't just affect that moment—it rippled outward, touching everything. My identity. My relationships. My sense of self. Birth and motherhood didn't just change me. They rearranged me. And honestly? They still are.

I know I'm not alone in that. I've walked this path, and now I walk it alongside other women too. I wish I had known back then what I understand now: postpartum doesn't just ask you to care for a baby. It asks you to meet yourself all over again.

And no one should have to do that alone. Whether it's family, friends, a postpartum doula, or even a neighbour who brings over leftovers—support matters. I didn't have that, and the loneliness nearly broke me. The panic and depression might still have come, but I wouldn't have been left to face them by myself.

What I didn't know then—but understand so clearly now—is that postpartum was only the surface. The deeper layers were still hidden, waiting. The fear, the panic, the belief that I had to survive it all alone... they didn't just come from becoming a mother.

They were rooted in something older. The unspoken parts of my story. The childhood I had spent so long trying to forget.

In the next chapter, I'll take you there. We'll explore how early trauma shaped me, how it resurfaced during birth and postpartum, and how, over time, I started to understand the connection between what I'd lived through and who I was becoming.

CHAPTER 3

My Trauma – The Shadows I Carried

> *"The wound is the place where the light enters you."*
> —commonly attributed to Rumi

In my early years, my childhood felt fairly ordinary—at least, that's how I saw it. But when I began talking about it with others over the years, especially therapists, I was often met with raised eyebrows and the occasional, 'How did you manage to turn out so normal?' And while that might sound like a compliment, it left me wondering if what I had lived through was far from *typical* after all. The truth is, normalcy felt like something I was always chasing—but never quite caught. For years, I lived in a constant state of apprehension and anxiety, even when everything on the outside looked fine.

I didn't realise then that what I thought was normal was actually survival dressed up as everyday life. It would take me years to understand just how much my past would shape the mother—and the woman—I became.

In hindsight, I can see it so clearly.

I grew up in what, from the outside, looked like a typical family. But underneath? It was anything but simple. A lot of that came down to my parents—two people who couldn't have been more different.

My mum was soft, hopeful, and rooted in the familiar. She craved safety, routine, and the steady rhythm of close family life. She wasn't adventurous—she was studying to be a nurse when she had my older sister, and her dreams were simple: a stable home, a clear path, a life with meaning.

My dad on the other hand was wired completely differently. He was intense, restless, always on edge. Where my mum found comfort in belonging, he seemed to come alive in movement and unpredictability. He chased success with a kind of desperation—more money, more recognition, more control. It wasn't just ambition; it was a constant need to prove something, to feel powerful. And when he couldn't reach whatever he was chasing, he grew agitated—dissatisfied. For him, money and control weren't luxuries; they were survival. Without them, he unravelled.

In my early memories, I can still see glimpses of affection and care from him. At least, I think I can. But over time, those images faded. I'm not sure if they were real or just what I wanted to believe. As I grew older, the mask slipped, and I saw the toll his ambition took. His hunger for control became all-consuming, tearing through not just the world around him but pieces of himself. That relentless drive didn't just shape him—it shaped us too, the ones growing up in his shadow.

Our lives were always in constant motion. We moved across continents like it was normal, chasing fresh starts that never really lasted. Looking back, it wasn't adventure we were chasing—it was escape. Most moves were sparked by stress or money trouble I didn't fully understand at the time. There was no real plan, just damage control—exhausting, relentless, and unpredictable. The moment life started to feel settled, something would tip, and we'd be packing up again. Each new place brought its own kind of instability.

Still, there was a brief stretch where things felt gentler—where the dust seemed to settle, just for a while, and life held a kind of softness I can still remember.

I was around six or seven. I remember sunlit mornings, easy laughter, the sense that our world—at least for a while—was holding together. That was the last stretch where I really felt like a kid. My family felt whole. There was warmth, rhythm, little moments that made things feel stable, even if they weren't. I hadn't noticed the cracks yet.

Later, when everything began to unravel, I'd go back to those memories like they were a secret place only I could reach. That time became my shelter—the calm before the storm, before everything changed and childhood faded into the background.

At the time, I believed that life was good then. It felt steady, even happy. But now I know it only looked that way because my mum was working overtime to hold it all together. She was doing everything she could to keep things from falling apart. Behind the scenes, though, things at home were already shifting beneath my feet. The tension kept building until it finally split everything wide open.

And then, the inevitable happened.

My parents' marriage collapsed under the weight of secrets, financial strain, and too many second chances. My mum eventually walked away from my dad's deception, but by then, the damage had already been done. He hadn't changed—just dragged the wreckage with him wherever he went. His personal and financial troubles finally caught up to him, and we all paid the price. That version of home had vanished.

The separation didn't just break their marriage—it split everything around it. My siblings and I were caught in the fallout, trying to find our footing while the ground never stayed still. What came next wasn't a clean break or a quiet exit—it was drawn-out, messy, and loud. Legal fights. Emotional warfare. So many versions of the truth, none of them clear.

I was too young to understand the details, and honestly, I don't think we were supposed to.

My sister and I were pulled into it anyway—caught in the crossfire, tugged back and forth like pawns in a game we never signed up to play. We kept searching for a side that felt safe, but there wasn't one. And when no one steps in to protect you, you start to believe the loudest voice. In our case, that voice was our dad.

He worked hard to win us over, twisting the story so we'd turn against our mum. He painted her as the problem. And she—hurt, overwhelmed, unsure how to cope—reacted in ways that only deepened the damage. We were absorbing it all. There was no middle ground—just pressure that kept closing in.

Things with our dad didn't slow down—they only intensified. We were coached on what to say, how to say it, when to stay quiet. Dragged into conversations we didn't understand. Made to sit in rooms where adult problems spilled over and somehow became ours to carry. Through it all, we were made to feel like it was on us—to hold the line, to protect him, to keep the story straight.

I couldn't make sense of any of it—but I felt it in my body. That constant tension, always humming in the background. That sense that if we got it wrong, something terrible would happen. We were just kids. But no one seemed to notice.

Caught between two people too broken to protect us from their own pain, we had nowhere to land. And no one else was stepping in.

Only years later did I realise that my mum was coming undone too. She couldn't manage the weight of what my dad was doing, and she didn't know how to shield us from it. As a mother myself now, I understand it better—not the choices she made, but the place she was in.

Still, even after everything we'd lived through, nothing prepared us for what came next.

We knew our dad was capable of drastic moves—but understanding that and living through one are two very different things. Everything broke open when he made one final, devastating decision: he took us away from our mum.

We didn't resist. We followed him—wide-eyed, uncertain, and carrying more fear than understanding. We believed him, because we had been made to. Because that's what kids do. He told us this was the only way. That life would be better. That it had to be this way. And somewhere inside, we wanted to believe him.

But it didn't feel like rescue. It felt like disappearing. And it was. What I didn't know then was that it would be the last time I saw my mum until I was an adult. No goodbyes. No contact. No communication. Just silence.

And eventually, that silence filled with questions I didn't know how to ask.

I've since come to question whether taking us was really about protection at all. Sometimes I wonder if it was about control—or revenge. Maybe having us with him was his way of rewriting the story—casting himself as either the victim or the hero. If anyone ever questioned him, he could say, "I did it for my kids," and believe it. That's the kind of story a man like him needed—one where he looked like the saviour, even if we were the collateral. Maybe we were leverage. Maybe we were a shield. Or maybe we were just the excuse.

Whatever the reason, the result was the same.

That was when a new kind of chaos began.

We became ghosts—constantly on the move, slipping in and out of places like we didn't belong anywhere. Sometimes it was a car. Sometimes a rental. Sometimes a stranger's house. There were brief stretches when we had money, and others when we were scrounging for a piece of bread. We never unpacked. Never got comfortable. We weren't just hiding—we were erasing ourselves in real time.

But even as we drifted from place to place, my mum stayed rooted in my mind.

Even with the fear drilled into me, some small part of me hoped she'd come. That she'd find us. That somehow, she'd bring us home—whatever "home" even meant anymore.

But I also knew what we'd been told over and over: if she found us, everything would fall apart. That my sister and I would be torn away from each other, or worse. I didn't know what was true. I only knew that longing and fear had tangled themselves so tightly inside me, I couldn't tell them apart.

Sometimes I'd close my eyes and slip into a dream-state where I could convince myself none of it was real. That I'd wake up to a warm house, a sense of safety, my whole family intact.

But I never did. Life kept going, and I had to learn how to survive without the safety I'd once taken for granted.

Survival became the only focus. Day by day, we stayed afloat in a life that barely made sense to us, let alone anyone on the outside. My dad was too caught up in his own mess to notice what we were carrying.

Through it all, my sister was my saving grace. She was the one person I felt safe with—the only one who offered me any sense of protection. In many ways, she stepped into the role of the mother I so badly needed. We were together constantly—just the two of us, all day, every day, for years. No friends. No distractions. We learned how to make each other laugh with the dumbest stuff. We'd whisper jokes under our breath or invent wild future scenarios where we were normal people with normal lives. "One day we're gonna look back and go, *how fucked up were they*," we'd say. And we'd *actually laugh*. Not from bitterness, but from this weird, beautiful place of knowing we were in it together.

But even she couldn't shield us from everything.

As my dad drifted through relationships with different women, his role as a parent faded further and further into the background. The lines between adult and child blurred in ways they never should have—emotionally and mentally. My sister and I were exposed to things no child should ever witness, and it changed how I saw him. There was no going back from that.

And with that unravelling, the last bits of routine slipped away.

School? That disappeared the moment our world shifted—when we were pulled from the only life we understood.

Education wasn't even part of the conversation anymore. There were no classrooms, no schoolyards, no teachers calling roll. No assemblies, no spelling tests, no art projects taped to the fridge. No first-day nerves or birthday invites. None of the little rituals that build a childhood.

BIRTHING WITH TRAUMA AND FEAR

I missed out on all of it. The friendships. The hallway whispers. The crushes and awkward first flirtations. The things most kids forget by adulthood were the very things I never got to have.

And the silence around it made it worse. It wasn't just that I didn't go to school—it was like the world moved on without me, and no one even noticed I was missing.

So I taught myself. I learned to read and write using whatever I could find. During the rare windows when we had money, I'd buy books and magazines—anything with words I could sink into. They became my teachers. My escape. My way of proving to myself that there was a world outside the one I was trapped in.

But knowing there was more didn't change what we were living. And always, there were the warnings. If anyone found out where we were, we'd be taken. Placed in shelters. Split apart. That fear lived in my bones. I'd freeze anytime I saw a police car. I didn't know what was real and what was manipulation—but it didn't matter. The fear was real enough to shape everything. It taught us to stay quiet, to be careful, to never share too much. We became actors in a life that wasn't ours, reciting lines we didn't write, playing roles in someone else's twisted movie. But that was our reality.

That life held on for years until the edge of adulthood, when I finally began to reclaim some control. But survival mode doesn't disappear just because you want it to.

Living in a constant state of alert became second nature. Always scanning, bracing, ready to run. That became my nervous system's default setting—and to be honest, parts of it still echo in me now. But that kind of adaptation comes with a cost. I carried the trauma. It rewired me. I never felt safe, even in safe places. I struggled to trust even in secure friendships, always waiting for the ground to fall out from under me.

Eventually, the panic settled, but the trauma never disappeared. It just lay dormant, buried deep, waiting for the right moment to rear its head.

As I got older, something inside me shifted. I didn't want to just survive anymore. I wanted to live on my own terms. So, I started to pull away.

Years passed. I didn't completely cut contact with my dad, but as I got older, I craved independence—anything that would let me be in control of my own existence.

I met my husband one month shy of my 20th birthday. Those two years between turning 18 and meeting him were still messy and unpredictable, but little by little I was rebuilding something that felt like a life. I was working and socialising for the first time. I was just being me.

I made a conscious choice not to think about my past. I boxed up my past tightly in my mind, convinced it didn't need revisiting. The panic attacks I used to have as a kid, caught in the middle of all that madness, stopped, and I thought, *I'm good. I've moved on.*

I thought I'd escaped it. I had built a life I believed was safe, predictable, mine. I had fallen in love, married, and we were expecting our first baby.

For a long time, I truly believed I could outrun the past. That I could draw a firm line between where I'd come from and the life I was creating. I was sure that having a baby would be my fresh start—the clean beginning I'd been craving.

But the body doesn't forget.

When it came time to give birth, the past didn't stay quiet. Fear, anxiety, and that familiar sense of not feeling safe crept back in and settled deep into my labour.

I recognised it instantly. I'd met that feeling long before—lying awake as a teenager, breathless and alone in the grip of panic. My dad had called it weakness. That belief—that struggling meant I was broken—had etched itself into me.

So I stayed silent, convinced I had to be strong, even when everything inside me was screaming.

My daughter's birth cracked something open in me. It brought my inner child to the surface—the one who had been screaming silently for years. Bella's birth was both the beginning of more struggle and the spark of something new.

In the years that followed, I began to see everything differently. Not just what I'd lived through—but what it had made me capable of. I started piecing together the fragments of my story, not to rewrite it, but to own it.

My father passed away years later, after a long period of disconnect that began a few years after Bella was born. There was no final conversation, no closure—just a quiet, unresolved ending I've had to learn to live with. I didn't get the goodbye I once hoped for, but I've made peace with the fact that some chapters close without neat endings.

Now, I own my story. All of it. The damage, the lessons, the resilience. I accept what brought me here. I see Bella's birth and my own childhood through new eyes—not with sadness anymore, but with clarity and appreciation. Because everything that hurt also shaped me.

And that, in the end, became my strength. Not from leaving the past behind, but from understanding it—and recognising trauma for what it is.

CHAPTER 4

Understanding Trauma - Unveiling the Impact

> *"Trauma is not just an event that took place sometime in the past; it is also the imprint left by that experience on mind, brain, and body."*
> — Dr. Bessel van der Kolk, The Body Keeps the Score

Most people think of trauma as something huge—a car crash, an assault, a devastating loss.

But trauma wears many faces. Sometimes it's loud and undeniable. Other times it slips in quietly, hiding beneath the surface, harder to name but just as real.

Trauma is the emotional response to a deeply distressing or disturbing experience.

Whether you notice it or not, it leaves a lasting imprint. It shapes how we see the world, how we cope, how safe we feel, and how much we trust the people around us—often without us realising.

And it doesn't just stay with the person who lived it. It ripples outward—through families, relationships, and the ways we love, protect, and respond to the world.

I've seen it. I've lived it. I know I'm not alone.

Yet for a long time, I struggled to find the words for what I was feeling. That understanding didn't come easily to me. I remember stumbling upon a book called *What Happened to You?*

by Dr. Bruce Perry and Oprah Winfrey and it was like someone had finally put words to what I'd been carrying for so long. Dr. Perry explained something I had always felt but could never quite explain: Trauma isn't just about what happened to me. It's about what happened inside of me because of what happened to me. (It's a lot, I know. Read it again—it'll click.)

It's not the event itself; it's the imprint it leaves behind. Dr. Perry, who's spent decades working with people affected by trauma, explains how early experiences shape the way our brains and bodies work. When kids grow up in fear—whether it's neglect, abuse, chaos, or just never knowing what's going to happen next—their bodies learn to stay on high alert.

That hyper-awareness doesn't magically disappear once things get better. It becomes the way we move through the world.

And for many women, especially those who've been through trauma early on, that survival mode never quite switches off. We stay braced. Always scanning, always preparing for the next bad thing. Even when we're technically protected, our bodies don't always believe it.

That relentless state of hypervigilance?

It's not a flaw. It's not weakness. It's a survival tool. And Once you start noticing how much women shoulder—how much we're taught to scan for danger, to be ready, to keep ourselves safe—you start to see it everywhere.

I was recently watching an Australian Netflix series called The Hunting in which a group of teen girls had explicit photos of them put onto a website online coined 'local sluts'. Even I, as a woman in my 40s, was surprised at how easily teen girls can be violated by having their male peers expose them online in such a way. And I'm sure this kind of traumatic experience—which can have such a huge impact on a woman's sense of safety and trust—barely even registers in the conversations we have about these offenses.

There was another part of the series that really stuck with me, something I hadn't really thought much about before. One of the teachers asked her male students a simple but powerful question "what do you do in your everyday lives to avoid sexual violence?"

There was no showing of hands from any of the boys, there was no one rushing to contribute a response. It was pure deafening silence.

Then this teacher posed the same question onto the teen girls. The overwhelming response was eye opening and saddening. As a mother to three girls, if there was anything that really keeps me up at night it's this. My daughters, like women everywhere, will always have to stay vigilant and protect themselves from sexual violence.

The girls' responses to that question said it all.

> "We always have to travel in groups."

> "Have triple zero (Australia's emergency number for police, fire, or ambulance) on speed dial."

> "Make guys feel better or smarter about themselves."

> "Always come up with an escape plan."

Sit with that for a moment. Take it in.

It's eye-opening, and if I'm honest, it's also pretty confronting. No, not every woman will experience trauma in the way we traditionally define it. But the truth is, as women we've been wired to live with a constant undercurrent of protection, whether we want to or not. And that has to emerge somewhere. For many of us, it shows up in the birth room.

Maybe it's feeling your whole body tense when a stranger walks in.

Maybe it's freezing when someone says, "I'm just going to examine you"—and suddenly you're lying there, vulnerable, exposed, naked in front of people you don't know.

Maybe it's something else entirely. That's the thing about birth: it asks you to surrender, and for women who've been taught to stay on guard, that can feel impossible.

That ever-present vigilance rewires our nervous systems, teaching us to stay on alert and distrust the people around us. It doesn't switch off when we enter the birthing room. For many women, labour becomes the moment when buried trauma breaks the surface.

But what happens when trauma has been pushed down, left to sit quietly in the background?

What happens when it cracks wide open during labour? How does it show up?

To understand it better, let's turn to those who've seen it firsthand.

My own story is just one example. And sadly, I know it's far from the only one.

> "A long time ago, I worked as a doula with a woman who had experienced sexual assault.
>
> For her, even the thought of someone—other than her very, very trusted long-term partner—putting anything inside her body was abhorrent and triggering. Unfortunately, at the time of her first birth, I did not know that this was something she had experienced. After her first birth ended in a caesarean, we debriefed, and I was able to provide some understanding for her.
>
> Her next birth I was also present for, and she chose to have a second doula present, who knew her situation. Unfortunately, that doula said something that triggered her and caused her cervix to close. That birth, although it had been an intended HBAC (home birth after caesarean), ended up as a repeat caesarean."
>
> ~ Phillipa Scott – Birth trauma
> and parenting therapist

I invite you to pause for a moment and ask yourself: Is there something tucked away in the back of your mind, something you've filed away, that might be worth revisiting? It doesn't have to be something extreme. Sometimes it's not a violation, but an unresolved hurt, an emotional wound, or a difficult memory you've quietly carried.

It's worth asking yourself this, not to stir up pain, but to gently process and heal—so you can walk into your birth feeling lighter, clearer, and more at ease.

I'm sharing this because you deserve to know you have a choice: to explore this, to look inward, and to prepare in whatever way feels right for you.

Not because you have to—but because you can. And that knowledge alone can be powerful.

Some people may never feel past experiences surface in birth. For many, labour unfolds calmly and safely, without old memories, emotions, or unresolved pain rising to the surface.

But if you know you carry something, you deserve the option to work through it before you walk into that birth. And you don't have to do it alone.

With the right care around you, birth doesn't have to feel unsafe or triggering. It can be grounding. It can even be healing.

And that's where trauma-informed care comes in. You've probably heard that phrase before—it gets thrown around a lot these days.

But what does it actually mean? And more importantly, are care providers really putting it into practice? At its core, trauma-informed care means understanding that your past may quietly walk into the room with you. It means your care team asks about your needs, your boundaries, and how you want to be supported—instead of assuming they know what's best for you.

It means they explain what they're going to do before they do it. It means they respect a "no" the first time you say it. It means creating an environment where you feel grounded enough to soften, to trust, to be fully present in your experience.

And really, this shouldn't be something reserved only for those they suspect have been through something. It should be the standard for every woman, every time. Because the truth is, far more people walk into birth carrying something than most realise.

And even if they don't, doesn't every woman deserve that level of respect and care in birth as a basic minimum?

When you consider how widespread trauma really is, it becomes even clearer why this should be the standard. The numbers tell their own story.

In Australia, it's estimated that around 75% of adults have experienced at least one traumatic event in their lifetime. That figure alone says a lot about the world we live in. Trauma isn't rare—it's something surprisingly many of us carry. Globally, research shows that by the age of 17, around 62–68% of young people will have faced at least one traumatic experience. In Australia, the numbers around sexual trauma are especially hard to take. According to the Australian Bureau of Statistics, around 2.2 million women—roughly 1 in 5—have experienced sexual violence, including both childhood sexual abuse and assault after the age of 15.

Even more confronting? Around 1 million women, or 11%, reported being abused as children, often by someone they knew.

These numbers aren't here to shock you. They're here because this is real. It's happening, and it matters.

And it's not just about sexual trauma. Abuse. Domestic violence. Emotional neglect. Mental abuse. Loss. Even growing up in an unsafe or unpredictable environment can have lasting effects.

For me, it wasn't physical abuse. It was the mental and emotional stuff—the stuff no one could see. But I felt it. I knew it.

I didn't realise how much of it I was still holding onto until I laboured with Bella. In her birth every contraction pulled something deeper than just physical pain. It was like parts of my past had slipped quietly into the room with me: old fears, childhood helplessness, that ache of not feeling safe. And underneath it all, I felt something even harder to name. I felt like my body was stopping me—as if it knew I wasn't ready. Not ready to become a mother. Not ready to let go of the girl inside me who still felt small, unprotected, and stuck in a past I hadn't fully escaped. I wasn't just bringing my daughter into the world—I was confronting parts of myself I hadn't faced in years.

Labour can do that, and it certainly has a way of stripping everything back, forcing a reckoning between who you are and who you've been. The vulnerability was overwhelming. Not because of birth itself, but because of what it surfaced.

And if that happens for you, it doesn't mean you've failed. It just means your body is asking to be heard.

But here's what I want you to know: we don't have to wait for birth to start listening. If we choose to get curious instead of scared, if we hold space for whatever our body is trying to say before labour even begins, we can start to soften the weight of what we carry.

And when we do, birth can become something else entirely. For so many women, birth becomes healing. They walk in holding the weight of their past, their fears, their doubts. And then, somewhere along the way, something shifts.

The work they've done—the hard stuff: processing, unlearning, preparing—makes room for something new to happen. They meet labour not drowning in fear, but steady in awareness.

They know what they've been through. They know what they need. They speak up. They trust their team. And even though the past may whisper, it doesn't get to take over. They come through not just with a baby, but with an unshakable sense of strength and ownership of their story. That's what I want for you.

This is why **preparation matters.**

Real preparation.

The kind that gives you knowledge, agency, and the confidence to feel grounded in your choices.

But I also have to tell you this: sometimes, even with all the preparation in the world, women are up against a system that wasn't built with them in mind. For many, birth becomes the trauma—not because of their past, but because of what happens to them in the moment. We need to talk about that too.

I know this has been heavy, and you've stayed with me—because this stuff matters. These are hard things to talk about, but naming them is how we start to change them.

So take a breath, grab a cup of tea if you need to—we're going to keep going, and I promise it gets better from here.

The next chapter isn't just about the pain of birth trauma—it's about reclaiming your power, understanding your options, and writing the next part of your story on your terms.

CHAPTER 5

Birth Trauma - When Birth Leaves Scars

"Birth trauma is isolating. Devastating. Real."
—*Birthtalk.org*

I couldn't write this book without talking about birth trauma. It's too real, too common, and honestly, too ignored.

I've seen birth trauma from both sides. I've lived it as a mother. And I've witnessed it as a doula, standing beside women as it unfolds in real time. That's why I couldn't leave it out. Let's get real for a second. One in three women walk away from birth traumatised. One in ten end up with posttraumatic stress disorder (PTSD). Read that again.

This isn't some niche issue or rare case. This is what's happening to women *all the time*—in hospitals, in birth centres, even in their own homes. For something that's meant to be one of the most powerful, transformative moments of our lives, way too many of us are coming out the other side feeling broken, confused, or just completely numb.

And those stats? They're not just numbers. They're real people. Real women. Each one with a story. Each one carrying pain they didn't expect from something they were told would be magical.

Behind every one of those numbers is a woman who did everything she could. She carried life, showed up, hoped, and prepared—only to be left with wounds no one warned her about.

What that looks like isn't always visible from the outside.

She's already carried a baby in her body for months—through exhaustion, nausea, worry, and hope. She's felt every kick, every shift, and built a bond with someone she hasn't even met yet. She's shown up to every appointment, made hard choices, and pushed through fears. She's prepared—mentally, emotionally, physically—for a moment that's supposed to change her life.

And it *does* change her life—but not in the way she imagined.

Instead of joy, the biggest emotion is often relief. Relief it's over. But under that relief, there's something deeper—confusion, fear, sadness. Trauma. A lingering heaviness that follows her into motherhood, even when everyone around her thinks the "hard part" is done.

This is what we're not talking about enough. That the way a woman *feels* about her birth experience matters. That birth trauma isn't just about something going physically wrong. It's how she was treated. Whether she felt heard, respected, or in control.

So how did we get here? How did we turn something so primal and powerful into something that leaves so many women feeling broken?

I didn't understand it at the time, but I know the feeling of birth trauma intimately.

When I gave birth to Bella, it was like I vanished. I wasn't a person anymore—I was a body on a bed. I remember lying there, cracked open by mental and physical exhaustion, when suddenly my legs were in stirrups. No one said a word. No one asked.

Then, without warning, the doctor—someone I had hired, someone I trusted—picked up the scissors and cut into me.

Just like that. No explanation. No consent. No pause. Just the sound, the shock, the tearing of flesh.

Then came the forceps. He pulled my baby out of me. And I lay there, stunned, hollow, unsure if what had just happened was normal or not.

I didn't say yes. I didn't even know I *could* say no.

And here's the wild part: I felt grateful. Because I'd been conditioned to believe that as long as the baby was healthy, nothing else mattered.

It wasn't until later—after I started training as a doula—that I began to unpack what had actually happened to me.

That's when I learned about the "cascade of intervention." It's real. I've seen it play out time and time again. One thing leads to another. Labour gets induced—most times without a solid medical reason. That brings on stronger, more intense contractions. So, an epidural follows. But the epidural can slow things down. Then up goes the synthetic oxytocin to speed it all back up again. And before you know it, you're being told you need a caesarean because your baby is in distress or your labour has "stalled" or as they like to pathologise it with the term 'failure to progress'. Again, even in those words, bringing the shift of blame onto the mother's body.

And while these steps that got her here are often explained as necessary, they're rarely talked about beforehand. No one says, "Hey, if we do this, it might lead to that." It's like you're on a ride you never agreed to. And the worst part? So many women come out of it not understanding what happened, just feeling numb. Confused. Traumatised.

What I've learned is that it's not always about individual doctors or midwives doing something wrong. Often, it's the system. It's how it's built. It's fast-paced, risk-averse, short-staffed, and focused on outcomes—specifically, whether mum and baby are alive when they leave the hospital. Which, of course, matters. But that shouldn't be the *only* way we measure healthy outcomes in birth.

Because what gets overlooked in that model is how women actually *feel* after birth. Not just physically, but emotionally. Mentally. Spiritually. This stuff goes deep. And when it's ignored, it doesn't just disappear—it festers.

This kind of unspoken trauma doesn't just come from what happens to us—it often comes from how it happens.

I've also seen a disturbing rise in what's now being called obstetric violence. It's a heavy term, but it fits. It's what happens when care crosses the line into control. When consent is bypassed. When women are coerced, dismissed, or outright ignored.

It took me around a year into working as a doula to recognise that what had happened to me—and what I was seeing far too often—was obstetric violence. I didn't have the language for it at first. Like so many others, I had been conditioned to believe that as long as there was a healthy baby, everything else was justified.

But then I started noticing the patterns. Midwives or doctors not stopping vaginal exams when a mother said no. Keeping their fingers inside her while instructing her how to push—without consent. Coercing her into procedures she clearly didn't want. And I was there, seeing it happen in real time.

And I now know this isn't rare. Around 1 in 10 women in Australia report experiencing obstetric violence during childbirth. Globally, research indicates that mistreatment during childbirth—including verbal abuse, non-consensual procedures, and neglect—is a widespread issue, affecting a significant proportion of women in various countries. These aren't isolated incidents; they reflect systemic issues within maternity care.

Witnessing these violations again and again early in my doula career changed me.

At some point, I realised I couldn't just be a witness to it anymore—because what was I, if not complicit in the abuse I stayed silent through? I found my voice. I started supporting women more actively—helping them say no, helping their partners ask questions, making sure they felt empowered in the room.

One birth in particular still stays with me—and not in a good way.

Years ago, I supported a woman who, from the very beginning, made it clear she wanted to guide her own birth experience. She'd done the work. Her partner was on board. They were informed, grounded, ready. Everything felt aligned.

She laboured at home first, and was doing beautifully—calm, connected, completely in her zone. But the moment we walked into that hospital, I felt it. The mood shifted. The energy in the room changed the moment the on-call obstetrician entered. You know when someone walks in and suddenly the walls feel tighter? That.

She barely glanced at the mother. She addressed most of her comments to the midwife and me—curt, dismissive, like she was annoyed we existed. When I calmly advocated for the mother's preferences—things we'd all discussed and agreed on—she shut me down. Publicly. Coldly. Almost gleefully.

I wasn't yelling. I wasn't demanding. I was doing exactly what a doula should do: holding space and offering informed support. But it was clear that, in her eyes, I was a nuisance. An outsider. A witness she didn't want in the room.

And the mother? She shrank. Every time she tried to speak up, the doctor spoke over her. Every time she tried to ask a question, she was met with a patronising tone or medical jargon meant to confuse, not inform.

This doctor—a woman, by the way—crossed a line I didn't even have words for back then. Now I do. It was obstetric violence.

She manipulated. She ignored consent. She controlled the entire birth like it was a procedure to get through, not a human experience unfolding.

I watched this strong, prepared woman be stripped of her voice, her power, her trust in herself. I saw her go from grounded to gaslit. From centred to silenced.

And I couldn't stop it.

That birth stayed with me—not just because of the mother's trauma, but because it rattled something in me too. I walked out of that hospital angry. Helpless. Haunted.

I've never forgotten her face. Or the way she looked at me afterward, as if to ask, *Was that supposed to happen?* It wasn't. It should never have gone that way. But sadly, it wasn't rare.

We can't keep acting surprised when women come out of birth feeling broken. Birth trauma can look like physical injury. But often, it's emotional. It's psychological. It's about not being respected. Not being heard. Not feeling safe.

We've got to stop telling women to just be grateful their baby is healthy. That's not enough. Survival isn't the only goal. Birth matters. *How* you give birth matters. It stays with you. It shapes how you step into motherhood.

I've spoken to so many women who carry the weight of their birth stories years later. It shows up in unexpected ways—dreams, flashbacks, anxiety. They're constantly on edge, like something might go wrong at any moment. Even if they're surrounded by support, they feel alone. Misunderstood. Like no one truly gets what they've been through.

Some feel a quiet disappointment that never really goes away. Others feel guilt for not being happier. Some feel nothing at all—just numb. And if that trauma isn't acknowledged, it can build into depression or make existing mental health struggles worse. It's exhausting to carry all that and be expected to just "get on with it." To smile, to function, to move on like nothing happened. But it shouldn't be that way. This is why trauma-informed care is so important. Why we need to listen better. Why we need to make space for women to tell their stories without judgement. Because healing starts when someone says, "I hear you. That shouldn't have happened to you."

And the stakes couldn't be higher. In places like the U.S. and France, suicide is now recognised as one of the leading causes of maternal death in the postpartum period. A 2024 JAMA Network Open study even found that many of these deaths are preventable with the right mental health care. That's how serious this is. We're losing women—not from childbirth complications, but from how unsupported they feel after. I know that feeling all too well.

Looking back, I can see how my postnatal anxiety was seeded in that birth room. It wasn't just the shock of new motherhood—it was the helplessness I felt when I was treated like a body, not a person. When decisions were made about me, not with me. That sense of being invisible, of having no voice, stayed with me long after the birth was over.

I've seen this pattern over and over—not just in my own story, but in the stories of countless women. Trauma doesn't always announce itself in the moment. It settles in quietly, then echoes later in ways you don't expect.

Trauma is messy. It's not linear. Some days you're okay. Other days, it blindsides you. That was my reality. And it's the same for so many women I've worked with. Sometimes all it takes to start healing is someone genuinely listening. Not fixing. Not judging. Just hearing you.

If you're reading this and you've had a traumatic birth, here's what I want you to know: you're not alone. You're not weak. And you're not broken. You don't have to pretend you're okay if you're not. Start by letting yourself feel what you're feeling. The anger, the sadness, the guilt, the confusion—even the relief. Whatever's coming up, it's valid. You don't have to justify it, and you don't have to push it down.

If you can, reach out for support. A therapist who understands birth trauma can make a huge difference. You shouldn't have to carry this on your own.

Connect with other women who've been through it too. Whether it's a support group, an online community, or just one honest conversation—being around people who *get it* can make you feel seen in a way that nothing else does.

Sometimes learning about birth trauma helps too. Understanding what actually happened—how and why—can be healing. It can help you make sense of it, and maybe even feel more in control if you ever choose to give birth again.

And once you start to understand what happened, the next step is learning how to care for yourself in it.

Please take care of yourself, in the little ways that you can. I know that can feel impossible in the thick of new motherhood. But even a few quiet minutes, a hot shower, or a deep breath can help you come back to yourself.

When you feel ready, if you want to, tell your story. Speak it out loud. Write it down. Share it with someone you trust. Your story matters—and it might be exactly what someone else needs to hear to feel less alone.

You've carried so much already. But this part—the healing, the reclaiming—this part is yours. There's no right timeline, no perfect way. Just your way. Step by step, breath by breath.

BIRTH STORY REFLECTION PRACTICE: EXPLORING YOUR EXPERIENCE

This reflective practice gently guides you through your birth story. It offers space to explore emotions, make sense of what happened, and identify any areas where healing or further support might help.

1. **Reflect on Your Emotions**

   - Find a quiet space where you feel safe and undisturbed. Have a journal or notepad ready.
   - Reflect:

   - How do you feel when you think about your birth experience?
   - Do any emotions stand out (happiness, sadness, confusion, relief, fear)?

2. **Explore Significant Moments**

   - Reflect:

   - What part of your birth story stands out the most?
   - Is there a moment that feels especially vivid or meaningful? How does it make you feel now?

3. **Review Your Support System**

   - Reflect:

   - How did you feel about the support you received?

BIRTHING WITH TRAUMA AND FEAR

- ☞ Consider the people who were with you—medical staff, partner, doula, family.
- ☞ Did you feel heard and supported? Were there moments you wished had gone differently?

4. Identify the Unexpected

✋ Reflect:

- ☞ Did anything unexpected happen during your birth?
- ☞ Were there any surprises or changes that affected you emotionally?

5. Consider Unresolved Feelings

✋ Reflect:

- ☞ Is there anything unresolved about your birth experience?
- ☞ Are there aspects that still feel confusing, distressing, or incomplete?

6. Recognize Your Coping Tools

✋ Reflect:

- ☞ What helped you cope during birth?
- ☞ Identify the people, tools, or inner strengths that helped you feel calm or grounded.

7. **Lessons and Preparation**

   ✋ Reflect:

   ☞ Is there something you wish you had known beforehand?
   ☞ What advice, information, or support would have helped you feel more prepared?

---

8. **Reflect on Your Postpartum Experience**

   ✋ Reflect:

   ☞ How did you feel in the days and weeks after birth?
   ☞ Were you well-supported? Did any surprising emotions surface?

---

9. **Your Transition into Motherhood**

   ✋ Reflect:

   ☞ How would you describe your transition into motherhood?
   ☞ Did your birth experience influence your early days as a mother?
   ☞ Did you feel empowered, or did challenges shape this time?

---

10. **Support for Moving Forward**

    ✋ Reflect:

    ☞ What support would help you now?

☞ If any feelings still linger, what kind of support (trusted person, professional, or time and space) might help you continue processing and healing?

Bringing It Together

- Take your time: There is no rush. Return to any question if it feels too hard right now.
- Talk to someone you trust: If strong emotions come up, consider sharing with someone who can offer compassionate support.
- Practice self-compassion: Be kind to yourself. It is normal to feel a range of emotions; there is no right or wrong way to process your story.
- Seek professional support if needed: A trauma-informed therapist or support group can offer guidance and understanding if birth trauma or anxiety feels overwhelming.
- You deserve the space to reflect, heal, and feel whole again.

CHAPTER 6

Fear -
Holding It Without Letting It Hold You

"Feel the fear and do it anyway."
—Susan Jeffers

I want to clear something up straight away: fear and trauma aren't the same thing. But I get why they get tangled.

Fear is like the smoke alarm going off. Loud, urgent, impossible to ignore. Your body goes, "Something's not right. Pay attention."

Trauma? Trauma is the smoke that lingers long after the fire is out. It hangs around in your body, your nervous system, your memory. Even when things are safe again, you can still smell it.

And how we experience either? That's personal. What shakes one person to their core might not even register for someone else. I used to drive myself crazy wondering, *Why does this throw me but not her?* Or, *why am I worrying about something she barely notices?* But here's what I've learned: it doesn't mean one of us is stronger or weaker. We've just lived different stories, carry different scars, and have our own ways of coping—and that's valid and okay.

So where does fear sit within birth? Let's talk about it. Fear and birth have always had a complicated relationship.

For so many women, the anxious thoughts start early. Doubts about pain. Worry over the unknown. Concern about losing control. The fear of not being heard or it not playing out the way you imagined it to go.

Sometimes that unease isn't even ours. It sneaks in through stories from your mum, your sister, your friends—the ones that quietly settle into your mind and shape what you expect birth to be. Sometimes it's passed down through generations, disguised as "helpful advice":

"Birth is terrifying, just get through it."
"Don't overthink it—you won't have any control anyway."

Unlike trauma, which is rooted in the past, worry often lives in the future. It's all the "what ifs" that pop up when we don't know what's coming or feel like we won't have a say when it does.

But here's the crazy thing most women don't realise: this feeling isn't the enemy. It's not something we have to fight or silence. Sometimes it's just trying to get our attention: Slow down. Check in. What do you need? When we actually sit with it—name it, unpack it—it can tell us a lot. And when we meet what scares us with the right tools? That's when things shift.

Education helps. Knowing how birth works, what your rights are, what your body is capable of—that knowledge eases the unknown. It doesn't erase the intensity, but it gives you something solid to stand on.

And support? That's everything. Your midwife, your doctor, your doula, your partner, your best friend—whoever's in your corner, it matters. When you feel safe, informed, and supported, doubt loosens its hold. It fades. Sometimes, it even turns into confidence.

I've witnessed that transformation many times, but there's one woman whose journey still stands out in my mind.

In my second year as a doula, I was hired by a woman for private childbirth education sessions. A big part of my classes is showing birth videos. I find it helps women, and their partners get familiar with the sounds, movements, and behaviours of labour—to normalise birth and start picturing their own experience.

But in our first session, when I suggested watching a birth video, she shook her head firmly. "I can't do it," she said. Even the thought made her lightheaded and faint.

I didn't push. Instead, we took a different path. We talked. We unpacked what was really sitting under the surface—her worries, her uncertainty, the "what ifs" that kept creeping in. We explored how those feelings might show up when she was in labour. I guided her through what I know best: education, simple research, and the gentle tools of HypnoBirthing® to help her start shifting her mindset. Slowly, she started to open up. I watched her confidence build session by session.

Before our final session, I gently asked, "Do you think you might be ready to watch a birth video now?"

She paused, thinking. Then she nodded. "I'm ready."

I held my breath as we watched. But what happened next amazed me. The fear I had expected wasn't there. Instead, she was wide-eyed, smiling, completely in awe. For the first time, she looked genuinely excited about her own birth. At the end of that session, she and her partner turned to me. "Would you be our doula?" they asked.

I smiled. I'd been secretly hoping they would. I was thrilled to say yes and support them through the rest of their journey. The day she went into labour, her partner called to let me know she was having mild early contractions, and they'd keep me posted. I waited, expecting the next call to tell me it was time to head over.

Instead, just a few hours later, the phone rang again. "She's already had the baby!"

She had done it. Calmly. Powerfully. Exactly the way she had envisioned—from beginning to end, completely on her own terms. She had always pictured it that way—just her and her husband, no one else. I was there as her safety net, just in case.

But in the end, she didn't need me. She had built that sense of safety for herself, from the inside out.

I still smile when I think about her. She showed me just how much power fear loses when it's tended to.

Her story leads perfectly into something I've come to believe: these worries need a voice. When a woman feels safe enough to say, "This scares me" or "I'm not sure I can do this," that's when things start to change. Not because the anxiety disappears, but because it stops quietly weighing her down.

The hardest part? Speaking it. Anxious thoughts thrive in silence. But the moment they're shared with someone who truly listens, they start to lose their grip.

That's why emotional support isn't just a bonus—it's essential. You don't need someone to fix it. You just need someone to sit beside you and say, "That makes sense. I hear you."

Because honestly, so much of what women carry into pregnancy isn't theirs to begin with.

And let's be real—the world doesn't make that easy. Women are bombarded with worst-case scenarios, horror stories, and not-so-subtle messages that their bodies won't measure up.

So of course anxiety shows up in pregnancy. How could it not? When everyone from your neighbour to your hairdresser has a "traumatic 47-hour labour story" to share, it's a wonder anyone sleeps past the third trimester. It's no surprise so many women feel on edge.

But beneath all that noise, there's often something quieter—and more important—trying to get through.

Here's what I've learned working alongside women: what scares us often shows us what matters. Sometimes that quiet pull you feel is just pointing you toward what you deeply value. I saw this unfold with another mother I supported named Sara—a story I always come back to. When she came to me during her second pregnancy, her voice carried that quiet fear.

"I want this birth to be different," she said. "But I'm scared it won't be."

She wasn't afraid of birth itself. She was afraid of being sidelined again. Of not being heard. Of history repeating itself. So, we started there.

We talked about what she wanted this birth to feel like. What safety meant to her. What control actually looked like. We talked about building a team that would respect her choices.

I encouraged her to write down every fear—not to dwell on them, but to get them out of her head. Naming them took away their power.

We practiced visualisation. Breathing. Imagining the birth space. The lighting. The people in the room. Her body in motion. Her voice, strong.

After one of our sessions together, she opened her eyes with tears on her cheeks. "I want that," she whispered. "But I don't know if I'm strong enough to get there."

The truth was, she already was. Strength isn't the absence of fear. It's choosing to move forward in spite of it walking right beside you.

When labour came, she was ready. I walked into the room and saw a woman in her power. She moved through her contractions with rhythm and purpose. She breathed deeply. She swayed. At one point, she looked up at me and said, "I feel it. This is mine."

Her baby arrived a few hours later. And the look on her face—that was the triumph. Not because it was perfect, pain-free, or easy. But because she had stayed connected to herself.

Her fear hadn't disappeared. But it had softened.

Another woman who reshaped how I understood all of this was Kate—a first-time mum who came to me carrying something heavy but hard to name. She kept saying, "It's not the pain I'm scared of." And it wasn't. What she was really afraid of was failing.

But even that word—*failing*—didn't fully hold what she was feeling. It wasn't just fear of things going wrong. It was fear of losing control. Of not measuring up. Of being seen as somehow less than.

That hit me hard, because I've seen that same quiet doubt in so many women. This idea that if birth doesn't go to plan, they've failed—as if their worth as a mother hangs on how "well" they give birth.

Kate's fear wasn't rooted in her body. It was rooted in something deeper: the fear of being powerless in a moment that's supposed to belong to her.

The turning point came during a conversation with her partner. He asked gently, "What would failing even look like to you?"

Kate paused, really thinking about it. Then she looked up and said quietly, "It's not that I'm afraid to fail. I'm afraid of feeling like I have no control."

From that moment on, everything shifted. We built a plan that wasn't about ticking every box or chasing the perfect birth. It was about making space for her voice. Centring her choices. Focusing on how she *wanted* to feel—strong, informed, involved.

Kate didn't enter labour without fear. But she walked into it prepared. Grounded. In her power.

What I saw in Kate, I've seen again and again—in so many different forms. The worry looks different, but the pattern is familiar.

It's human nature to think ahead and start second-guessing what's to come. But those doubts don't have to run the show. Sometimes what we call fear is actually something else—a signal, not a warning. It might show up as nerves or hesitation, but underneath, it's asking you to slow down. To pay closer attention.

It's easy to confuse the two. Fear is loud and chaotic. It pushes you into worst-case scenarios and makes everything feel urgent. But that deeper voice—the one worth listening to—is usually quieter. It feels calm, clear, grounded. It doesn't rush. Even when it's asking you to face something uncomfortable, it does it with steady conviction —that's intuition, not fear.

So instead of trying to silence the noise, try to sort through it.
Ask: *What is this really about?*

That's where trust begins—not in having all the answers, but in being willing to listen for the right questions. You'll start to tell the difference. That's where real confidence begins.

And even when the nerves show up (because they naturally will), what matters most is what we do next.

We name what's scary. We keep going anyway. We trust that we're stronger than we think—even when the path feels messy and uncertain. But strength doesn't just appear. We build it.

And that's exactly what we're about to do.

I've seen what makes the biggest difference for women heading into birth. It's not luck. It's preparation.

Not the vague "just go with the flow" approach because let's be real, you wouldn't just wing your wedding day—and birth deserves way more intention and attention. I'm talking about deep, deliberate preparation—the kind that puts the power and the plan back in your hands.

That's what The Essential 10 is: a straight-talking guide to getting yourself ready—mentally, physically, emotionally, spiritually, with your support crew, and for anything else this wild birth journey throws your way. Ready? Let's go.

CHAPTER 7

The Essential 10 - Foundations for an Empowering Birth

"Success is where preparation and opportunity meet."
— Bobby Unser

We've finally made it—The Essential 10.
If you've read this far, you've walked with me through some big stuff. I know it's been heavy in places (necessary, but heavy). So let's take a breath together.

This next part? It's the good stuff we've been building toward. The part where we shift from unpacking the past to what you can actually *do* to feel supported, prepared, and empowered as you move toward birth.

You might be thinking, *"Do? What can I actually do?"* I get it—I asked the same thing when I first started this work. Birth felt like this wild, unpredictable thing, and I couldn't see how anyone could possibly prepare for something that seems so out of your hands.

But over time, after supporting hundreds of women through pregnancy and birth, something became really clear: the women who walked away from birth feeling strong—really strong—were the ones who had done the work. Not just the practical prep, but the emotional work too. The inner work. The kind that asks you to look at what you're carrying, get honest about how you want to show up—and what you really need to make this birth yours.

A lot of these women had lived through something heavy—grief, trauma, anxiety, disconnection. Some had really shaky starts to motherhood or felt like their bodies had let them down in the past. And yet, when the moment came, they met it with a kind of strength and calm that didn't come from luck. It came from intention.

They didn't cross their fingers and hope it would all work out. They showed up for themselves before the birth even began. They reached for tools. They asked for support. They created space to feel, process, and prepare. And I watched as they leaned into certain themes—mindsets, practices, pillars—that helped hold them steady when things got big.

This wasn't a one-off thing. I saw it again and again. In birth rooms. In conversations. In those raw, beautiful debriefs where women shared what helped and what didn't. In the little moments that sneak up on you and stay with you for years.

Eventually, the pattern was too clear to ignore. These weren't just helpful ideas. They weren't just "extras" or optional bonuses. These were the things that helped women move through birth feeling calm, connected, and in their power—even when things didn't go exactly to plan.

That's when I started calling them *The Essential 10*. They're not a checklist. They're not a formula. But they're real. They're solid. And they've made a difference—for women I've supported, and in my own births too.

You've already seen little glimpses of them woven through these pages. Now we're going to take a closer look—so you can see how each one can support you as you prepare for what's next.

They are: Safety, Intuition, Oxytocin, Continuity of Care, Doula Support, Therapeutic Healing, Community, Mind–Body Connection, Birth Planning, and Resilience.

And because I'm all about keeping it real, you'll find real-life stories sprinkled throughout—stories from women I've supported, births I've witnessed, experiences that were shared with me, and moments from my own journey too. I leaned on these essentials in a big way during my second and third births. Honestly, I don't think I would've had the experiences I did without them. Now I get to pass them on to you. And that feels pretty special. Let's dive in.

Safety

She'd planned a home birth—because all her friends had. But hours into pushing, something wasn't shifting. The room was warm, quiet, supportive, but her body was holding back. The midwife suggested a transfer. As soon as she walked into the hospital room, her shoulders softened. Her eyes met mine, and for the first time, I saw her settle. Within the hour, her baby was born. Safety had never been about the setting—it was about how she felt inside it.

Safety is personal.

It's what lives inside you, around you, and holds you steady when everything else feels big.

It's the feeling that lets your body exhale and do what it knows how to do.

Intuition

At her 36-week appointment, the midwife said everything looked perfect. Baby was in position, heartbeat strong—no concerns. "I'll see you in a few weeks," the midwife said. She nodded, smiled, thanked her—then walked out feeling unsettled. Not panicked. Just… off.

That night, she repacked the hospital bag she'd already packed twice. Added extra snacks. Changed clothes three times before bed. She told her partner, "I don't know why, but I think I need to be ready."

Her waters broke at 4 a.m.

By 6 a.m., contractions were strong.

By 9 a.m., she was holding her baby.

No signs, no warnings. Just a feeling.

That's Intuition. It's the quiet nudge you can't explain, but you know it's there.

A whisper in your gut that says, "pay attention." It's not guesswork. It's a remembering.

A knowing that doesn't wait for permission.

Oxytocin

She was swaying by the bed, lights low, music humming softly. Her partner was rubbing her back with slow, steady hands. Every few minutes, he'd whisper something—small, tender things: "You've got this." "You're amazing." "I love you."

The monitor showed what we already knew: her contractions were growing stronger, closer, more rhythmic. No one rushed her. No one hovered. And in that quiet, undisturbed space, labour unfolded like a wave rolling in.

That's oxytocin.

Not just a hormone—a rhythm. The quiet current behind it all. It rises in calm. It disappears under pressure. And when we let it flow, that's when the magic happens.

Continuity of Care

At her final antenatal appointment, the same warm smile was waiting—the one that had been there since week twelve. The same midwife who remembered her daughter's name.

The same voice, steady and present in labour.

"You're doing beautifully," she said softly.

And the woman believed her—because trust had already been built.

That's continuity.

Not about titles. Not about perfection. It's about someone who knows you. Your story. Your hopes. Your fears. And shows up—again and again.

Doula Support

The room was starting to fill—the midwives checking monitors, someone adjusting an IV, voices moving fast. Her eyes went wide. "I can't do this," she whispered.

Her doula knelt beside her, took her hand, and met her gaze.

"You already are."

One slow breath together. Then another. The chaos faded. She found her rhythm again.

That's what doulas do.

She's there for one reason: you.

Not to give you power, but to remind you it was always yours.

When you say, "I couldn't have done it without her," what you really mean is:

"I did it. She just helped me remember I could."

Therapeutic Healing

It started as a passing thought—maybe I should talk to someone. As the due date crept closer, the thought got louder. Old fears. Unspoken grief. Things she hadn't yet dared to say out loud, even in her own mind.

One night, after another wave of emotion hit out of nowhere, she booked the session. Just one. But it was a start.

Therapeutic healing doesn't mean having it all figured out.

It's giving yourself a soft place to land.

A moment to exhale.

A reminder that healing isn't a finish line—it's a kindness you offer yourself along the way.

Community

She was the first in her group of friends to get pregnant. Her family lived hours away. Her partner tried, but he didn't fully understand the emotions she was moving through. Then one night, wide awake at 2 a.m., she posted in an online forum:

"Anyone else feel like they're falling apart for no reason?"

Replies came within minutes.

"Same."

"Totally normal."

"You're not alone."

She cried reading them. Not from sadness—but relief.

That's community. It wraps around you quietly, showing up when you least expect it but most need it.

Mind-Body Connection

Every night before bed, she practiced breathwork and visualisation. Not because she thought it would make labour easy—but because it made her feel present.

During labour, when contractions surged and doubt crept in, she closed her eyes, went to her safe place, and breathed the way she had in her bedroom. Her shoulders dropped. Her jaw softened. She wasn't trying to escape it anymore—she was with it.

Your mind speaks. Your body answers.

In birth, they move as one. Your role is to embrace it and listen.

Birth Plan

She almost skipped writing one. "Birth plans never go to plan," everyone said.

But something nudged her to do it anyway. Sitting at the kitchen table late one night, she wrote it—not as a list of demands, but as a list of what mattered. The small things. The big things. The things that made her feel calm, safe, and seen.

When labour took a sharp left turn, the plan didn't stop the detour. But she knew what it all meant, and she was part of the choices she made.

That's the power.

Your birth plan is not a script.

It's a voice.

A way to say: this matters to me.

It won't control the twists and turns,

But it gives you something solid to stand on when things shift.

Resilience

After what happened last time, birthing again felt impossible. But here she was: pregnant, afraid, and determined to do things differently.

She hired support. She spoke up sooner. She shook through parts of her labour. She cried through others. But she never backed out. And when she held her baby she didn't say, "I wasn't scared." She said, "I did it—even though I was."

Resilience is not loud.

It's not perfect.

It's choosing to keep going even when the outcome feels uncertain.

You bend, but you don't break.

That's resilience.

And now you've met them—or at least had a taste of them—the pillars that have stood steady for so many women, through so many birth journeys. They didn't come from theory. They didn't come from textbooks. They came alive through real women, real experiences, real births.

As you explore them, I want you to think: *Does this speak to me? Could this help me on my path?* Some will instantly feel right, like they were always meant for you. Others might not fit right now—and that's completely fine.

This isn't about applying all ten to "get it right." That's not how this works. What makes these pillars special is that even just one or two can create real change. I've seen it, time and time again. When women lean into even a few of these elements, their journey shifts in powerful, unexpected ways.

Along the way you'll find reflective practices too, so you can figure out what works for *you*, in your own way, on your own terms.

This is your journey. You get to choose what you take with you.

And if there's one place to begin, it's with safety—the kind that tells you *you're held here*. Not just physically, but emotionally, spiritually, completely supported. Because only when you feel truly secure can your body soften, can you open, can you move through this.

From there, everything starts.

Let's take that first step, together.

CHAPTER 8

Safety - Redefining Safety in Childbirth

"Whenever and however you give birth, your experience will impact your emotions, your mind, your body, and your spirit for the rest of your life."
—Ina May Gaskin

In the middle of the chaos of the 60s and 70s—when the world felt loud, uncertain, and divided—there was this gentle man in a cardigan who quietly became a source of comfort for millions of children. Fred Rogers, the creator of Mister Rogers' Neighbourhood—a long-running American children's show known for its warmth and honesty—understood something powerful. Kids don't just need entertainment. They need to know they're safe, even when the world around them isn't. Emotionally safe. His show was the opposite of what we see on screens today. It was slow, calm, and full of reassurance. He'd look into the camera and say, "I like you just the way you are," and somehow, you believed him.

He didn't shy away from the hard stuff either and he did it with such care that it made children feel seen and protected.

There's a reason Mister Rogers felt so comforting. He created safety—not by fixing things, but by acknowledging them, gently and honestly. And in many ways, that's exactly what women need in birth too. Not just for things to "go to plan," but to feel like they're seen, supported, and held—emotionally, physically, spiritually. Because just like children navigating a big, uncertain world, women in labour aren't just looking for outcomes. They're looking for safety they can feel.

WHAT DOES SAFETY MEAN TO YOU?

Take a moment. Your answer will be different to mine. It's different for everyone.

I've asked this question more times than I can count—in birth prep classes, in whispered conversations, and in the unspoken moments when a woman's eyes search the room for this. Sometimes women know straight away: "I need to feel listened to." "I need to trust myself in this." Other times, they sit with it for a while.

I've witnessed all kinds of births over the years—calm ones, chaotic ones, fast ones, and ones that took days. And through it all, one truth keeps rising to the surface:

When something in her doesn't feel right—when her body is bracing, her breath is shallow, her energy scattered— birth feels harder than it needs to be—her body is telling us she doesn't feel safe anymore.

But when the tension lifts, when she starts to exhale and sink into herself, something else begins to unfold. I've seen it happen—not just physically, but deep in her bones. It's not something you can measure or chart. It's in the way her shoulders soften, the way her eyes stop scanning the room and she starts turning inward. That shift—that quiet returning to herself—is what real safety looks like.

It's in that quiet moment when she no longer needs to ask, Is this okay?—because something inside her already knows: You're held. You're okay.

And it doesn't always happen in the places you'd expect. Not always in the softly lit rooms with the birth ball and fairy lights. Sometimes it happens under fluorescent lights, with machines beeping in the background and the hum of a hospital corridor just outside the door.

Because safety isn't always about the space—it's about what's happening inside her. I saw that truth come to life in a birth I'll never forget—one of the first I ever attended as a doula.

I supported a mother planning a VBAC (vaginal birth after caesarean). Her first birth had been what we call a "cascade of interventions"—one intervention leading to the next until she was in theatre, disconnected and disappointed. She didn't just carry the scar of a surgical birth; she carried a belief that her body had failed her. As we worked together, that belief began to shift. She started to realise that it wasn't her body that failed—it was a system that didn't support her. That reframing gave her new strength. She was a quiet woman. Soft-spoken, gentle—not someone you'd expect to roar in labour. But when the time came, she did. It wasn't chaos—it was instinct. A fierce, guttural sound that didn't come from fear, but from power. She laboured at home first, and the moment I walked in, she let out this deep, releasing sigh—like just having someone there who believed in her made it safer to let go.

When we got to the hospital, everything changed.

With every surge, she began to chant: "Mama, mama." Over and over again. It was primal and beautiful.

I found out afterward that she was calling for her own mother, who had passed away years earlier. That was her anchor. Her safety. Not the hospital. Not me. Not a plan. But that deep, instinctive reaching for love.

That birth reminded me that safety can come from places we don't expect. It can be a person, a memory, a word, or a feeling. It doesn't have to make sense to anyone else. It only has to feel true to her.

And while that experience was powerful, it was also rare. Because for many women—especially in clinical settings—that kind of deep, personal safety doesn't just emerge.

It has to be fought for.

Not because they're not capable of finding it, but because it's hard to stay inward when the space around them keeps pulling them out.

I've seen that play out in so many different ways. But here's what I've learned: most of the time, the environment doesn't create safety—she does. Often in spite of the space, not because of it.

Now, don't get me wrong—I'm not here to bash hospitals. Okay, maybe just a little... but let me explain myself.

It's not that safety can't exist in those settings—it absolutely can. But the space itself doesn't exactly make it easy. Sterile rooms. Harsh lighting. Strangers walking in and out with clipboards. Language that makes women feel like visitors in their own experience. It all adds up. And without the right kind of presence—without someone anchoring her—it's easy for a woman to feel like birth is happening around her, not with her.

And the space itself? It often mirrors that disconnect.

Before a word is spoken or a hand is laid, the environment is already speaking. And most of the time, it's not saying: *You're safe here.*

The décor? Honestly, it hasn't changed much since the early 2000s—same blank walls, same stiff chairs, same generic art that looks like it was stolen from a dentist's office. The only real update? The monitors beep louder.

Then there's the gear. Foetal monitors. IV poles. Metal trays of instruments. Screens blinking out data. Nothing is hidden. It's all right there, front and centre. Women see it. They might not name it, but they feel it—that quiet message running beneath it all: *Birth is something to be managed. Measured. Controlled.*

And when the equipment becomes the focus—not the woman—it's no surprise that something important gets lost. Her ease. Her presence. Her sense of ownership in the space.

I remember once walking down a hospital corridor after a birth, off to grab the mum something to eat. On the wall, hanging like it belonged in a gallery, was a large self-portrait of a senior obstetrician—grinning, holding up a pair of forceps like a trophy.

I don't know about you, but that's not exactly the kind of thing that makes my ovaries feel warm and fuzzy.

It was a reminder—loud and clear—of what's been celebrated in those spaces... and what hasn't. Not women's bodies that's for sure.

Still, in Australia at least, hospital birth remains the norm for most. Around 97% of women give birth there.

And whether that choice comes from trust, habit, pressure, or lack of other options, the space is often already set. But here's the thing—while you might not be able to change the room, you *can* prepare for how you feel inside it.

That's where your power is. You don't have to control every detail. You just need to know what helps you feel steady.

Is it the scent in the room? A song that calms your body? Something from home that grounds you—soft lighting, a photo, a familiar texture? A birth partner who knows how to hold space? Because the real work isn't about creating the perfect space—it's about shaping one that reflects *you*. And that starts with letting go of what safety is *supposed* to look like, and owning what it actually feels like for you.

And once you're in that space—your space—it's easy to assume you have to keep it all together. Be calm. Be quiet. Be still. But birth doesn't work like that. It moves. It builds. It surges, softens, swells again.

So maybe safety isn't about staying composed. Maybe it's about having full permission to do what your body needs—To move how you want. To make noise. To fall apart and find your way back again. To speak up, change your mind, be messy, be human. Be unedited.

Because feeling safe doesn't always look peaceful. There's no one formula. No universal blueprint.

We're told safety at birth looks a certain way—like essential oils and affirmations.

But honestly? Sometimes, it looks like dirty jokes, loud music, and a midwife who doesn't flinch when you swear. So maybe the real work isn't matching someone else's idea of safety. Maybe it's being radically honest about what *you* need—even if it's not what anyone else expects.

Whatever it is, honour it. Own it. Make space for it.

Because when a woman feels safe, she taps into a strength she didn't even know she had. The quietest among us can roar when the space allows it. That's what safety makes possible.

So, take the time to ask yourself what safety means to you. Trust that your instincts are wise, and your body knows the way. Because it does. And you do.

And once you've created that safety—once the noise quiets and the fear softens—you can hear something else. That inner voice. The one that's been there all along, whispering what you need, guiding you towards what feels right.

In the next chapter, we'll explore that voice—your intuition—and how to trust it, especially when the world tells you to second-guess it.

EXPLORING YOUR SENSE OF SAFETY

Inner Work: Tuning Inward

Use these questions to explore what safety really means to you so you can shape a birth environment that feels grounded and right for you.

---

1. What does safety feel like to you?

- ☞ Think back to a time when you felt completely safe—physically, emotionally, or both. Where were you? Who was with you? What made that moment feel secure?
- ☞ Try to describe the *feeling*, not just the situation. Did your body relax? Did your breath slow down? Did you feel held, seen, or protected?
- ☞ Understanding how safety feels in your body can help you recognise and recreate it in your birth space.

---

2. What helps you feel physically safe during birth?

- ☞ Do you feel more at ease in a quiet, private space or with people around you?
- ☞ What physical elements—lighting, sounds, smells, help you soften and relax?
- ☞ How do you feel about medical support? Does a hands-off approach help you relax, or do you feel more grounded knowing medical options are available if needed?

3. **What helps you feel emotionally safe?**

    ☞ What kind of emotional support grounds you?
    ☞ Is it being fully informed, having a calm presence beside you, or knowing you can express yourself freely?

4. **How do you respond when things feel out of control?**

    ☞ When you feel vulnerable or overwhelmed, what helps bring you back to centre?
    ☞ What anchors or practices help restore your sense of calm and control?

5. **What fears or anxieties do you hold around birth?**

    ☞ Name them honestly. Where do they come from?
    ☞ What might help ease those fears and create more space for trust?

6. **Who helps you feel anchored and cared for?**

    ☞ Who do you want by your side during birth?
    ☞ Who helps you feel emotionally safe, steady, and truly seen?

7. **How will you communicate your needs during labour?**

☞ Do you feel confident speaking up?
☞ What would help you feel heard and respected by your care team?

Action Steps: Applying Your Insights

Create your space

Whether you're birthing at home, in a birthing centre, or hospital, shape the space to support your calm. Consider lighting, scents, sound, privacy, and the overall energy of the room.

Choose your people

Surround yourself with those who help you feel emotionally safe—your partner, doula, midwife, or trusted family members.

Name your needs

Talk with your care team about what matters to you. Share your values. Speak up if something doesn't feel right—your voice matters.

Plan for the unexpected

Think about what will help you stay grounded if things shift. It might be breathwork, a mantra, a memory, or someone holding your hand and reminding you: *you're safe*.

KIMMY'S STORY

Kimmy's first birth, with her daughter, Amity, was nothing like she had hoped or imagined it to be. At the time, she was in a toxic and emotionally abusive marriage, which left her feeling unsupported and disconnected. While Kimmy knew that her pregnancy and birth with Amity would be challenging—due to her endometriosis and three broken vertebrae in her lower spine from a car accident nearly 10 years earlier—nothing could have prepared her for what was to come during the birth, or for how the cascade of interventions left her feeling like control over her body had quietly slipped away.

Kimmy's labour with Amity was filled with challenges. It began with an artificial rupture of membranes, which led to Amity not descending properly. An epidural followed, and eventually, an episiotomy was performed. By then, Amity's heart rate had started dropping dangerously low and wasn't recovering between contractions.

Kimmy felt powerless, as though all control and decision-making had slipped out of her hands. She loved the idea of birth and just wanted to hold her baby in her arms—but after nearly 40 hours of labour, she was left with both emotional and physical scars.

She still remembers the sting of her now ex-husband leaving shortly after the birth to celebrate with friends, adding to the sense of abandonment and hurt that lingered long after that day.

5 years later, Kimmy found herself in a loving and supportive relationship with her new partner, Dan. When she became pregnant with her second baby girl, she was determined to have a completely different experience. Kimmy committed to preparing for a birth that would heal her past trauma and leave her feeling empowered, to be able to rewrite her birth experience. She chose a team of midwives she trusted and felt connected to and hired myself as her doula initially to provide emotional support to Dan, however, he didn't need my support, especially as the labour intensified and Kimmy needed more from her birth team.

Dan was amazing in holding space for Kimmy to be able to bring their baby into the world. He was everything Kimmy needed him to be, and this allowed the birthing team to be what Kimmy needed for her.

Feeling supported in this way gave Kimmy the space to focus on her own preparation.

She approached her second birth with a deep sense of purpose. She practiced HypnoBirthing®, which helped her redevelop a strong mind-body connection and trust in the birthing process and her body.

She also worked on physical preparation, regularly visiting an osteopath and a pelvic floor osteopath to ensure her physical body was ready. Emotionally, Kimmy revisited the trauma of Amity's birth, sharing her story with Dan as a way to process and heal. She also debriefed her story with her midwives and me, so we all knew what she was aiming to get out of this birth, which was a more supported, more loving, more calm, more connected labour and birth.

She was mindful to surround herself with positive birth stories and filled her mind with affirmations, empowering videos, and images of the birth she wanted. She created a peaceful and welcoming environment in her home, transforming her bedroom and ensuite into a calm, welcoming sanctuary. With fairy lights, affirmations, and her favourite playlist, and a diffuser emanating the scent with Clary Sage.

The space reflected her vision for the birth she wanted. That night after setting it up, she wrote a heartfelt letter to her unborn baby, giving herself permission to welcome her baby into the world on her own terms.

Early the next morning, Kimmy woke up to find her waters had started to come away. She alerted her midwife and me and she began the day with a sense of calm anticipation. She even found time to nest in her own unique way, preparing snacks for friends and organising her home, a reflection of her grounded and calm mindset. As mild contractions began, she leaned into her preparations. She walked around her neighbourhood with Dan, soaking in the fresh air and keeping her body moving.

As labour intensified, Kimmy's support team gathered around her. Dan, I, and her midwives were present, each playing a vital role in holding space for her. Her ten-year-old daughter Amity and Dan's mum Carole were also present for almost all of it, bringing a beautiful sense of connection and continuity to the experience. It created a full circle moment. She leaned on her team, Dan, me, and her midwives who supported her every step of the way. She moved instinctively, using abdominal lifts and squats to help her body move and to assist with labour progress. At one point, when the possibility of transferring to a hospital was mentioned, Kimmy looked to me for reassurance. With calm determination, she declared, "I'm not going to the hospital," and her team rallied around her, affirming her strength.

As labour progressed, Kimmy experienced a powerful moment of connection. She described it as stepping into the universe to bring her baby earthside. She felt surrounded by the strength of all the women who had come before her. This deep sense of connection carried her through the final stages of labour. Moving into the bath, which in this moment, was a birthing pool, Kimmy surrendered fully to the process. With Dan by her side and her team providing calm, steady support, she birthed her daughter, Sadie Darling, into her arms and was held with such gratitude.

Kimmy's home birth was deeply healing and empowering. It was everything her first birth was not, peaceful, transformative, and filled with love. She often reflects on how life-changing it was, saying, "If every woman had the kind of birth I had with Sadie, no one would give birth in a hospital unless absolutely necessary."

CHAPTER 9

Intuition - Listening to Your Inner Guide

"The only real valuable thing is intuition."
— *Albert Einstein*

Before we dive into how intuition shows up in birth, I want to take you somewhere unexpected — into the mind of Albert Einstein.

Yes, that Einstein. The one known for his wild hair, complex theories, and genius-level thinking. But what many people don't realise is that some of his greatest breakthroughs didn't begin with logic — they began with intuition.

As a teenager, Einstein imagined himself riding on a beam of light, exploring the nature of time and space. No equations. No data. Just a vision that lived in his mind long before it lived on paper.

He once said, "The only real valuable thing is intuition." And for him, it truly was. He trusted that inner voice — the one that nudges you towards something long before you can explain it. The numbers came later. The insight came first.

And if someone like Einstein, who lived and breathed science, trusted his gut — why shouldn't we?

Einstein trusted his intuition to unlock the mysteries of the universe. I wasn't exactly trying to bend the laws of physics—but something similar was happening inside me. That same quiet inner knowing began to stir long before I ever stepped into labour.

When I was getting ready to have my first baby, there was a moment that's never really left me. My husband and I were out to dinner with his parents. Nothing dramatic. Just a quiet, familiar restaurant and the kind of evening that's meant to feel normal. But somewhere in the middle of small talk and comfort food, something shifted in me. I suddenly felt off—uneasy in a way that didn't make sense.

It wasn't physical. It wasn't about the baby or labour signs. It was deeper. Not a Braxton Hicks in sight. No dramatic movie moment where my water breaks in a fancy restaurant and someone yells "Call an ambulance!" Just me, my gnocchi, and a rising sense of something I couldn't quite name.

A kind of internal tightening. A whisper inside that said, *Something's not right.*

I'd felt it before—years earlier. That same quiet dread that used to creep in when I was younger, especially at night, especially when things felt uncertain. Back then, I didn't have space to sit with it. I just pushed it down and carried on. And that's what I did that night too.

I quietly excused myself, went to the bathroom, and stood there looking at myself in the mirror. I could feel the pressure building. But instead of asking myself what I needed or giving space to whatever was rising, I told myself to hold it together. There wasn't time to fall apart. I was about to become a mother. I needed to be strong. Because apparently the bathroom of a suburban Italian restaurant was not the place for an emotional breakthrough—who knew? So, I pulled myself back into line, fixed my face, and walked back out as if nothing had happened.

But something had happened.

At the time, I didn't have the language for it. I wouldn't have called it intuition. I wouldn't have said, *my body's trying to tell me something.* But that's exactly what was going on. My inner voice was nudging me, gently but clearly, asking me to stop and pay attention. It was pointing me towards something unprocessed, something real. I just wasn't ready to hear it yet.

That moment wasn't about panic. It wasn't even really about fear. It was about a part of me trying to speak—and me doing what I had always done: quieting it so I could keep going.

Only now—after years of motherhood, experience, and doing this work—can I truly see it for what it was. A moment of instinct. A moment of inner knowing.

My intuition wasn't broken—it was loud and clear. I just hadn't learned how to listen to it yet. And that's the thing: our intuition doesn't always come in with fanfare or clarity. Sometimes, it shows up as discomfort. Or tension. Or a quiet sense that something's off. We don't always know what it means right away, but it's still worth noticing. Especially in moments where we're about to cross thresholds—like birth, like motherhood, like anything that changes us.

When I reflect on it now, I wonder—if I had paused long enough to listen, would I have felt more ready? More grounded? I'll never know.

But here's what I do know: our intuition is powerful. It's always there, even when we choose to ignore it.

You've probably felt it too—that quiet voice, that strange gut feeling that nudges you when something just isn't right. We call it women's intuition, but really, it's a kind of deep inner wisdom.

The hard part? We're taught to silence it. We tell ourselves we're overthinking, being dramatic, or just worrying too much. But intuition isn't "just noise." It knows more than we realise.

Over the years, I've seen how intuition plays a role in the decisions women make, especially during pregnancy, birth, and postpartum. Many women have the experience of meeting highly recommended medical care providers who seemed to do and say all the right things—yet something about the interaction just didn't sit right. That gut feeling told them this wasn't the person they wanted to guide them through their birth. Sometimes they listened to that voice; sometimes they didn't. But the voice was always there, trying to steer them towards what was right for them.

Maya was one of those women. As a nurse, she was trained to trust evidence over instinct—logic over feeling. So when she became pregnant with her first child, she approached it methodically: researching, planning, and choosing a well-recommended obstetrician. Everything looked fine on paper. But something didn't feel right.

It wasn't that anything was blatantly wrong—her doctor was well-known and admired, her tests were normal, and her pregnancy was progressing smoothly. And yet, deep in her gut, a quiet unease stirred. She couldn't explain why, but each time she left an appointment, she felt disconnected from her own experience, like she was just going through the motions rather than actively participating in the journey of bringing her baby into the world.

One evening, Maya found herself unable to sleep. Lying in bed, she placed her hands over her belly and thought to herself, What am I missing? A wave of emotion washed over her, and in that moment, she knew: she needed to shift something. She didn't have a logical reason, no medical emergency prompting a change—just an undeniable inner knowing that the path she was on wasn't the right one. Despite her discomfort with making a decision based purely on intuition, she listened. At 30 weeks pregnant, she sought out a midwifery-led practice and a doula for support. It felt like stepping into unfamiliar territory, but from her very first conversation with her new team, something inside her settled. She felt seen, heard, and truly involved in her own care for the first time. Over the next few weeks, that feeling only deepened. She began to feel more grounded in her decisions, more connected to her body, and more trusting of the process ahead.

When labour began, there was no rush, no pressure—just space. Space to move, to listen, to be with what was happening. Her team supported her without interfering, reminding her to trust her body and follow her instincts.

As the hours passed, she stayed grounded—even with the growing intensity. Then, just as she was reaching the point of pushing — which lasted for several hours — she felt a strong, undeniable urge to shift positions. Even though her support team reassured her that the position she was in was fine, something deep within her said otherwise. There was no logical reason, just a knowing. Trusting herself, she moved onto her hands and knees.

In that moment, something changed. Her body responded instinctively, and with a few powerful urges to bear down, her baby arrived — smoothly, powerfully, and completely in her own rhythm.

Maya's logical mind would have questioned that shift. But her body had known. Her intuition had guided her to the exact position she needed.

I've seen this kind of moment more times than I can count—when a woman listens to that quiet pull inside, even when everything around her says to ignore it.

It wasn't a thought—it was embodied knowing. That experience transformed not just how she viewed birth, but how she moved through life—no longer dismissing her inner voice but honouring it as the quiet wisdom it had always been.

What Maya learned is something that shows up more often than you'd think. When we start tuning into our intuition during pregnancy—whether it's a whisper that something feels off, or a pull towards a different kind of support—we lay the foundation for a more connected birth. It's like a muscle. The more we listen, the stronger it gets.

By the time labour begins, we're not strangers to our own inner voice—we've been building a relationship with it. So, when that moment comes—when logic goes quiet and the body speaks—we don't freeze or second-guess. We trust. We move. We listen. And more often than not, the body responds.

Intuition also shows up in powerful ways when we're facing fear or carrying trauma. It becomes a quiet compass—not always loud, but steady. It helps us move through big emotions, protect our energy, and find the people who truly get us.

Sometimes it says: *slow down. You're not behind. You're right where you need to be.*

And in the harder moments—the ones where everything feels too much—it's often your intuition that whispers, *Breathe. Go outside. Call someone. Let it out.*

Sometimes, it just says: *You don't have to carry all of this alone.*

Looking back on that dinner, I know now my intuition was trying to reach me. Not to scare me—but to bring something to the surface. It was asking me to pause, to pay attention, to heal. I didn't listen then. But that moment taught me something. It reminded me that the quiet voice inside me has always been there — waiting, trustworthy.

Years later, during my second pregnancy, my doula said something that has stayed with me ever since.

She told me that when a woman is deeply connected to her intuition during pregnancy, she can tap into it even more powerfully during birth — often sensing if something isn't right with her or her baby long before anyone else in the room does and I think that is so profoundly true.

As women, we have this deep, often unspoken ability to sense what's right for us. Our intuition isn't always dramatic. It doesn't need to be. It's a thread we carry—connecting us to ourselves, to others, and to the truth we may not have words for yet.

Learning to trust it can take time, especially in a world that tells us to put logic first and doubt our instincts. But when we start listening, really listening, we find it's more than a guide. It's a gift.

And when we don't trust our intuition—especially after trauma—it can ripple into so many parts of our experience.

As birth trauma and parenting therapist Phillipa Scott explains so powerfully:

"One of the biggest repercussions associated with previous trauma in birth is the lack of confidence. This comes from several things, including unconscious beliefs held by the woman. Often women take on ideas about themselves when experiencing traumatic events. That traumatic event contributes to how they feel about themselves and their capabilities. Birth requires a woman to dig deep, it requires faith in self and the ability to sit with oneself and have confidence. When women have experienced trauma, they often don't trust their own intuition, which makes leaning into the feelings of birth very difficult. It means that they often look for outside validation and give their authority and power away, because of that lack of trust in self.

When the maternity system isn't designed to empower women, but rather to support them in giving away their power and treat them as though they don't know what they're doing, the issue is compounded. The flow on effect is that in their mothering and in their relationships, they also feel this lack of confidence."

This is why it's not always easy to *'just trust your gut.'*

Trauma can blur the lines between fear and instinct. But when we do begin to trust ourselves again—when we let that quiet inner voice lead—something opens up.

We make space for more than just insight. We make space for connection, for presence, for love.

And that's where oxytocin comes in.

Often called the love hormone—but it's more than that. It's the chemistry of connection, of safety and surrender.

In the next chapter, we'll explore how oxytocin shapes the way we give birth, the way we bond, and the way we feel held—by others, and by ourselves.

CONNECTING WITH YOUR INTUITION FOR BIRTH

Inner Work: Tuning Inward

Use these prompts to explore how your intuition speaks to you and how to trust it through pregnancy, birth, and beyond.

1. **When have you trusted your intuition in the past?**

   ☞ Think of a moment—big or small—when you followed a gut feeling.
   ☞ What happened? What did it teach you about listening to yourself?

2. **How does your body speak to you?**

   ☞ Notice the physical signals you get when something feels right—or off.
   ☞ Do you feel it in your chest, your belly, your breath?
   ☞ How does your body guide you?

3. **What helps you reconnect to your inner knowing?**

   ☞ Are there rituals or practices—like journaling, meditation, quiet walks, or breathwork—that bring you back to yourself?
   ☞ How could you bring more of this into your pregnancy?

4. **What is your intuition saying about your birth?**

- When you slow down and tune in, what are you drawn toward?
- What feels essential to honour in your birth experience?

---

5. **How do you balance intuition with outside advice?**

- Pregnancy often comes with opinions from every direction.
- What helps you hold space for your own voice when advice doesn't align?
- How do you come back to what feels true for *you*?

---

6. **What role does intuition play in your decision-making?**

- How is your intuition guiding the choices you're making for birth—like your plan, your setting, or your care team?
- What helps you know when something feels right for you?

---

7. **How do you navigate the unknown?**

- Birth is unpredictable.
- How can you lean on your intuition when things don't go to plan?
- What helps you stay grounded in those moments?

Action Steps: Strengthening Your Intuition for Birth

Listen to your body

Make space each day to check in. Gentle movement, breathwork, or stillness can help you hear what's underneath the noise.

Set intentions

How do you want to feel during birth? Let your intentions come from your inner wisdom—not external expectations.

Choose people who trust you

Build a support team that respects your instincts. Surround yourself with those who reflect your trust back to you.

Stay flexible

Birth doesn't always follow a script. Trust that your intuition can guide you through the unknown with clarity and calm.

SVENJA'S STORY

Svenja so courageously shared her story with me, and it speaks volumes about the power of intuition and inner knowing. She loved and lost her baby girl, Luna, at birth—and the ripple effects of that trauma, and the depth of grief that followed, shaped a powerful trust in what was to come. Her story is one of love, deep inner wisdom, and immense strength.

> "I'm originally from Germany and moved to Australia almost 23 years ago. My career began in the film industry, but eventually I made a significant change and have been working in natural therapies ever since. I started with remedial and pregnancy massage, and it didn't take long to realise that pregnancy and childbirth were the areas that I felt most connected to and passionate about. Wanting to deepen my knowledge and skills, I pursued acupuncture, focusing again on pregnancy, prenatal, and postnatal care. Yet, despite these advances, it still felt like I was missing something, the most crucial element: the birth itself. This realisation led me to become a doula and childbirth educator, which gave me the opportunity to be part of the entire journey of bringing life into the world.
>
> During this time, I ran my own business, co-founded a natural therapies clinic with a friend in the inner west of Sydney and met my partner, Jason. My work as a doula exposed me to a wide range of experiences. While many were positive and uplifting, others were deeply challenging and stressful. I supported families through early pregnancy losses and accompanied couples to the hospital for experiences that were far from

ideal. Witnessing these challenges reinforced the importance of respectful, compassionate care throughout pregnancy and birth.

Before my firstborn, Luna, I experienced two miscarriages. When I fell pregnant with Luna, I knew immediately that I wanted to give birth at home as the hospital system didn't feel safe to me. Luna wasn't a planned pregnancy, and at the time, I had just started a 350-hour yoga teacher training program, which I continued throughout my pregnancy, finishing at 37 weeks.

Luna was due around Christmas and New Year, which made it a bit more challenging to find a private midwife, as unfortunately, the one I wanted wasn't available during this time. A different midwife agreed to take me on, yet regrettably our relationship wasn't quite right and as connected and trusting as I hoped for, which became increasingly evident, and we parted ways when I was 38 weeks pregnant.

Thankfully, I was able to find a new private midwife, who was everything I needed, and the difference was felt immediately. After my first meeting with her I cried, overwhelmed by what I had missed in my earlier care. She provided the compassion, understanding, and support that I needed during this vulnerable time. Her care and presence made a profound difference not only in my remaining pregnancy but also in my postpartum recovery and mental health.

Although I had been a doula since 2008, being pregnant myself brought so many new insights and challenges. My studies in acupuncture, with one of its emphasis on cycles of life, Qi,

Blood, Yin, and Yang helped me process the unpredictability of pregnancy and birth. As a self-confessed control freak, I don't always like the uncertainties of life, but I was and am still learning to accept them. Preparing for Luna's birth was a deeply intentional process. Beyond attending prenatal yoga classes, I immersed myself in body and breath work as part of my yoga teacher training and also attended a wonderful three-day Shamanic Dimensions of Pregnancy workshop with Jane Hardwicke Collings. During this incredible time, we all sat in circle together and I could deeply connect to my pregnancy, Luna and also explore the impact of my own birth on my life, amongst other things.

Throughout my pregnancy though, I had a persistent feeling that something was not quite right with Luna. Despite reassurances from my care providers and clear test results that everything was fine, I couldn't shake this intuition.

Around 40 weeks, I went into labour with Luna, which progressed smoothly at home lasting six and a half hours. Most of my pushing phase I spent in the birthing pool. At one point, I asked my midwife about possibly using a catheter as I wasn't sure if I had urinated in a while. She suggested moving on to the bed, and as I wanted to lie down, a massive contraction came along. I shifted into a horse stance and a couple of pushes later Luna was born. Jason caught her, but we instantly realised something was wrong. Luna appeared to be born sleeping.

The two midwives acted immediately, giving Luna oxygen and CPR while calling an ambulance. What followed was a disastrous ordeal that added so much more trauma to our already devastating birth. The ambulance took longer than expected to arrive, and when it did, the paramedics didn't instil any confidence in me, in how they handled the situation and treated Luna. Shortly after I arrived at the hospital and was reunited with Jason & Luna, we were put up in a little kitchenette to have some time with her. The hospital called the police, saying that this was their normal procedure. As a result, I had a police officer standing in front of my door continuously and Luna was considered "property of the state coroner". This horrendous treatment would never happen to anyone experiencing a stillbirth in a hospital setting. We were allowed only a few hours with her before we had to hand her over and she was taken from us. The hospitals' actions led to a police investigation, accusations, and immense emotional strain for Jason, me, and the midwives who had supported us. Losing Luna was traumatic in itself, but the added legal and medical challenges compounded the pain immensely.

Six months later, Jason and I were invited to a yoga retreat in Bali by a dear friend who encouraged us to take time to heal. Little did we know that it would be there that we unexpectedly conceived Arlo. His pregnancy became a massive opportunity for healing.

Arlo's pregnancy and birth was a stark contrast to Luna's for so many reasons. One of them being that this time, I was giving birth in a birth centre. My care team included our already trusted private midwives from Luna's birth, plus the birth centre midwives and a maternal foetal specialist. Together, they provided me with the utmost gold-standard care, ensuring I felt safe and supported throughout.

As with Luna, I approached this pregnancy with intention and preparation on all levels: body, mind and spirit. Given her stillbirth though, my awareness and anxiety were obviously heightened. Therefore, spirituality became an even more important aspect of my journey, along with being able to lean on my village of women for emotional support and taking time out for myself and the pregnancy. I connected with Arlo and also myself through taking the time for various practices like yoga, acupuncture, massages, chiropractic care, time in nature, reiki, intuitive communication with him and more.

At 36-37 weeks, we had a meeting with my entire care team—Both my private midwives, my maternal foetal specialist and my primary birth centre midwife—to go through my birth plan in detail. I wanted to ensure that my choices were respected and that I had full autonomy over my experience. I had to sign waivers because I refused continuous monitoring, insisting on the freedom to move and only allowing doppler checks when necessary. I also made it clear that I wouldn't birth in a labour ward. Having these discussions ahead of time gave me confidence, allowing me to focus on labour without the stress of advocating for myself in the moment. In that room, I felt heard, respected, and reassured that my birth would unfold on my terms.

Labour began unexpectedly after a morning swim, a cherished ritual I had also done with Luna. I felt a bit off at the beach and had the urge to go home to have some food. When I got up from our lounge, my waters broke. I started to clean up, so I wouldn't slip on the wet tiles, called my team and packed my bag as I was asked to come in for some monitoring. It was such a special moment as we called my mum overseas and she could hear Arlo's heartbeat with us over the phone. Within the hour I was in established labour cycling through exactly the same labour stations as I did in Luna's birth. Starting on the toilet, moving to the shower, then the bath but ultimately, giving birth on land three and a half hours later, supported by my private and birth centre midwives, Jason and our dear friend Jerusha. At one point, fear and anxiety crept in as I worried about the possibility of losing Arlo too. These thoughts flooded my mind, but one of my midwives seemed to sense what I was feeling, knelt in front of me and said, "I know." Her words validated my fears and allowed me to fully let go.

As I entered the final moments of labour, my midwife physically supported me, holding me up from behind while Jason helped guide Arlo into the world. Even though Arlo arrived crying, I still asked, "Is he okay?" It took a moment for me to trust that he was safe. When they handed him to me, the relief and gratitude I felt were overwhelming. Arlo's birth was a healing experience that reminded me of the strength and courage I carry as a mother and the importance of trusting myself and my intuition.

Looking back, I've learned so much but most importantly, to trust my instincts and prioritise love over fear. Birth is transformative, and even in the face of trauma, we hold incredible strength and wisdom within us. My journey has taught me the value of preparation, community, and deep self-trust. I encourage every woman to find her village, listen to her intuition, and approach birth with the confidence that she already holds everything she needs within her."

CHAPTER 10

Oxytocin – The Love Hormone in Action

"Oxytocin is love. Oxytocin is within you."
— Paul J. Zak

In the late 1970s, neonatal doctors in Bogotá, Colombia faced a crisis. Hospitals were overcrowded, and there weren't enough incubators for the number of premature babies needing care. Without warmth and constant support, these babies were at serious risk— hypothermia, infection, and poor development were taking too many lives. Out of necessity, Dr. Edgar Rey and Dr. Héctor Martínez came up with a different kind of solution: Kangaroo Care.

Instead of relying on machines, they encouraged mothers to hold their premature babies skin-to-skin, tucked against their chests, where the warmth of their own bodies could regulate the baby's temperature and offer continuous care.

At first, kangaroo care was seen as a temporary fix. But the results were remarkable. Babies held skin-to-skin breathed more easily, their heart rates stabilised, and they showed fewer signs of stress. Over time, research confirmed what those doctors had seen firsthand— These physical changes were accompanied by a surge of oxytocin, the 'love hormone,' released in both mother and baby. A powerful force was at work, binding them in ways machines never could.

What started out of urgency has now become standard practice in neonatal care around the world. Kangaroo care is recognised not just for its ability to save lives, but for something just as powerful: its ability to deepen emotional connection. That flood of oxytocin during close, uninterrupted contact doesn't just support survival—it builds love, safety, and trust. The very things that make birth not just bearable, but meaningful.

There's a sacred vulnerability in labour—a moment where a woman's body and soul are cracked open to bring new life into the world. This isn't just about the physical process of birth; it's a deep transformation.

As a baby is born, so is a mother. Mentally, emotionally, spiritually—she expands. She stretches in ways she never has before, stepping into a role that will reshape her forever. On the other side, she holds her baby in her arms, changed, standing at the edge of a new chapter. And while this turning point is undeniably profound, it's also deeply biological—a hormonal dance guiding her through the process. At the heart of it all is oxytocin—often called the "love hormone," but that barely scratches the surface. Oxytocin is the thread that runs through it all: the contractions, the connection, the surrender. It's the hormone of love, yes—but also of power, presence, and deep physiological change.

Dr. Sarah Buckley, author of *Gentle Birth, Gentle Mothering* and *The Hormonal Physiology of Childbearing*, calls oxytocin *"one of the most important and best-studied hormones"*. She explains, *"Oxytocin was first discovered as a hormone that promotes a fast (oxy) birth (tocin). We now know that oxytocin is also important for other aspects of reproduction in all mammals, including sexual activity, labour and birth, and maternal behaviours and bonding."*

That's what the research tells us. But how do you make that real—something that actually lands in a childbirth class?

How do I explain the importance of this hormone—this quiet force behind labour—to the partners sitting in front of me, some half-engaged, clearly unsure why they're even there? They fidget, glance at their phones, and I can almost hear their inner dialogue: *Why am I here? What does this have to do with me?* And I get it. At the birth, they figure their job is to hold a leg, fetch a sandwich, maybe say *"you're doing amazing, sweetie"* once or twice—like a coach in a Netflix drama—and otherwise try not to faint. What could they possibly offer? This is her gig, right? But that's before they understand what oxytocin is really doing. Until then, it just sounds like another science term. But it's not. It's the heartbeat of the whole journey—from conception to birth to bonding. And that's what I try to show them. It's a love story—one that's been present from the very beginning of this baby's life. It's the thread that weaves through connection, creation, and becoming a parent. And who doesn't want to hear about that?

So, I start there. I explain that oxytocin has been a part of this journey all along. Whether this baby was conceived through lovemaking, assisted reproduction like IVF, or brought into the family through other loving paths, oxytocin played a role. It's the hormone that builds trust, deepens emotional closeness, and helps sustain life in the womb. And as labour approaches, oxytocin steps forward again, ready to guide the birthing process.

But here's the part that lights people up—this mother has the power to influence one of the most vital hormones in her body. Not through effort or willpower, but by leaning into what makes her feel good. Together, we explore how oxytocin isn't just something the body releases—it's something she can gently invite in.

It rises when she feels safe. When she's wrapped in warmth, held with kindness, or simply not rushed. Oxytocin flows best in calm, connected spaces—in quiet moments where she feels loved and seen. A soft light. A familiar voice. Music that soothes her nervous system. Laughter that breaks the tension. The hush of being emotionally held.

This isn't about doing more. It's about allowing more of what helps her soften.

That's when partners begin to see their role differently. They realise they're not just there to witness birth—they're helping shape the space it unfolds in and influencing how it unfolds within her. Their presence, words, and actions help shape her sense of safety—and with it, her body's ability to release more oxytocin.

That's when we start looking at the other side of the coin: how stress and fear can slow things down, how labour can stall when the nervous system shifts into fight or flight. From there, I introduce what I call the *'oxytocin toolkit'*—ways to support her nervous system, bring her back to centre, and help labour flow.

I've seen the power of this firsthand.

Years ago, I supported a client whose pregnancy had taken a sharp and unexpected turn in the final weeks. She'd developed pre-eclampsia that progressed into HELLP syndrome, a rare and serious complication. Her birth needed to be highly medicalised, carefully managed, and closely monitored. This wasn't the birth she had imagined, and by the time labour began, she was already moving through it with a heightened sense of vulnerability.

The hospital room was full—machines, monitors, staff moving in and out, updates being delivered in clipped clinical language. The midwives weren't unkind, but they were focused on risk, on protocol. At one point, they spoke directly over her body about possible complications, using terms that were cold and frightening. I watched her face change. Her whole body tensed. Her blood pressure spiked. The baby's heart rate started to fluctuate. The monitors told the story clearly: her nervous system was moving into fight-or-flight.

And then, we stepped in—her husband and I. Gently, we brought her back. He held her hand. I whispered steadying words. We rubbed her back, stayed close, softened the space with presence and warmth. Within minutes, we saw the shift. Her breath deepened. Her shoulders dropped. The monitors settled. Her blood pressure came down. The baby's heart rate returned to a reassuring pattern.

That moment said everything: who is in the room, and how they speak, touch, and respond—it all matters. It's not just about comfort. It's about chemistry. The body listens closely to its environment. Oxytocin and adrenaline are like the hormonal equivalent of oil and water—they don't mix. One says *relax, we've got this*, the other yells *run!*

What she needed wasn't to feel more in control—it was to stay in oxytocin, not be pulled into adrenaline.

I share this story often in my classes. And when I do, I watch the shift. I see eyes lift from phones, bodies lean in. The partners in the room start to feel it. Now they see it—they have more presence, more influence, more of a role in birth than they ever realised.

It's not just about being there. It's about how they show up. And with that comes purpose. They're listening now. They're curious. Something clicks.

They begin to understand—it's not just comfort, it's hormonal. The way they speak, touch, and respond can actually shape the hormonal landscape of birth. That's when I connect the dots more deeply—explaining how in labour oxytocin acts like a rhythm builder, each surge strengthening contractions and bringing the baby closer. As Dr. Buckley describes, *"During labour and birth, oxytocin is released from the brain into the bloodstream, and it travels to the uterus where it promotes the rhythmic contractions of labour. At the same time, oxytocin is also released into the brain, where it helps the labouring female by fostering calm and connection as well as providing natural pain relief."*

But its work doesn't end there. It's also the hormone behind the euphoric feeling at birth. Oxytocin fills the room when a baby is placed on their mother's chest. That rush of connection—it's not just emotion. It's chemistry in motion. The body's way of saying: *I'm here. I'll take care of you.* A surge of protection and presence—the beginnings of the maternal bond.

I've seen mothers who've just laboured for hours—sweating, shaking, exhausted—suddenly light up with something almost otherworldly. Their eyes shine. Their skin glows. They're flooded with oxytocin, and you can feel it in the air.

As midwife and birth advocate Ina May Gaskin once said, *"If a woman doesn't look like a goddess in labour, then someone isn't treating her right."* And she's right. When a woman feels seen, supported, and safe—when she's been held through the intensity and met with love on the other side—she radiates something powerful. That's oxytocin in action. The glow isn't a myth. It's biology lit up by love.

Once the baby is born, oxytocin keeps working. It supports the birth of the placenta and helps reduce bleeding. But even more than that, it lays the groundwork for lasting attachment. In the brain, oxytocin triggers a deep sense of protectiveness and care—laying the foundation for the bond that continues long after birth.

Dr. Buckley explains, *"Oxytocin release in the brain during labour, and particularly the very high peaks at birth, also activates the maternal dopamine-related reward centres, preparing the labouring female for pleasure and reward as she meets her offspring for the first time at the moment of birth. This will imprint a positive connection, rewarding and motivating the new mother to give the dedicated maternal care that every newborn mammal needs."*

And when you really take that in—everything oxytocin is doing, everything it's creating—you realise you're witnessing something far bigger than just a set of bodily functions. This is nature at its most intelligent and intuitive. It prepares a mother to fall in love. To protect. To care. You can't help but feel part of something ancient, powerful, and deeply magical. This isn't just science at work. It's nature's way of supporting something sacred. And like any deep connection, it needs the right conditions to thrive. That's why understanding what supports—or disrupts—oxytocin matters so much.

One of the most important things to understand is that oxytocin is sensitive—what Dr. Sarah Buckley calls a "shy" hormone. She explains: *"Just as we need to feel safe in our environment to release oxytocin with sexual arousal, we also need to feel safe to release oxytocin in labour. Like all mammals, women will usually choose the relative safety of a small, quiet, dark place to labour and birth, if that is available to them."* She emphasises, *"Feeling safe—ie; being with familiar people in a familiar place, is generally the most supportive environment for oxytocin release and labour progress."*

Here we come back to the first and most fundamental element of the Essential 10: safety. For women approaching labour—especially those carrying fear or a history of trauma—creating a safe, supportive environment isn't just helpful. It's essential. Safety is what supports the flow of oxytocin—the hormone deeply tied to how labour begins and unfolds.

And the body knows when it's safe. That's why so many women go into labour in the quiet hours of the night. There's a reason for that.

As the world slows down and the lights dim, the body begins to release melatonin—the same hormone that helps us wind down, feel drowsy, and slip into sleep.

It's in the softness and stillness that the body feels safe enough to open. As melatonin rises in those quiet hours, it helps "wake up" oxytocin—prompting it to flow from the brain into the bloodstream. The two hormones work in rhythm, feeding each other in a quiet biological loop that gently signals labour to begin. But as morning light breaks and melatonin fades, oxytocin can fade with it. Even the soft light of sunrise is nature's way of saying, *you're visible now*. Movement, stimulation, and the feeling of being watched or exposed can chip away at the sense of safety a woman's body needs to keep labour going.

It's not that oxytocin suddenly shuts off with the sunrise. But the hormonal environment becomes less favourable. The shift in light, energy, and attention signals the body to be more alert, more outward-facing—less surrendered. And labour, by nature, asks for the opposite.

Just like other mammals, the labouring body is wired for survival. If something feels off—if there's tension, noise, or a subtle sense of threat—her body may pause the process.

In nature, that threat might be the sound of a predator nearby. In modern birth settings, it can look different—but the body doesn't always know the difference. A bright light. An unfamiliar voice. Even something as simple as a string of questions or being asked to lie back for an exam can pull her out of her body and into her thinking brain—signalling the primal brain that now isn't the time to let go. That subtle shift is often enough to slow things down.

And yet, this is still the norm. Bright lights. Strangers. Timelines. An environment that often asks a woman to perform, not surrender.

Humans are the only mammals who give birth under observation—under fluorescent lights, often with people watching. No other mammal chooses to labour in the open. Birth happens in the dark, in quiet, in privacy—because the body knows that safety is what keeps labour moving. And it's safety that allows oxytocin to rise. But in our system, that knowing is often overridden.

Take, for example, the woman who comes into hospital early in labour. She's having contractions, she's excited, maybe a little anxious—so she heads in, thinking it's time. But once she arrives, everything changes. The lights are bright. The energy shifts. She's asked questions, hooked up to monitors, maybe told it's still "too early" to admit her—but now she's under observation. She can't settle into her rhythm. The oxytocin that was building at home starts to stall. And without that natural flow, her labour slows.

And when those conditions aren't there, it's no surprise that rates of induction and augmentation are so high. So often, we disrupt the very physiology we then try to medically restart or speed up. In response, many women turn to natural methods—trying to encourage labour on their own terms.

As birth approaches, it's common to see a flurry of preparation: drinking raspberry leaf tea, eating dates, scheduling acupuncture, bouncing endlessly on a birth ball, and checking off every task on the let's get baby out to-do list.

But here's the thing—how can your body truly prepare for labour when, by 40 weeks, you feel like a ticking time bomb, pressured to "evacuate" your baby as soon as possible?

I get it. By the end of your pregnancy, you've forgotten what your ankles look like. You're dodging the "Any signs yet?!" texts. And you can't sneeze without a strategy. And the pressure builds with every passing day.

But stress and urgency don't just make you feel off—they send your body the signal that now isn't the time. Labour doesn't respond to pressure; it responds to presence. That slow, inward rhythm that gets things moving can only rise when you feel unhurried, undisturbed, and safe in your space. I see it all the time: women with houseguests who only go into labour after everyone leaves, or mothers clinging to unfinished to-do lists who finally let go—and then their body does too.

It's not just timing. It's biology. And if biology sets the rhythm, then your role is to create the conditions for it to unfold.

So, how do you invite oxytocin into your body during pregnancy? By doing the things that light you up and bring you joy. I always gently tell my clients: towards the end of pregnancy, it's time to stop "doing" and start "being." Forget the deadlines and pressure to "make labour happen" and instead focus on what fills your heart and makes you smile. Labour will come when you and your baby are ready, your job is to create the right conditions for oxytocin to flow.

Simple Ways to Boost Oxytocin During Pregnancy

Do what you love

Whether it's painting, baking, gardening, or dancing in the living room—make time for the things that light you up from the inside.

Spend time with your favourite people

Laughter, hugs, and heartfelt conversations with people who lift you up are powerful oxytocin triggers.

Pamper yourself

Take a warm bath, enjoy a prenatal massage, or curl up with a soft blanket and a good book. Simple comforts matter.

Get moving

Gentle yoga, a walk in nature, or floating in water can help your body feel nourished and your mind slow down.

Laugh and play

Watch a comedy, tell old stories that make you giggle, or play with your pets. Joy is medicine.

Create your sanctuary

Dim the lights. Add textures you love. Use scents that soothe. The environment you create can support your inner calm and sense of safety.

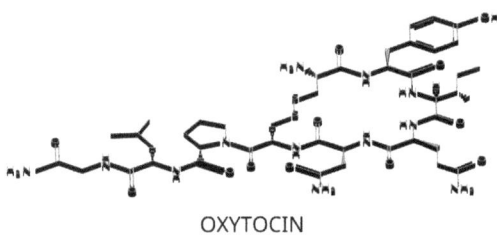

OXYTOCIN

And don't forget your partner! They can play a vital role in supporting oxytocin during these final weeks, and in labour too.

How Your Partner Can Help Boost Oxytocin

Set the mood

Dim the lights, put on relaxing music, and create a warm, inviting space for connection. And if you're up to it—yes, sex and orgasm can naturally stimulate oxytocin and help get things moving.

Be hands-on

A gentle back rub, a foot massage, or simply holding hands can help you feel grounded and loved. Physical touch is one of the most effective ways to release oxytocin.

Make you laugh

Watch a comedy, share old stories, or just be silly together. Laughter reduces stress and supports your nervous system—exactly what you want during this time.

Cook something comforting

A home-cooked meal you love can bring a deep sense of care and comfort. The smell, the familiarity, the effort—it all matters.

Protect your peace

Let your partner manage visitors, phone calls, and well-meaning texts like "is the baby here yet?" Their job is to be your buffer and help create a space where you feel safe, calm, and uninterrupted.

This is the partners' chance to shine. By prioritising calm, connection, and comfort, they're not just offering support, they are actively helping your body prepare for birth.

And remember, labour isn't something to rush or force. It's a delicate dance between mother and baby, happening when both are truly ready. For some, that might be 38 weeks for others, it's closer to 42 and potentially beyond. Let go of the pressure to 'make it happen.' Focus instead on nurturing your heart, mind, and body. The magic of oxytocin isn't just in its role during labour, it's in how it allows us to slow down, connect, and feel deeply supported.

But that kind of support doesn't just happen—it's built. And one of the most powerful ways we build it is through continuity. Being surrounded by people we know and trust changes everything.

In the next chapter, we'll look at how continuity of care lays the groundwork for trust—and why that trust matters more than we've been led to believe.

CONNECTING WITH YOUR OXYTOCIN FLOW

Inner Work: Mapping Safety and Calm

Use this reflection to create your personal oxytocin map to return to throughout pregnancy, birth, and postpartum.

1. **Imagine a Day in Oxytocin Flow**

   - Close your eyes and picture a day where you feel completely at ease.
   - Where are you?
   - What time of day is it?
   - What sounds do you hear?
   - What do you see around you?
   - What textures, smells, or movements are present?

   - Jot it down as a short story, a list, or free-flow sentences. Let this guide how you shape your days and your birth space.

2. **Identify Your Anchors**

   - Create a simple map—on paper or in your mind.
   - Start with: *"I feel safe when..."*
   - Surround it with your personal anchors:
     - A person who helps you feel held
     - A scent that calms you
     - A song that centres you
     - A space that feels grounding
     - A ritual that slows you down

- Sketch or list your anchors—this is your *oxytocin compass*.

---

3. **Anchor Into Birth**

- Reflect on your upcoming birth:
    - Which elements from your oxytocin day or map could support you in labour?
    - What small comforts or rituals help you feel safe and open?
    - Who do you want beside you to protect your peace?
    - What can you bring into your birth space to help you stay soft, focused, and connected?

- Write a short birth intention or mantra, like: *"I feel safe. I am supported. My body knows."*

EMMA'S STORY

Emma's journey into motherhood was shaped by her deep connection to health and wellness. Much of her early adulthood was spent studying occupational therapy, traveling, and exploring holistic and alternative medicine. She entered pregnancy with a blend of curiosity and caution. Although she believed in birth as a natural process, her time working in hospitals and the tragic birth stories she'd heard left her with a quiet fear of the unknown. From the outset, Emma envisioned a hands-off, natural birth. Still, shaped by societal norms and her own inner doubts, she chose a hospital setting under the care of a Midwifery Group Practice (MGP) midwife—an option that offered both continuity and clinical reassurance.

Her research into doulas, however, opened new doors. Through me, her doula, Emma and her husband joined a childbirth course that completely shifted their perspective. For the first time, Emma learned about the rising rates of hospital interventions and how these could often steer birth away from a mother's original plan. She also discovered how her natural biology could work with her—and for her—to help her body not only go into spontaneous labour but also shape the positive experience she deeply hoped for.

Emma took these insights to heart, drawing on mind-body practices and evidence-based tools to build trust in her body's ability to birth her baby. Even so, it was clear early on that birth still held a tight grip on her—mentally and emotionally.

She asked the most questions about risk—not in a fearful way, but in a deeply analytical, thoughtful way. She listened with intent, absorbing everything, clearly determined to implement what she was learning. I could see her weighing the evidence with care, but I also quietly wondered whether her brilliant, questioning mind might stand in the way of the powerful birth experience she hoped for.

Seven months into her pregnancy, as COVID-19 began to disrupt daily life, Emma found herself reconsidering her decision to birth in a hospital. The restrictions and uncertainty made her dream of a home birth resurface, but she doubted whether she was relaxed enough to pursue it.

Despite her fears, Emma embraced preparation and support with intention. She immersed herself in meditations, educated herself through research and resources, and actively worked to normalise the idea of natural birth. She also placed mindful focus on nurturing oxytocin in her daily life, creating the ideal conditions for her body to initiate the natural hormonal orchestration of labour.

She describes a pivotal moment the night before her labour began: "I validated and accepted myself and my fears. It was okay to be fearful. Optimistic, yes, but equally okay to admit that pushing a few kilos out of my body was scary. And as the next 24 hours proved, it didn't need to be."

When Emma messaged me that morning, she thought she might have a stomach bug. I gently mentioned that she could be in early labour, but she seemed unconvinced. Her husband said she was calm and coping well, so I headed over—not expecting to find her in active labour, but simply to check in and maybe offer support with active birth positions.

What I didn't expect was to arrive and see paramedics in the driveway. I walked in to find Emma sitting on the floor, baby in arms, with the most radiant, peaceful smile on her face. That moment will stay with me forever. After all the questions, all the preparation, all the effort she put into facing her fears—there she was, having birthed her baby at home, in her power, in her peace.

To understand how we got there, we have to go back to that morning.

Emma's labour began subtly on the morning of July 4, 2020, with the loss of her mucus plug and a sense that something was shifting. She followed her body's instincts, moving between her ensuite and bedroom in a quiet, private space. As her labour intensified, she entered what she called "labour la-la land," a deeply primal and unobserved state.

By midday, Emma's husband found her in the ensuite, where he saw their baby's head emerging. With their midwife and paramedics on speakerphone, Emma remained calm.

At 12:20 pm, Emma birthed her daughter into her husband's arms. This most certainly wasn't the birth she had imagined and because she remained so calm throughout she actually didn't fully realise how far along she was in her labour and unexpectedly birthed her baby at home. Emma recalls the experience as nothing short of euphoric: "The hours after this were the most precious, sacred, and empowering moments of my life. It wasn't pain-free, but it was manageable, and I felt in control."

Reflecting on her experience, Emma describes her birth as a profound moment of learning to trust her body and intuition: "It's okay to know the risks and have the research. It's also okay to lean into your intuition and give yourself a chance."

Now 29 weeks pregnant with her second baby and planning a home birth, Emma carries forward the lessons from her first birth. While she respects medical interventions if needed, she deeply trusts her body and baby to work in harmony. Her hope for her next birth is simple: "I just want it to be as beautiful, empowering, and insightful as my first.

OLIVIA'S STORY

"Coming from a long line of home-birthing women, I always believed that experiencing a beautiful birth was simply part of my ancestral heritage. How wrong I was.

I had a very traumatic hospital birth just three days after my 23rd birthday. The experience caused immense physical and emotional pain. I was left needing a blow-up donut pillow to sit on for over six weeks. I was shocked by what had happened and struggled for a long time to understand why. I felt sorry for myself, and even today, the scars remain, both physically and emotionally visible.

Physically, my recovery took almost a year. My whole lifestyle had to change, and I needed a great deal of help during my postpartum period. Deep fear of giving birth again took root, leaving me vulnerable and confused.

This birth experience profoundly shaped my understanding of birth and pushed me to seek alternatives. For my second birth, I moved away from the hospital system and systemic approaches to birth, beginning instead to research home birth. I had to completely shift my perspective on what birth could look like. I kept telling myself that my first birth was just one story, it didn't have to be the story of my second. It was a lesson that led me towards alignment and a new path.

After my first birth, my life transformed completely. I began exercising and practicing yoga. I spent time connecting deeply with my inner self and my baby during my second pregnancy. I slowed down and, by the time I gave birth again, my body was strong and ready.

I did significant work both physically and emotionally and found a midwife who truly aligned with my wishes. This continuity of care was what I had needed all along. I also built a village of support for my transition from one to two children, a stark contrast to my first experience, where I had struggled alone in the transition from zero to one. Having a village of mothers around me made all the difference.

Oxytocin also became a vital part of my journey. Educating myself about the powerful hormones that drive birth was something I continued to explore even after my second baby was born.

All this immense preparation led to what became the most magical, unintended freebirth. I am forever grateful that my midwife forgot to save my partner's number, so when he called, she didn't answer. As a result, she didn't make it in time.

I had experienced prodromal labour for four or five nights before the birth. Despite all the work I had done, emotionally, I knew something was stuck. I was waiting for my mum to arrive, flying in from Germany. Just two hours after she walked through the door, bringing with her the safety I needed to let go, my baby arrived. Little did she know she would catch my baby while still wearing her airplane clothes. My partner barely made it home from work, arriving with just ten minutes to spare. He began pumping up the birth pool, but it was already too late. I felt something in my pants and asked my mum to check. She could see my baby's head. I started walking to the couch to find a comfortable position, but my walk turned into a crawl. I ended up on all fours, unable to move further. Kneeling on the tiled floor, I experienced the foetal ejection reflex, my baby was coming.

The membranes hadn't yet broken. Her head emerged, still in the amniotic sac, while my pants were still on. Before the next surge, my mum tried to take a photo. She managed one blurry shot before tossing her phone aside to catch my baby. Three generations of women were together in that moment.

The midwife arrived after my placenta was birthed.

This was my redemption birth. It was the most euphoric high I have ever experienced. It changed my life and my career, making me feel like I could do it over and over again.

For mothers who have experienced trauma, I encourage you to do a fear release. Don't hold on to the trauma, work through it, face it, and let it go. It does not define you. You are capable of magic. Trust yourself!"

CHAPTER 11

Continuity of Care - The Foundation of Trust

"In any society, the way a woman gives birth and the kind of care given to her and the baby points as sharply as an arrowhead to the key values of the culture."
—Sheila Kitzinger

We're creatures of comfort—but not just in the soft blanket, cup-of-tea kind of way. It's deeper than that. It's the comfort of being known. The ease of stepping into a space—or a moment—where you don't have to explain yourself. Where someone already gets you.

Like when you step into your regular café, and they already know it's an oat latte with a little cinnamon on top. Or when you sit in your usual seat at the hair salon and your stylist just gets it—no small talk, no overexplaining, just "same as last time?" and you nod, feeling safe in the rhythm of being remembered.

You know that feeling—like in that old show Cheers—where everybody knows your name? (Yes, I'm showing my age.) That's what real continuity feels like. Familiar. Easy. Safe.

Even kids do it. They want the same bedtime story every night, told the same way, with the same silly voice. Not because they don't like surprises—but because predictability feels safe.

Familiarity says: I know you. I see you. You don't have to start from scratch.

Now imagine that same sense of familiarity—not in a café or a salon—but in your pregnancy, your birth, your care.

New Zealand gets it. Most women choose their midwife early in pregnancy, and that same midwife (or one of a small known team) walks beside them through it all—pregnancy, birth, and postpartum. One relationship. One thread of care. And it shows—lower intervention rates, higher breastfeeding success, and a deep sense of being supported by someone who truly knows you.

The Netherlands: Another country that gets it. Their system is built on trusting women and trusting birth. Midwives are the primary care providers for healthy, low-risk pregnancies. Obstetricians only step in if complications arise. Many women choose to birth at home—not because they have to, but because they feel safe to. Home birth is common, well-supported, and fully integrated into the healthcare system. It's not treated like a backup plan—it's simply one of the plans. And it works—because it's built on trust, education, and a continuity model that honours birth as a physiological, not pathological, event.

What these models show us is simple: when care is continuous, women feel held. They feel confident. And more often than not, they walk away not just healthy, but whole.

Because for many women, having someone consistent throughout their pregnancy isn't just a luxury—it's everything. It's not about charts or checklists. It's about being truly seen. And when you are, something unlocks.

That kind of support can change everything, especially in a time as raw and transformative as this.

You're entering one of the most vulnerable, life-changing seasons of your life. Maybe it's your first pregnancy. Maybe it's your fifth. Either way, the questions pile up. The unknowns feel big. You're navigating a thousand emotions at once.

Now imagine walking into your next appointment—and not needing to explain a thing.

You don't have to recap your history. You don't have to worry about being misunderstood. Because the person across from you? They already know. They've been walking this path with you since the beginning. They know your story, your hopes, your hesitations. They remember the tears you brushed away at twelve weeks, the excitement in your voice at twenty, and the unspoken fears you haven't dared to say aloud.

That's continuity of care. It's not just support—it's stability.

And as the weeks pass, that bond deepens. These check-ins aren't just about your blood pressure or your fundal height. They're little moments of connection. You might talk about how excited you are to meet your baby. Or how scared you are to give birth. Or how you ate an entire jar of pickles with a spoon and called it lunch. No judgment. Your midwife has probably heard it all. Over time, they become more than a care provider. They become your anchor. And when labour begins, that trust becomes your strength.

But let's be honest—not all care models give you continuity or the same kind of time (or vibes).

Now don't come at me if your setup looks different—I'm speaking from the Australian system here. If your care model is pure gold and running like a dream, consider yourself lucky and carry on with a satisfied little smirk.

Take private obstetric care. Most—though not all (there are unicorns out there)—mean more time scrolling your phone in the waiting room than actually talking to the doctor.

In the public system, hospital-based midwives are often warm, skilled, and doing their absolute best—but they're stretched thin, managing shift work and caring for several women at once. You might only see the same midwife once or twice during your whole pregnancy, and it's usually whoever's rostered on that day.

Some women find a better rhythm with Midwifery Group Practice. You're more likely to see the same few midwives throughout your care—which can offer a stronger sense of continuity. But even that isn't always a sure thing. In Australia, access is limited, and it's not uncommon for your primary midwife to change—or leave—late in pregnancy.

And birth centres? They can feel a little more personal, and you might get more face time—but even then, appointments can still be a bit "in and out."

Now home birth midwives—that's a different kind of care altogether. These appointments? They're the good stuff. They sit with you in your own space, cup of tea in hand, asking how you *really* are—not just how your baby's heart rate is sounding. You talk birth, life, fears, hopes, and probably your favourite Netflix binge. These sessions can last an hour or more—and not because anything's wrong, but because that kind of care is normal in this model.

And then there's doulas. We're like the long-haul flight attendants of the birth world—there for the whole journey: pregnancy, labour, and postpartum. And while I'm totally not biased (okay, maybe just a little), doulas might not take your blood pressure—but we do take your emotional temperature like pros.

That kind of steady, grounded presence—whoever it comes from—can change everything in labour. You don't forget it. You feel it.

Picture this. You're in labour. The room is dim. You're breathing through another wave, and it's intense. You lock eyes with the person beside you—and they don't ask what you need. They already know. Maybe it's a hand on your back, a whispered reminder, or just their quiet presence anchoring you. They know your birth preferences. They know what you hoped for, what you feared, what you said mattered most. You've built trust over months. You've laughed, cried, unpacked your fears. And now, in this moment, you're not alone.

That doesn't just happen by accident. It's not about luck. It's about continuity.

And it doesn't stop once the baby is born. If anything, it matters even more. You're bleeding, leaking, raw in every sense—and they show up again. They ask how you are, not just how much the baby weighs. They remember the things you shared before the birth—the worries, the wishes, the things that felt big to you.

That kind of care changes things. It turns uncertainty into trust, and a clinical experience into a human one.

And sometimes, it changes how that experience stays with you. Not just during birth—but in how you carry it, years later.

I remember once sitting outside the entrance of a birth centre, waiting for a mama and her partner to arrive in labour. It was quiet, early morning, and this older woman—maybe in her late 60s—sat down next to me on the bench. She seemed up for a chat, and when she asked what I was doing there, I told her I was a doula, waiting for a client in labour.

Now, if you've ever told a woman you're a doula, you'll know—it's like a secret handshake. Nine times out of ten, you're about to hear a birth story. And that's exactly what happened.

She shared hers right there on that bench, decades after it happened—and she told it with such emotion. But what stood out wasn't what went right or wrong, or even the birth itself. It was the way she was made to feel. She lit up as she spoke about the midwives who stayed with her, who spoke gently, who didn't rush her. She said, *"They made me feel like I could do it. Like I mattered."*

That's what stays. Not the timing or the centimetres—but the *impression it leaves.* The people. The presence.

When someone has walked the journey with you—knows your story, respects your pace, and stays by your side—it becomes part of how you carry the experience.

Without it, the experience can feel disconnected.

But midwifery-led continuity of care isn't just about feeling emotionally supported—it's linked to better outcomes too. Fewer caesareans, less need for pain relief, fewer episiotomies and instrumental births, and a lower risk of preterm birth. And the impact goes even further. Some research suggests that if more women around the world had access to this kind of care, we could see fewer maternal and newborn deaths—especially when midwives are properly trained and supported.

But what really stays with women is the *emotional imprint* of the care they received. Those with a known midwife consistently report higher satisfaction than those in standard hospital care. The message is clear: when women are supported by someone they know and trust, they walk away from birth feeling more empowered, more seen, and more in charge of their story.

On the flip side, I've heard from women who didn't have that consistency—who walked into labour rooms full of strangers and felt like they had to explain themselves mid-contraction. One mother told me, *"They were kind, but I felt like I had to prove myself the whole time."* That kind of emotional load can be heavy—and it's avoidable.

And sometimes, the consequences of fragmented care go beyond emotional weight—they force women to make huge decisions mid-labour, just to protect their autonomy.

I remember a client who booked me as her doula, doing everything she could to prepare for the birth she envisioned—calm, natural, and undisturbed unless truly needed. She was due right around Christmas, so finding an obstetrician who aligned with her values and wasn't heading off on holiday was a task in itself. Eventually, she found one who assured her he was supportive of her birth preferences and would be available.

She did HypnoBirthing®. She stayed active. She worked hard to prepare emotionally, physically, and mentally. When labour began, I met her and her partner at home, and we laboured there until she felt ready to head in. By the time we arrived at the hospital, she was in full active labour—calm, focused, on all fours and moaning through her surges like the absolute powerhouse she was.

As we got her settled in, the midwife—who knew I was her doula—pulled me aside. She told me quietly, *"Her obstetrician is actually away. He never passed on her birth plan. The backup doctor isn't going to go for any of this. He'll want to manage the whole thing."* Then she looked me in the eye and said, *"Off the record: if she wants a natural birth, she shouldn't be here. You should leave and go to the nearest public hospital."*

So, I went back into the room and gently told her partner, he agreed that we should go as he didn't want this on call obstetrician to sabotage her birth by her staying there. He blinked and said, *"Yeah... I think you should tell her."* (Understandably dodging that one!) His face said it all—the universal look of a man who'd rather fight a bear than explain this to his labouring partner.

She was still deep in labour, eyes closed, working through each wave on all fours. I crouched beside her and whispered, *"We're going to take you somewhere safe to have your baby."* That was all she needed to hear. She nodded. No drama. No panic. Just trust.

It was nearly midnight. We got her down the hall, into the lift, into the car—eyes still closed the entire time, trusting us to guide her—and then we flew down the motorway to the nearest public hospital. She was admitted through emergency and birthed her baby not long after we arrived.

She did everything right. She prepared. She asked the questions. She built her team. But the lack of continuity in the system meant she had to make a huge decision mid-labour just to protect the birth she'd worked so hard for. That's the cost of fragmented care.

That moment shouldn't have fallen on her shoulders. But when the system drops the ball, it's the people around you who make the difference. That steady support you need? It doesn't always have to come with a title.

Sometimes it's none other than your incredible partner.

Sure, they might forget where they parked the car or pack six muesli bars and no baby clothes—but they've been by your side through it all. The appointments. The waiting. The weird cravings. When they really show up—with presence, patience, and love—they are continuity. They might not have clinical skills (unless Google counts), but their consistency, the inside jokes, the knowing look when you raise an eyebrow—that matters. Don't underestimate the power of someone who knows your story because they've lived it with you.

And of course, speaking of steady support... Yep, doulas again. What can I say? When someone shows up like that, they earn a second mention.

You've got the medical care covered—but the one making sure you don't get lost in the system? That's your doula. The grounding presence. Just there for you.

In the next chapter, we'll dive into what doula support really looks like—and why having someone by your side who's there *just* for you can make all the difference.

REFLECT & EXPLORE: BUILD YOUR CIRCLE OF CARE

Choosing your care team isn't just about logistics—it's about safety, trust, and feeling seen.

This isn't a checklist to complete. It's a conversation to have with yourself.

Go slow. Be honest.

There's no right answer—just the truth of what *you* need.

---

1. **Start with what you need**

   - What matters most to you in your care?
   - What kind of birth experience do you want?
   - What kind of emotional support helps you feel safe?
   - Have you had care in the past that made you feel truly supported—or unsupported? What made the difference?
   - If you've been through trauma, or if certain fears are still sitting with you—honour that. Your needs are valid.

---

2. **Ask around**

   - Talk to friends, family, or support groups in your area.
   - Listen not just to what happened, but *how they felt*. Empowered? Rushed? Heard? That feeling is often more revealing than the details.

3. **Do some digging**

- ☞ Look into potential providers—background, approach, reviews.
- ☞ Do they seem to share your outlook on birth? Do they treat it like a medical event or a physiological one?
- ☞ You're not just looking for experience—you're looking for alignment.

4. **Meet a few**

- ☞ Book some consults. These conversations aren't just about what they offer—they're about how you feel with them.
- ☞ Did they listen? Did you feel like you could exhale?
- ☞ Were they present—or rushing through? Did they make space for your questions?

5. **Ask about trauma-informed care**

- ☞ If this is part of your story, it's okay to ask directly:
- ☞ "Do you understand how trauma can show up in birth? Do you work with that in mind?"
- ☞ You deserve care that's aware—not just clinical.
- ☞ This might feel bold to ask. That's okay. Your safety matters more than their comfort.

6. **Trust your gut**

- ☞ How did you feel after the conversation—more grounded or more tense?

- ☞ Did you feel truly heard? Did something feel off?
- ☞ Your body knows. Pay attention.

7. Be open about your story

- ☞ If you feel ready, share your history or your fears early on.
- ☞ Not just the facts—but the feeling. What do you want your care team to *understand* about you?
- ☞ It helps them show up in the ways that matter most.

8. Check the vibe of the place, too

- ☞ Look into the culture of the hospital or birth centre you're considering.
- ☞ Do they support personalised care? Are birth plans respected?
- ☞ Do you feel *welcomed*—as you are? Not just your birth preferences, but your identity, your values, your voice?

9. Find someone who'll work *with* you

- ☞ Look for care that feels like a partnership.
- ☞ Are they open to plans changing? Or do they seem set on one "right" way?
- ☞ Shared decision-making isn't a bonus—it's the baseline.

10. **Think about adding a doula**

- Maybe what you need is someone who's just there for *you*—through it all.
- Someone steady. Someone who brings calm when things feel uncertain.
- If that idea makes your shoulders drop a little… it might be worth exploring.
- Sometimes, just knowing someone will really *be there* changes everything.
- This isn't about finding the "best" provider—it's about finding the right *fit*.
- The one who backs your choices. Who listens to your gut. Who meets your needs.
- Go gently. Be curious. Take your time.

Because in the end, birth isn't just about what happened.
It's about how you felt as it unfolded.
Were you safe? Heard? Respected?
That's what lingers. That's what becomes part of your story.

And with the right support, you'll carry that story with strength, not regret.

ALY'S STORY

"I'm from the UK originally. I came here 11 years ago, and I'm a neonatal nurse, which impacted my understanding of birth and the hospital system, not necessarily in a good way. I came to Australia with the intention of traveling but only ever bought a one-way ticket. I think it was meant to be, I was supposed to come. I met my husband in 2014, and we got married in 2018. Pretty quickly, we fell pregnant on our honeymoon. We had our first baby, Joe, in 2019, and then Theo, our second, in 2021, during the COVID lockdowns. Now, I'm 36 weeks pregnant with baby number three.

In my childhood, as wonderful as my parents were, they were very British, a little bit caught up in their own stuff to notice what was going on with their daughter. Unfortunately, our family was infiltrated by a man, a family friend, who groomed and sexually abused me from the age of six for about six years. I then blocked the memory out. When I came to Australia, I started remembering the sexual abuse. I had quite a tumultuous adolescence, filled with alcohol abuse, drug use, many partners, and a pregnancy in my early 20s that ended in a distressing termination. I was also in an abusive relationship as a teenager with an older man. I went through various bits of therapy but never really got to the bottom of things until I moved to Australia. Then, all these memories resurfaced.

When I first started to remember, I felt like my whole life had been shaped by this early childhood experience. I didn't know who I was. I felt robbed of over 20 years of my life. It was overwhelming. I was 27 when I came here, and everything began to unfold. I'm a Christian, and I started seeing someone through the church. It was the first time I experienced a caring, non-sexual relationship. He was nurturing and, when I shared my views on sex, he said, 'I don't think this is normal.' He encouraged me to see someone, and that's when I began therapy, and the memories truly surfaced.

It was awful. I had constant nightmares, flashbacks—PTSD that felt inescapable. Some days, I would have 20 flashbacks. I overdosed one Monday after work. My boyfriend sensed something was wrong while on the phone with me, called an ambulance, and I was admitted to a psychiatric unit for nine days. It was horrible but, fortunately, it was the beginning of my healing journey. I started with an awful psychiatrist but was later referred to a great one who diagnosed me with complex PTSD. He connected me with a psychotherapist I've now been working with for nine years. I was also prescribed antidepressants. It was a long, difficult road to recovery. I didn't want my parents to know I was in the hospital. I carried a lot of hurt and betrayal, believing they should have protected me. At the same time, I felt a strong determination to heal. I shut everyone out and told myself, I'm going to get better.

I met Ben, my husband, not long after that. I was still early in my healing and kept pushing him away. I thought it was a terrible time to meet someone, so I tested him by telling him shocking things, expecting him to run. But he didn't. He stayed.

When it came to thinking about kids, I worried about how I would cope if I had a little girl. But I didn't think about how pregnancy and birth might bring up trauma related to the bodily changes and loss of control. My understanding of birth was quite medicalised, based on my NICU experience. My mum was a midwife, but birth wasn't something we talked about. I assumed it was something that would just happen. It wasn't until I was pregnant that I thought, Oh shit.

I was lucky during my first pregnancy because I worked in a hospital that focused on women-centred care. I didn't initially get into MGP (Midwifery Group Practice) because I didn't realise you had to book at conception. But a colleague stepped in and connected me with an amazing midwife, Tammy. From our first appointment, I shared my past trauma, and Tammy understood how it could affect my pregnancy and birth. She was the perfect midwife for me, even studying trauma-informed care at the time. She suggested I continue seeing my psychotherapist, consult with the hospital psychiatrist, and consider hiring a doula.

At first, I didn't want a doula because I subconsciously wanted to avoid talking about my past. But eventually, I connected with a doula at 30 weeks. She listened to my story with kindness and helped me prepare for every scenario. I felt reassured knowing she and my husband would support me through the birth.

I was also fortunate to meet with a well-known, women-centred OB in Sydney. He asked, 'How do you want this to happen?' My husband and I were surprised, expecting him to tell us what to do. Instead, he empowered us to make informed choices.

I also consulted the hospital psychiatrist to create a plan in case I dissociated during labour. We drafted a document giving Ben authority to make safe decisions if I couldn't. It was one of the hardest things to do, but it gave me a sense of control. My protective instincts kicked in; I didn't want to put my baby at risk if I lost control. I worked with Ben and my doula, Jerusha, on grounding techniques to keep me present during birth, like using sensory cues and affirmations to remind myself, This is 2019. I am safe. I have choice. One of the most helpful techniques was Ben holding an iPhone in front of me. Seeing the phone brought me back to the present moment because iPhones didn't exist when I was a child. We also used sensory cues, like Ben talking to me about mundane things, questions like, "What's your favourite sandwich at Subway?" He reminded me that I wasn't six years old anymore and helped anchor me in the here and now. The combination of these techniques kept me from becoming trapped in past trauma.

My birth preferences were clear: no unnecessary interventions, no strangers in the room, and no one standing over me. I wanted everyone to respect my space and announce their actions. We had a plan in place to support me in case I entered fight, flight, or freeze mode, ensuring that everyone knew what I needed at any stage.

My birth started with some contractions at around 4 a.m. on a Saturday morning. I just went back to sleep and carried on with my day. By Saturday afternoon, the contractions became a bit more regular. I used my birthing ball, and they were coming about every 15 minutes. It was a bit of a challenge because we didn't live in Sydney and knew we had to travel down for the birth, so we were trying to time it. We booked a hotel room in Sydney, thinking we wouldn't be there long. However, the drive down to Sydney slowed everything. We ended up staying in the hotel room from Saturday night until around 2 a.m. Monday morning. He wasn't born until 9 a.m. Monday.

That whole pre-labour phase was a lot harder than I expected, so much harder. The contractions kept fluctuating, slowing down, then picking up, and back again. I wasn't really sleeping. I vomited a lot, so I couldn't eat or drink anything. We were crunched up in this little hotel room, which in hindsight was a terrible choice. My doula, Jerusha, came and went. At one point, she suggested we go for a walk. I remember thinking, Are you fucking kidding me? I can't walk for months! But it turned out to be the best idea. It helped, although the contractions slowed again after that. I asked Jerusha, "Can it slow down again?" She gently reassured me, saying, "Yes, it can," which frustrated me because I felt like I couldn't keep doing this anymore.

By early Monday morning, I must have been transitioning because I suddenly got up and said, "Okay, enough now. We're going to the hospital. I can't do this anymore." When we arrived, I told Ben, "I'm going to have an epidural and a caesarean now." I had always told him before the birth, "If I ask for an epidural, make sure you ask me three times to confirm if it's what I really want." He did exactly that, and I said, "Ben, don't ask me again. This is what we're doing."

Tammy, my midwife, happened to be on call, which was amazing. She gave me options, saying, "Of course, you can have a caesarean if you want. Or maybe we can try giving you some morphine first." I told her, "I just can't keep going. I'm so tired." She then offered to do a vaginal examination, saying it might reassure me about how far along I was. Even though I loved and trusted Tammy, I was still nervous. I remember my legs shaking uncontrollably from the adrenaline. I asked, "What's happening? I can't stop my legs from shaking." Tammy calmly explained, "It's just the adrenaline. It's okay."

I was about 7 to 8 centimetres dilated at that point, which reassured me. Knowing how far along I was gave me the strength to keep going. If she had told me I was only 2 or 3 centimetres, I think I would have felt very differently.

They got the bath ready for me. In my mind, I thought I was only in the bath for about 20 minutes, but Ben reckons I was in there for two hours. At this point, time felt distorted.

The hospital itself felt like a safer space for me. Coming from the cramped hotel room, I suddenly had more room to move. I could sit on the birthing stool and walk around freely. I don't think I even got on the bed once. I stayed completely in my zone. I laboured for about two hours, pushing hard and just knuckling down to get through it. Tammy stayed with me, even though her shift had ended. One of the other midwives from my MGP team was in the room, but Tammy was there as a secondary midwife. The only moment I experienced panic or dissociation was when I was in the bath. It happened when I felt the involuntary pushing start, and the baby's head began descending. I freaked out for a second, caught off guard by the muscle memory of that sensation. Tammy immediately recognised my fear. She looked me in the eyes and said, "You're safe. You're safe. Look at where you are."

After two hours of pushing, my baby was born. It was such a beautiful moment. Tammy later told me, "Your birth is why I became a midwife." Her words meant so much to me.

The value of having the right support team cannot be overstated. If it weren't for my doula, Jerusha, we would have gone to the hospital much earlier than needed. She normalised what I was experiencing and gave me guidance and reassurance when I needed it most. She also helped support Ben, teaching him how to care for me throughout the process. That's where I see the true value of a doula, supporting both the mother and her partner.

I believe everything I did to prepare for my first birth enabled me to come out of it with this lovely oxytocin glow. I felt so healed and empowered. It was such a transformative and euphoric experience that I wanted to do it again and again."

SAM'S STORY

"My dad used to play hockey, and we spent hours on weekends cheering him on. Sometimes the games were in stadiums, but often they were on grassy fields surrounded by trees. On this particular day, we were at a big grass oval lined with trees on two sides. Asking young kids to sit and cheer for the whole game is a big ask, so a couple of friends and I whose dads were also playing were allowed to play in the trees nearby. We decided to play hide and seek. There were only three or four of us, and we didn't wander far from our parents.

I can't remember if I was hiding or seeking, but while we were playing, a man walked through the trees and said "hello." My brain has protected me, so I can't recall exactly what happened next. I don't think I was forced to touch him, but he showed me his penis and asked if I would show him what I had. I don't know why or how we were interrupted, but I didn't have to answer, and he walked off. I remember him leaving, not rushing or hiding, just walking away.

At the time, I didn't think much of it. He was just a weird old man who asked me a strange question, and he disappeared. It didn't feel like something I needed to worry about.

Later that day, when we got home from hockey, mum and dad sat me down. They explained that my friend's parents had called to tell them a man had approached their child while we were playing and had put his hand down her knickers. My parents asked if I had seen him.

Suddenly, I felt scared. It was clear to me now that this was serious. I said "no." My parents gave me a big hug, relieved but clearly shaken by how close I had come to something terrible. I didn't tell anyone what had happened to me for another 10 years. It wasn't until my parents asked me that day that I realised something had been wrong, and only as I grew older did, I understand the full seriousness of it.

I justified it to myself by thinking, "There was no physical contact, so it wasn't as bad for me as it was for her."

I remained fairly innocent compared to my peers, but I think my brain protected me by clinging to the belief that "private parts" were private and didn't need further acknowledgment.

As I got older, especially as a late teenager, I became anxious. I struggled to connect with myself, and in hindsight, I think it was because I forced myself to ignore the fact that I was growing up. "Private parts" were more than just another body part, they were an integral part of who I was, and I wasn't ready to accept that. I joined a youth group, which helped for a while because sex wasn't discussed there either, but I eventually outgrew it. I felt like I was constantly fighting myself.

I had always been friends with boys as a child, but those friendships became harder to maintain. I was a people pleaser and let some friends take advantage of me, not by doing anything "wrong," but by thinking that if I pleased them, I could win back their friendship or make them like me more.

I hated the thought of touching a male's "private parts," which felt embarrassing, even to myself as I entered my twenties. I didn't really like being touched either, and all hands stayed at or above the waist.

I did a lot of counselling in my late teens and early twenties. While I never directly addressed my inability to touch a penis, the deeper issues that contributed to my anxiety eventually

brought me clarity. Through therapy, I gained self-confidence, respect for myself, and the ability to make decisions for me, not just to please others. Only after this did I meet my (now) husband.

When I became pregnant with my first baby, I didn't connect my childhood trauma to the challenges I faced during pregnancy until much later. My midwife made all the difference. A friend encouraged me to apply to the family birth centre, and I was assigned a midwife who was compassionate, patient, and non-judgmental.

I remember when the topic of vaginal exams came up, I panicked. The thought of someone needing to look at or touch me filled me with embarrassment and stress. I worried about how I would "compare" to others. Should I have hair or not? Was I doing the "right thing"? I regretted not being a "girly girl" who knew what was normal or expected. In hindsight,

I realise my brain was protecting me from addressing the deeper issues.

I didn't intentionally seek out strategies or support because of my trauma history, but I am so thankful I had them available. For my first birth, I went into it relatively naïve, with no deep knowledge of the system or process. I had heard great birth stories from my mum and friends, and I stayed in that innocent mindset, which worked for me. Still, I knew my biggest triggers would be being touched and feeling out of control. I worked through the anxiety around those feelings by asking questions and ensuring I felt informed throughout my pregnancy.

I read books, something I don't usually do. Birth Skills by Juju Sundin and Birth With Confidence by Rhea Dempsey were game changers for me. One provided practical tips, while the other focused on mindset. I had expected Birth Skills to be the most helpful, but Rhea's book about mindset changed everything. I began to see birth as something I could relate to all the hard things I had already done, survived, and even enjoyed.

Labour started on a Monday when I was 40 weeks and 1 day. My mum and I had been getting foot massages three days in a row, laughing with the staff as mum asked them to press harder to "get the baby out." We had been doing everything, side-stepping while watching Harry Potter, massaging trigger points, and eating dates for weeks. That evening, I used some clary sage oil, putting a drop or two on the back of my hands to smell. I felt some strong Braxton Hicks contractions, but after three nights of false alarms, I tried not to get my hopes up. I paced around the house for a while before going to bed, just in case this time was different.

I woke up at 11:30 p.m. needing the toilet but quickly realised my waters had broken.

Contractions began, so I woke my husband, and we called the midwife to let her know. I used a TENS machine, which became my lifeline during labour. Every time a contraction started, I pressed the button, it gave me something to focus on and helped me manage the pain. My husband supported me by pulling on my legs during contractions while I focused on deep breaths and counting things in the room to distract myself.

By 2:45 a.m., I felt like it was time to go in. My midwife told me, "It's your decision," and I remember overthinking her words. I didn't want to disappoint her, so I doubted myself. But after the next contraction, we decided to go. I prayed I hadn't made the decision too early, worried it would be embarrassing if we were sent home.

We arrived at the family birth centre at 3:45 a.m., and I was 9 cm dilated! The vaginal exam was the hardest part of my labour. I screamed and cried through it, but it wasn't traumatic because my midwife had told me it wasn't mandatory, I had chosen it. Even though I regretted that decision, I was proud I had made the "right call" to come in.

The TENS machine wasn't helping much anymore, so I tried the shower, but I didn't like the water spray. It wasn't until I got into the bath that I felt any relief. I hadn't planned a water birth, but once I was in, I refused to get out. My husband held my hands, talking me through each contraction.

At 5:45 a.m., just over six hours after labour started, our daughter was born in the water. I remember looking down and seeing her eyes open. I yelled, "She's a girl!" followed by, "She's so big!" She was huge, and I was instantly in love.

The birth felt peaceful and serene to me, though my husband reminds me I probably didn't sound peaceful to anyone else. Still, that's how I remember it.

My takeaway for women is this: Do the work. Even before pregnancy, it's never too early to address the emotions and triggers that will surface through pregnancy and birth. Avoiding triggers completely can leave you vulnerable to them reappearing unexpectedly, which is when they can become overwhelming or re-traumatising. Work through them so you can take control of your decisions and trust yourself."

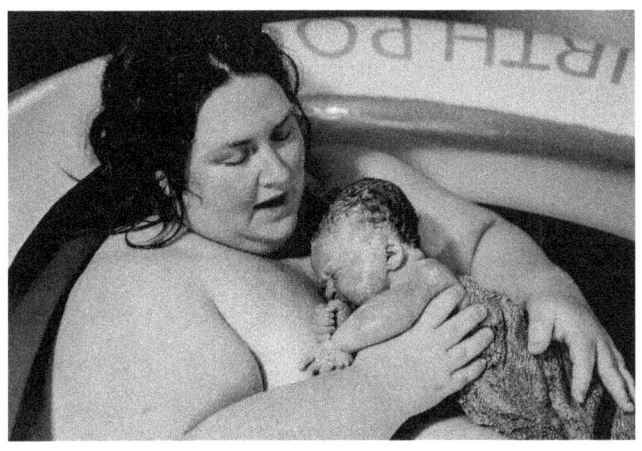

Ashley's Birth

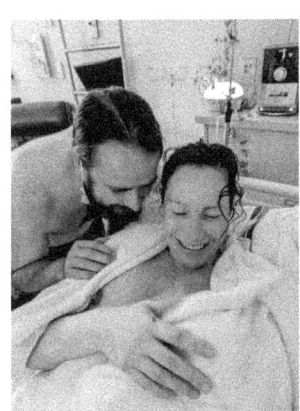
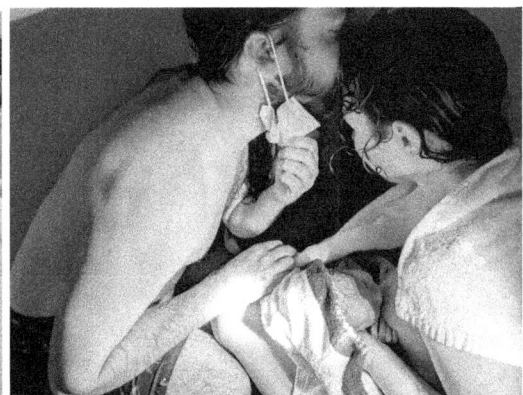

Donna's Birth

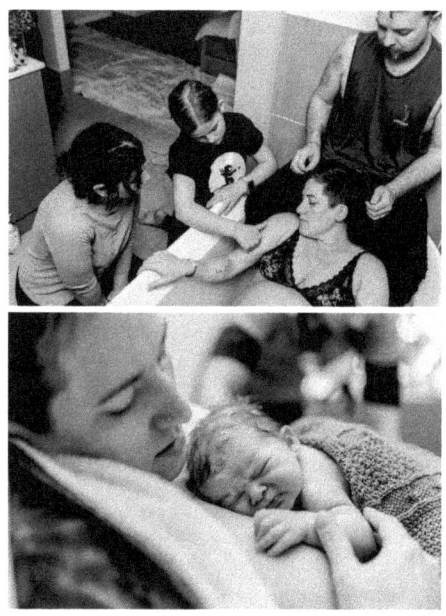

Kimmy's Birth

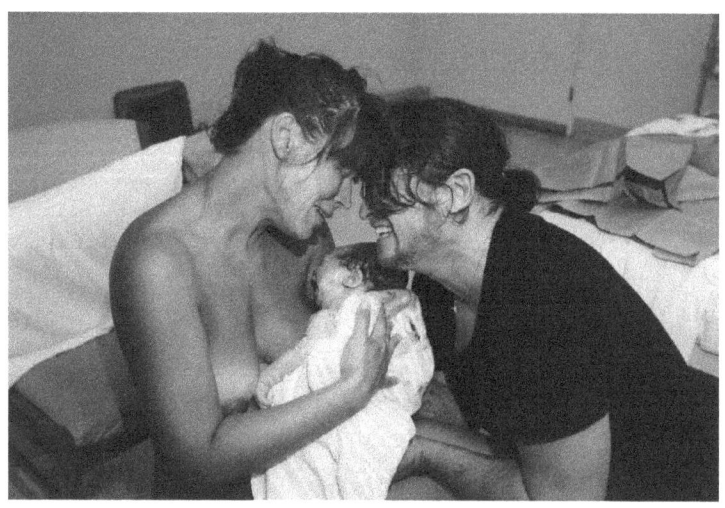

Svenja's Birth With Arlo

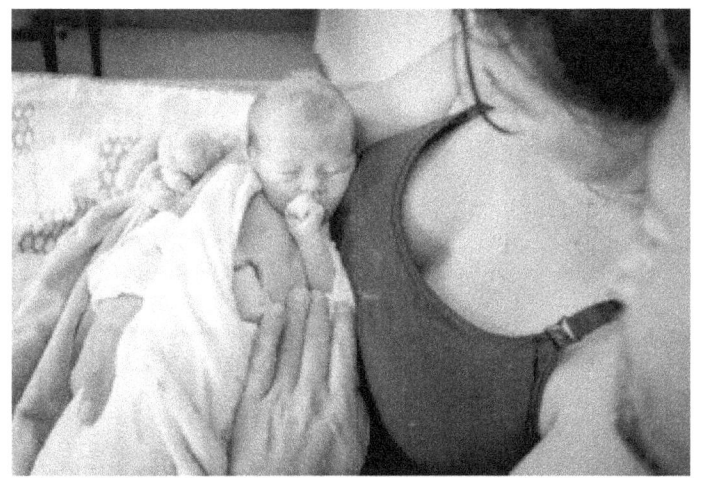

Svenja's Birth With Luna

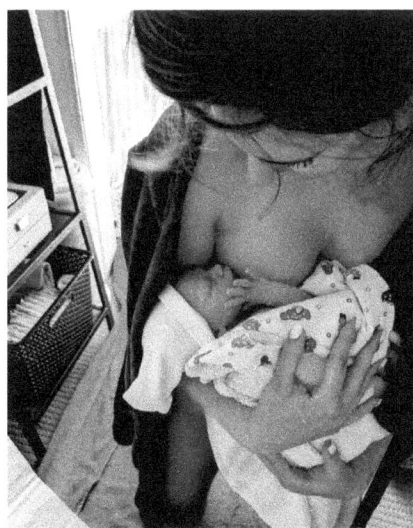
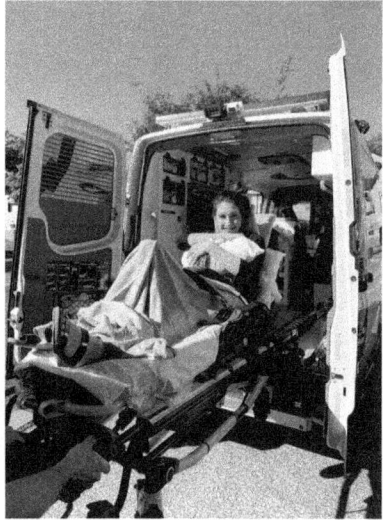

Emma's Birth

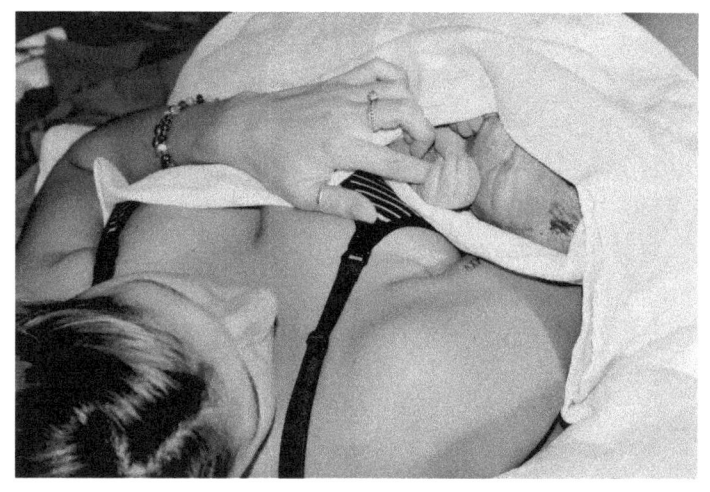

Olivia's Birth

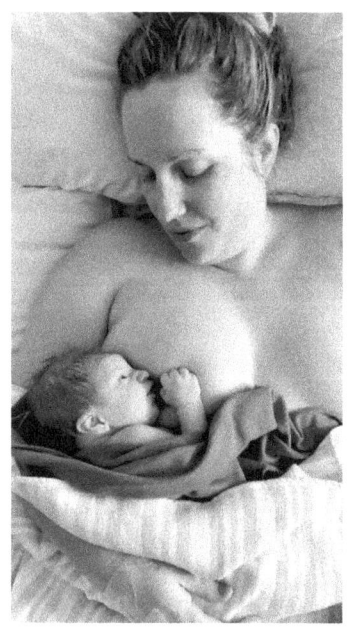

Aly's Birth

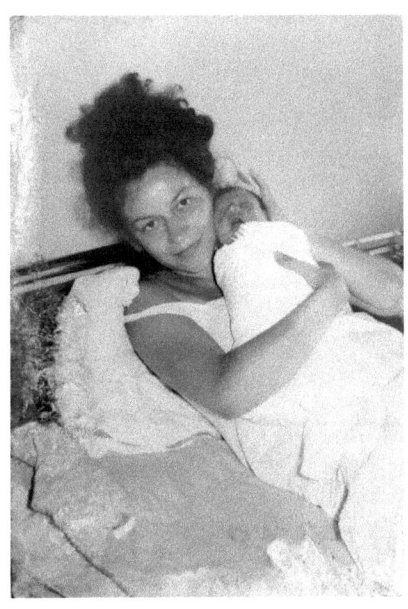

Steph Pictured With Her Mum

Steph's Birth & Steph With Her Second Son

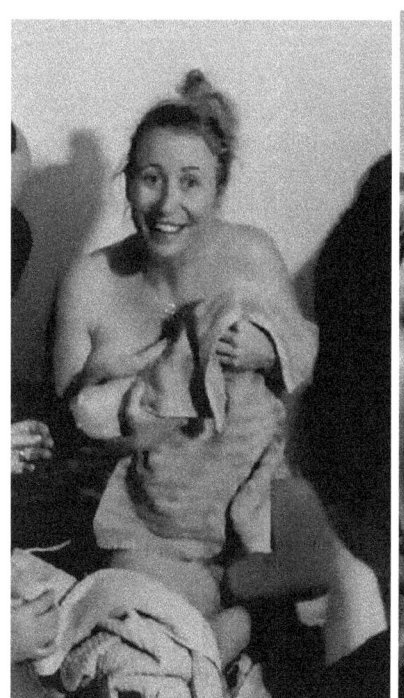
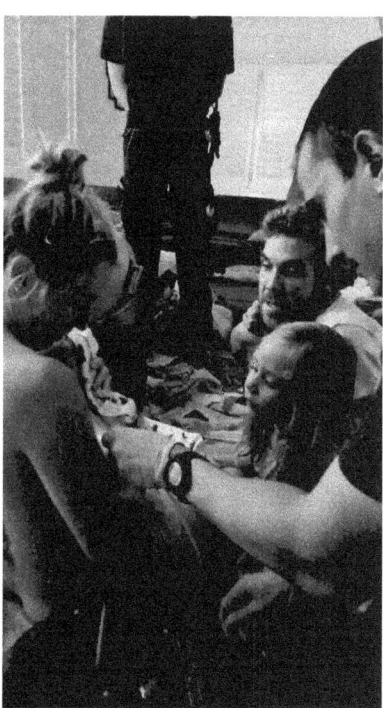

Emilie's Birth

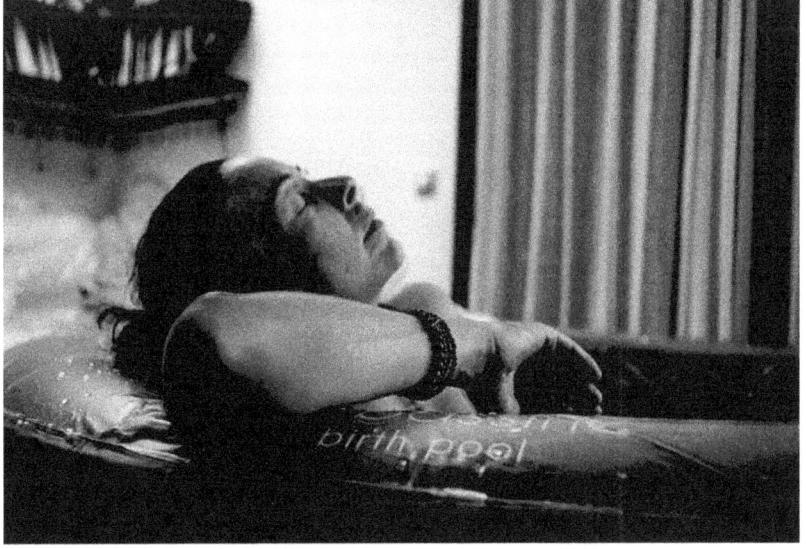

Agathe's Birth

Tanya's Birth

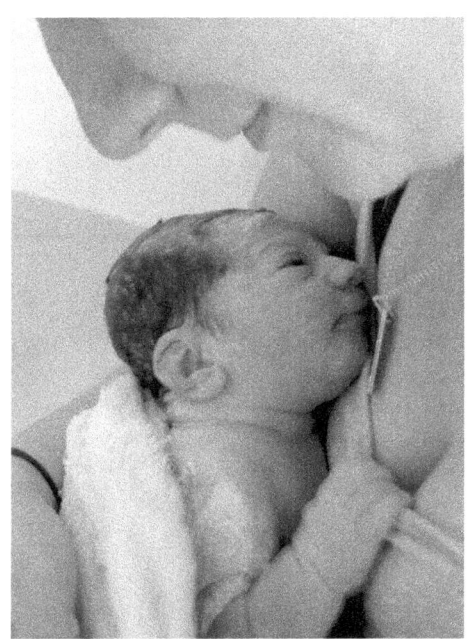
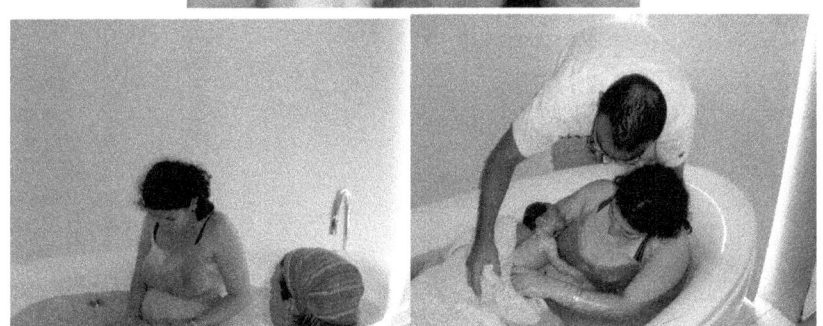

My Birth With Portia

CHAPTER 12

Doula Support – A Steady Hand Through the Journey

"The mind of a doula is clear and calm.
The arms of a doula are supportive and strong.
The soul of a doula is generous and gentle.
The heart of a doula is bigger than you could ever imagine.
And the mommy that is supported by this magical.
being is blessed beyond words."
—Shani

In the early 1970s, during the wave of the feminist movement, Ina May Gaskin and a group of self-described hippies founded The Farm, an intentional community in rural Tennessee. They arrived in a convoy of converted school buses, looking to live by their values of peace, self-sufficiency, and community. As babies started to arrive, Ina May and the women around her taught themselves midwifery, eventually setting up The Farm Midwifery Centre—one of the first out-of-hospital birthing centres in the United States.

Their approach was simple: they stayed. Through long labours, slow progress, and endless position changes, they stayed. They weren't rushing between rooms or checking charts in the hallway. They sat, they listened, they encouraged. They were there to support.

Midwives have always understood the power of staying close, and many still offer that. But in today's busy systems, continuity isn't always possible. That's where doulas come in. We're not medical, we're not in charge, we're not there to "run the show." We're the extra pair of hands, the steady support, the person who doesn't clock off at shift change.

Having someone in your corner from start to finish? That's the game-changer.

This is what doula support really looks like.

A woman on all fours, breath catching. The air thick with effort. She locks eyes with the person beside her—not a midwife, not her partner, but someone who's been quietly watching, attuned to every shift in her energy.

The doula leans in. Matches her breath. Offers a hand without asking. Nothing flashy. No grand gestures. Just presence—calm, steady, human.

And somehow, with just a whispered word or a shared rhythm, something returns. Strength. Clarity. Power.

That's the heartbeat of doula support. It's not about directing anything. It's about protecting the space around her, so she stays at the centre.

This kind of presence shows up in all kinds of places, in all kinds of ways.

You'll find doulas in hospitals, birth centres, and homes. Sometimes holding a hand, sometimes holding silence. Maybe offering a heat pack. Maybe rubbing a tired back. Maybe just sitting quietly at the edge of the room, watchful and calm, while the work of birth unfolds.

No two births are the same. No two women need the same thing.

But the role? It stays steady:

To back you. To see you. To help you stay connected to yourself when everything else feels like too much.

That belief—that women deserve to feel safe, supported, and in charge of their own story—has been carried forward by many. One of them is filmmaker and advocate Ricki Lake. In 2008, she co-produced *The Business of Being Born*—a documentary that cracked open the conversation about maternity care. When it was released, she said most people hadn't even heard the word "doula."

Fast forward to now. There's still work to do—but doulas are no longer on the fringe.

More and more, they're being recognised. Welcomed. Seen not as a sidekick, but as a real part of the circle. A steady presence that even care providers—some, not all (unfortunately)—are happy to have in the room. That shift didn't happen by accident. It came from voices that challenged the norm, from women who spoke up, from families who said, "this made all the difference."

And now? Doulas aren't just showing up at home births or water births or any one kind of birth. They're showing up wherever they're needed.

They're not a trend.

They're not a luxury.

They're often the missing link—the quiet strength that helps everything else fall into place.

But it's not just emotional support. Doulas bring practical skills too—talking through comfort measures, pain coping techniques, and tools like Spinning Babies® to support optimal positioning and ease in labour. They help you work through fear or past trauma, and they advocate alongside you, making sure your voice stays at the centre of your care.

They've moved from the margins to the middle, becoming a trusted part of birth for women everywhere. Not because they take over, but because they make space.

Not because they replace your partner, but because they lift the whole team—partner included.

Some roles are hard to define—but this one's been named for centuries.

The word *doula* comes from ancient Greek—'a woman who serves.' And if you've ever had one with you, even for a moment, you'll know... it's a kind of service that feels like sanctuary. They don't enter with fanfare. They arrive quietly. Calmly. Right in the middle of it all. They bring heart. Skill. Stillness. They bring themselves.

And the real magic? It's not just in the hip squeezes or heat packs. It's in how they learn your rhythm. How they attune. How they hold the space so you can move through the biggest threshold of your life feeling held—not handled.

I know this not just because I've witnessed it. I know it because I've lived it. When I was pregnant with my second daughter, I was already carrying fear. The kind that doesn't sit on the surface—but lives in your body. Bella's birth had left a mark.

The memory of it—the parts that felt out of my hands—was still there. Quiet, but heavy.

Even the thought of labour again made me tense. I didn't want a repeat of last time. I knew I needed support. I just didn't know what kind—or who to even ask.

One day, I finally opened up to a friend. She listened with that kind of gentle understanding that only comes from someone who's been through something of her own.

We talked—different stories, different paths—but she understood what it meant to want more support the second time around. Then she said something that stopped me mid-sentence:

"Have you thought about hiring a doula?"

I remember thinking: what's a doula? I'd never even heard the word.

She told me about a friend's positive birth experience with a doula, and something clicked. I got curious. I started researching, reading, trying to figure out what a doula actually did and whether it could help me.

And then I thought—how would that even work with my husband already by my side? Would it feel awkward? Would she take over? Would it help? I wasn't sure. But I was curious enough to keep looking.

If I'm honest, part of me had this image of doulas as a bit too "earthy" for me. I pictured dreamcatchers, sage, sound bowls, and someone quietly drumming in the corner. (And if you knew me then, you'd know drumming was definitely *not* my love language.)

But even with that impression stuck in my head, I couldn't shake the feeling: I wanted something different this time.

I reached out to the doula my friend had recommended—and from our very first meeting, something clicked. It felt meant to be. She wasn't the drum-beating, incense-waving hippy I'd secretly envisioned. No dreamcatchers, no chanting—just a grounded, warm, real woman who somehow made me feel instantly calmer. She opened the door to a completely different way of seeing birth. She shared videos of women from all around the world embracing birth in their own power, their own way. It wasn't just about physical labour—it was emotional, cultural, and spiritual.

And then she recommended I watch *The Business of Being Born*, the documentary by Ricki Lake and Abby Epstein. Watching it for the first time felt like a veil had lifted. My entire perspective shifted—from birth being something I had to get through, to something I could own. It was a revelation. A well-kept secret that so few women seemed to know about. I remember thinking, why didn't anyone tell me this before? I wanted every woman to see that film. That's how much it changed me.

And working with my doula kept that shift going. During my pregnancy, I met regularly with her. I was finally ready to unpack what had happened with Bella's birth—and I told her everything. My fears, my worries, my grief, my hopes. She listened with genuine care, never rushing, never judging.

With her, I had space to process and heal. We talked about my triggers and how they might show up again during labour, and together we made a plan to meet them with calm and confidence.

More than anything, I wanted to feel like I had a voice in my birth—to have a say, to not just watch it unfold from the outside. My doula helped me reclaim that. Her support gave me the clarity—and the belief—that I could actually have it.

Looking back now, I know without a doubt: her presence during both of my subsequent pregnancies and births was essential. It was the missing piece. With her by my side, birth became something beautiful. Something transformative. Something I will always carry with pride.

I always joke with my husband that if I'd been pregnant during the COVID restrictions—when hospitals were only allowing one support person—he would've definitely lost that spot to our doula. I'm only half joking. No hard feelings, of course… but she had the skills. And the touch.

From the start, she made it her mission to understand us—both of us. She got to know my husband too—not just as my support person, but as part of the team. Because birth isn't a solo act. It's a shared space. And when it all kicked off, we were already in sync.

That's the thing about doulas—they don't take over. They lift the whole team. A good doula supports the partner too: helping them feel present, confident, and connected. It's not about stepping in. It's about creating a rhythm where everyone moves together.

And when labour hit, that rhythm mattered. She could read the room—and read me.

That moment stayed with me—because it showed me just how powerful an anchoring presence can be. There can be moments—no matter how much you've prepared—when it all starts to feel like it's slipping. Your breath quivers. Your body tightens. And that's when a doula can quietly bring you back. With a grounding word. A steady hand. A look that reminds you: you're still in this.

But that presence doesn't just happen. It works because there's been trust built beforehand. You've talked. Shared what helps. And they've listened—really listened. So when it matters, they meet you exactly where you are.

That kind of connection? It's not something most people find in the system. Appointments can feel rushed. Surface-level. It's easy to nod, smile, and say "all good" even when it's not.

Doula care isn't clinical or by-the-clock. It's real. It's steady. And often, it fills a space you didn't even realise was empty—until something finally filled it.

And look, I know some women think, "I don't need a doula—I've got my mum, my sister, my best friend. They'll be there." And maybe they will. They might be a beautiful part of your support team. But it's worth gently asking: what are they also bringing into your birth space? It's not just their care and good intentions (which are lovely). It's also their own stories, their own births, maybe even their own trauma. And unless they've taken the time to unpack that, it's coming with them—right into your birth room. Sometimes what feels like protection is actually fear in disguise. You might want calm presence, and instead you get someone trying to rescue you from pain the moment things get intense.

And then there's the sibling or friend who's never witnessed a birth before. Would they know how to advocate for you if something didn't feel right? Or would they pause, unsure whether it was their place to speak up? That's the difference.

A doula isn't there because you don't have people who love you. They're there because they're trained, grounded, and not carrying your birth—or anyone else's—on their back. They're not emotionally tangled in your story. They're there for *you*, full stop.

To really understand a doula's impact, you need to hear from the people who've been supported by one.

I once shared a post on Instagram, asking mothers and their partners to reflect on how their doula shaped their birth experience. The responses were raw and real.

Leila, a first-time mum, wrote:

"I was terrified of giving birth after hearing so many horror stories. My doula, Mara, changed that for me. She worked with me throughout my pregnancy, helping me reframe my fears and teaching me how to breathe through the contractions. By the time labour began, I felt strong and ready. I'll never forget the way she looked me in the eyes during a tough moment and said, 'You've got this.' That was all I needed."

Adam, whose wife Sarah hired a doula, admitted he wasn't sure at first.

"I thought, why do we need another person in the room? But as soon as labour started, I realised how much I needed her too. Nina, our doula, taught me how to really support Sarah, how to hold her, how to advocate for her wishes, even how to stay calm myself. She made me feel like I wasn't just there watching; I was part of the process."

Olivia, a mum of two, shared:

"When the doctors said we needed to head to surgery, I felt completely overwhelmed. Tara held my hand and explained everything as it was happening. She kept me calm and grounded in the scariest moment of my life. I don't know how I would have coped without her."

Stories like Olivia's say more than any definition ever could. And if you're still asking yourself, "What does a doula actually do?"

She reminds you who you are—at a time when it's easy to forget.

Not by telling you, but by reflecting it back. That's the work. That's the magic.

And here's the wild part: the research backs it up

We're not just talking warm and fuzzy vibes—there's solid research behind the power of continuous support in labour. The 2017 Cochrane Review (often called the gold standard for birth research), which looked at over 15,000 women across 26 studies, found that when someone is there just for you—not hospital staff, not a friend or partner, but someone whose only role is to support you, like a doula—you're more likely to have a shorter labour, use less pain relief, and avoid unnecessary interventions, including a lower chance of a Caesarean.

And beyond all that? You're more likely to feel supported, in control, and actually satisfied with your birth experience.

The message is clear: this kind of care really works.

But honestly? I don't need research to tell me that. I've seen it, felt it, and lived it. Studies only tell part of the story. What stays with women long after the baby arrives is walking away from birth not just relieved it's over—but simply proud of themselves.

It's why so many women say having a doula completely changed how they experienced birth.

Dr. John Kennell once famously said, *"If a doula were a drug, it would be unethical not to use it."*

Because when a woman feels truly held, something awakens—not just in her heart, but in her body. That's not just poetic—it's physiological.

Birth isn't just emotional. It's physical. The mind and body are in constant conversation during labour, quietly shaping how it unfolds. And when that connection is supported—not interrupted—it can change everything about how you move through it.

In the next chapter, we'll explore how to work with that connection—so your mind and body aren't just along for the ride, but fully engaged in the birth you deserve.

REFLECTION PRACTICE: IS A DOULA RIGHT FOR YOUR BIRTH

Inner Work: Exploring Whether Doula Support Feels Right for You

This exercise will help you decide if working with a doula fits your needs and expectations for pregnancy, birth, and postpartum support.

1. **Why Are You Considering a Doula?**

   ☞ What type of support are you looking for—physical comfort, emotional reassurance, information, advocacy?
   ☞ Is there a specific challenge or concern you want a doula to help with?
   ☞ Write a short list of what you want most from doula support.

2. **What Role Do You Want Your Doula to Play?**

   ☞ Do you want a doula involved during pregnancy, birth, postpartum, or all three?
   ☞ Would you prefer someone hands-on (e.g. massage, position changes) or mainly offering emotional support and reassurance?
   ☞ Note what feels right for you.

3. **How Do You Feel About Adding Another Person to Your Birth Space?**

   ☞ Would a doula's presence help you feel calmer and more supported?

☞ Or would it feel like too many people in the room?
☞ Jot down any thoughts.

4. What Qualities Matter Most in a Doula?

☞ Think about personality, communication style, experience, values, cultural understanding.
☞ What would make you feel safe and supported?
☞ List the top qualities you want in a doula.

5. Are You Prepared to Interview and Choose?

☞ Doulas vary widely. Are you ready to meet a few and ask about their approach?
☞ Do you know what boundaries or expectations you'll want to set?
☞ Write down any key questions you would ask a doula.

6. How Does Your Partner Feel About Having a Doula?

☞ If you have a partner, have you talked with them about the role of a doula?
☞ Would they feel supported by a doula, or unsure about including someone else?
☞ Note any thoughts or concerns you or your partner may have.

☞ When you're clear on what you want from a doula, you'll be better prepared to choose the right person—or to decide you don't need one. Either way, the choice is yours.

ASHLEY'S STORY

Growing up in a home marked by domestic violence and alcoholism, Ashley was determined to break the cycle and become a mother who offered her children the stability and love she herself longed for. Haunted by her own mother's harsh criticisms and predictions, she was driven by a deep desire to prove those doubts wrong.

However, Ashley's first two births left her grappling with trauma and feelings of failure. Her first birth ended in a C-section, leaving her with immense shame, guilt, and a sense of unworthiness. She felt like she had failed before her journey into motherhood had even begun. Her second birth was an attempted VBAC that turned into a traumatic emergency C-section due to a uterine rupture. Left awake on the operating table as the medical team worked to save her life, Ashley emerged with PTSD and overwhelming despair. The trauma weighed heavily on her, leaving her feeling disconnected from her children and doubting her ability to mother.

Determined to heal and reclaim her birth experience, Ashley spent years preparing for her third birth. Safety and autonomy became her priorities, and she chose a freebirth (a birth intentionally planned without a medical care provider present) to regain control over her body and the birthing process. Her preparation was deeply rooted in therapeutic healing and mind-body connection. Ashley worked with a psychologist and a mindset coach to address her trauma and rebuild her confidence. She immersed herself in birth courses, read extensively, and joined homebirth and freebirth communities. These connections gave her a sense of belonging and a supportive network to lean on.

Ashley embraced hypnobirthing, practicing meditation, visualisation, and affirmations to calm her mind and foster oxytocin, which helped her feel safe and grounded. Surrendering to the natural process of birth became a central focus for her, as she learned to trust her body's instincts.

While she sought a midwife, Ashley couldn't find one who would support her circumstances, including a high BMI and a history of C-sections. Therefore, she carefully chose a doula experienced in freebirth instead so that she has someone there who is able to provide her with the emotional and physical support she needed. She also created a birth plan that respected her wishes, ensuring her authority would be honoured and her space would remain free of coaching or interference.

On the day of her third birth, Ashley felt a profound sense of safety and support. She trusted her body's innate wisdom, allowing the process to unfold naturally and instinctively.

Surrounded by people who respected her autonomy and shared her values, Ashley experienced a birth that was calm, empowering, and deeply healing. For the first time, she felt whole, reclaiming her authority and belief in herself as a mother.

NATA'S STORY

"I was living my life, enjoying the simple pleasures, and being as present as I could be. I have always followed my inner compass, which led me down an unconventional path. In the past, I struggled with depression, but I resolved it through years of deep inner work. Later, I studied occupational therapy but, after encountering the limitations of the medical system, decided to become a mindset and life coach to help others. I experienced some difficult times in my life but was able to overcome them through my ability to feel deeply and my naturally positive outlook on life.

Before any trauma entered my life, I was living the dream. When I was young, I knew I wanted to build my life in Israel. So, after my studies, I moved there. I had a fantastic job, lived in the most beautiful part of the desert, with the love of my life, and I was 38 weeks pregnant.

Then, one Saturday morning, while cuddling in bed with my husband, we heard a rocket siren. It was October 7th, 2023. Our phones buzzed, and we quickly realised something was wrong. A horrific war had broken out. Within an hour of hearing the siren, my husband was drafted to the army reserves. He left immediately, and I didn't know when I'd see him next—if he'd make it to the birth, or whether he'd come home at all.

That same day, I had to leave my house for a safer area. Every day, I was confronted with horrific news, too cruel to believe, but painfully true. There was no way to escape what was happening. In an instant, I was ripped from my life, my home, my safe space, with my husband far away.

As I neared my due date, I endured never-ending prodromal labour. My body wanted to give birth but couldn't. The nesting instinct kicked in full force, but I wasn't home. I didn't feel comfortable or safe, even in this "safer" place. Every day, I worried sick about my husband, praying he was alive. Physically, mentally, and spiritually, I wasn't in a place that would allow my body to feel ready for labour. I tried every trick in the book, but nothing worked.

I can't even begin to describe how horrifying the war was. I knew I wasn't going into labour because I didn't feel safe where I was. I needed to go home, but my husband begged me to stay in the safer area. By week 41, I was physically and mentally exhausted. I couldn't take it anymore, so I moved back home. Within a few days, labour began, but I was stuck in the latent phase for two days.

Thankfully, my husband was released from the army and was with me. At 42 weeks, I was utterly drained. With his support, I decided to move things along and got admitted to the hospital for a Cook catheter (a device used to manually prepare the cervix for labour). That was the most painful and horrible part of my labour. After six hours of intense contractions, I had a breakdown. I was sure that this birth would become the most traumatic experience of my life, worse than the war itself.

Nothing was going to plan. I had wanted an unmedicated hospital birth and to go into active labour naturally. But all the conditions that support labour, oxytocin, safety, and comfort were missing. I didn't feel safe! My labour and delivery room were literally a bomb shelter.

I did my best to separate what was happening in the world from what was happening to me. I accepted the situation for what it was, focusing on what I could control. I turned my attention to my husband, his support, his love, his voice, his hands holding me. In that connection, I found home.

When I hit my lowest point, I called my doula, and her presence became the turning point of my birth. She has a special energy; the moment she walked into the room, everything felt calmer and more grounded. I felt safe and cared for in her presence. We did bodywork to help me stay present and connected to my baby and the sensations of labour. It kept me from thinking about anything else.

In preparation for this birth, I had done a hypnobirthing course with my husband and worked closely with my doula throughout pregnancy. Her support was continuous, helping me face every challenge, even during the war. She provided counselling, craniosacral therapy, and physical massage treatments that were invaluable.

I also leaned on my years of coaching experience and my deep belief that everything happens for a reason, even when I don't understand it. I held onto my faith that everything would be okay. I've always believed that whatever I set my mind to, I can achieve. One of my strengths is that I don't get attached to bad thoughts or feelings. I feel them, yes, but I don't dwell or get stuck. I keep moving forward.

The moment my doula looked into my eyes; I felt a deep reassurance. It was as if her soul whispered, You're going to be okay. We immediately began Spinning Babies exercises, and within 15 minutes, my water broke. I was already six hours into labour by then, but now I could finally let go and fully enter that deep "labourland." I was so in tune with my body, sensations, and the journey. Nothing else existed.

I laboured on the ball and in the shower, working with the pain and pressure. At one point, I had a setback when my midwife said that not all of my waters had broken and suggested helping them along. After the procedure, I went from 8 cm back to 5 cm. It was a lot to take in, but I reminded myself I'd get back to 8 cm faster this time. My doula stayed by my side every second.

After 20 hours of active labour, I was beyond exhausted. I asked for a cervical check and told myself that if I was at 10 cm, I would consider giving birth without an epidural. The midwife said I was at 9 cm, but I was so physically drained that I opted for the epidural. I laboured with it for another 2-3 hours. Twice, my baby's heart rate dropped, almost resulting in an emergency C-section, but my doula guided me through bodywork to prevent it.

After around 23 hours of labour, I had to push or risk needing a vacuum-assisted birth. I pushed for 20 minutes, and then my baby girl came into the world. It was the most surreal experience of my life.

Everything felt so natural, the way I held her, the way she latched. I felt like a mother from the very first moment. After an extended golden hour, I left the delivery room feeling the

proudest I've ever been. I felt like I could conquer the world, because nothing is as powerful and miraculous as giving birth.

To other mothers, I encourage you to treat each birth as a new experience, free from the attachments of the past. Be present with what's happening in the moment. Work with your body and nervous system. Explore ways to regulate yourself and create a birth experience that is beautiful and empowering. And please, look into hypnobirthing, it can make all the difference!"

CHAPTER 13

Mind-Body Connection – Aligning Mind and Body for Birth

> *"It is the mind that makes the body rich."*
> —William Shakespeare

Olympic swimmer Michael Phelps is known for his intense visualisation practices, often rehearsing every aspect of his race — including what might go wrong. During the 2008 Olympics, his goggles filled with water mid-race. Because he had mentally trained to stay calm under pressure, he continued swimming blind and still won gold — even breaking a world record. While we may not all be Olympic athletes, this kind of mental preparation can be incredibly powerful — especially in birth. His story reminds us of a powerful truth: the mind and body are deeply connected, and when they work together, incredible things can happen.

But let's be real—most of us aren't swimming blind toward gold medals. Still, if visualising a smooth birth works even half as well as it did for him, sign me up for the mental Olympics.

And while birth is a very different kind of endurance, the principle holds: when the mind is steady, the body can do incredible things.

That realisation put everything in a new light for me.

This mind-body connection isn't just theory—I've felt it in my own body.

For years, I was on a mission to understand how the mind works—mainly because I needed to help myself. I devoured everything I could find, trying to understand how our thoughts shape not just our feelings, but our physical experience too. And what I discovered blew me away. It wasn't just about learning. It was about reclaiming my power.

When I realised I could change not only my mindset but the way I experienced birth, something clicked—deeply.

Healing wasn't a straight line for me (spoiler alert: it never is). But it gave me something invaluable: real, deep, *"I get it"* understanding when I sit with someone else carrying the same weight.

I'm not a therapist or a doctor, and I'm definitely not here to hand out diagnoses. But I can spot when survival mode quietly takes the wheel—and I know how it can twist birth into something it was never meant to be.

That's why I pay attention when I sit with women preparing for birth. I notice the little ways fear sneaks in—a nervous laugh, hesitation in their voice, shoulders tensing just talking about labour.

I remember it from my own first birth. Fear doesn't politely stay in your head—it sets up camp in your whole body. When your mind freezes, your body follows. It's like your brain says, *"Panic mode, go!"* and your uterus replies, *"Copy that. Shutting down."*

I've seen how much it matters to have a safe space—somewhere you can go inward, process what's there, and meet birth with clarity. Because birth doesn't just happen in the body—it moves through your whole being.

Your birth hormones know what to do. But stress? It throws a spanner in the works. It tightens muscles, ramps up pain, and can stall labour altogether. Meanwhile, doubt creeps in, and instincts get second-guessed.

This is where so many women get stuck—not in their bodies, but in their minds.

There's a space between what our bodies are capable of and what our minds are still holding onto. That space? That's why the mind-body connection matters.

It's not just about getting your body "ready." It's about softening the mind, loosening the grip of what's holding you back, and helping both sides trust each other.

When your mind steps back and lets your body do what it already knows how to do, things tend to flow more easily.

Birth works best when you and your body are on the same team.

And here's the thing: none of this is new. For thousands of years, healers around the world understood that true health comes from balance—the mind, the body, and the spirit all working together. Ancient traditions like Ayurveda in India and Chinese medicine were built on this idea. Even Hippocrates, the guy we call the 'Father of Medicine,' believed in treating the whole person. He famously said, *"Natural forces within us are the true healers of disease."*

While these traditions continued in many cultures, western medicine eventually took a different path.

Around the 1600s, during a time called the Enlightenment—when science and reason were taking centre stage, thinkers like René Descartes came along with this idea that the mind and body were totally separate. That thinking shaped modern medicine for centuries. The body became something to fix—like a machine with broken parts. And sure, that mindset led to some incredible breakthroughs, but it also came with a cost: the emotional and mental sides of health got boxed up and pushed aside.

Imagine if we'd never lost that connection. If we'd always seen the mind and body as inseparable. Maybe we would've built a system that cared for the whole person, not just their parts.

Thankfully, by the late 1800s, some people started to question that split. American psychologist William James argued that emotions and physical reactions are linked. A racing heart, tense shoulders—they're not just random; they're part of how we experience stress or fear. Around the same time, Sigmund Freud suggested that buried emotions and unresolved conflicts could show up in the body as physical symptoms.

And modern science is catching up. Our thoughts and emotions don't just stay in our heads—they show up in our bodies, too. Take stress, for example. It doesn't just leave you feeling drained. It can weaken your immune system, fuel inflammation, and slow down healing. That's why practices like mindfulness, meditation, and yoga have found their way back into mainstream healthcare—they help restore the balance ancient healers always knew was essential.

One of my favourite mind-body examples comes from World War II. Doctor Henry Beecher noticed something wild: soldiers who thought they were getting morphine—but were actually given saline—still felt pain relief. Saltwater. It worked because their brains believed it did, flipping the body's natural "feel better" switch. If that doesn't tell you how powerful your mind is, I don't know what does.

The bottom line? Your mind and body aren't separate. They're in constant conversation, shaping how you feel, heal, and move through life. And when it comes to birth? That connection becomes everything.

One of the best real-world examples of the mind-body connection in birth comes from the stories I've heard (and seen) from women who've used HypnoBirthing®. Developed by Marie Mongan, it's helped countless women approach labour with calm and confidence—turning what most expect to be overwhelming into something empowering.

The roots of this approach trace back almost a century to Dr. Grantly Dick-Read, an English obstetrician who started asking a question no one else was asking: why do some women experience unbearable pain in labour, while others don't?

In the 1920s, Dick-Read was called to assist a woman in a poor neighbourhood. Expecting to find her doubled over in agony, he was stunned to see her calm and composed, birthing her baby without the intense pain he thought was inevitable. When he asked her how she managed it, her answer stopped him cold: *"It didn't hurt. It wasn't supposed to, was it?"*

That one sentence flipped everything he thought he knew about labour. As he studied birth more closely, he noticed a pattern. Fear triggered tension, muscles tightened, labour slowed, pain increased—and so the vicious cycle repeated. He named it the *Fear–Tension–Pain theory*.

Dick-Read believed that removing fear allowed labour to progress naturally, with less tension and less pain. His insight laid the foundation for the natural childbirth movement.

HypnoBirthing® builds on exactly that understanding. It teaches women how to break free from the *fear–tension–pain* cycle using guided relaxation, visualisation, and breath. The goal isn't to eliminate sensation, but to shift how it's experienced. When the mind stays calm, the body follows: endorphins flow, tension melts, and labour unfolds with less struggle.

That's the power of the mind in birth—but it also shows the flip side. When fear, anxiety, or trauma sneak in, they can quietly raise walls that slow or stall the process. Understanding how our minds work—and how past experiences shape our reactions—is key to unlocking a smoother birth.

But this connection doesn't stop at the emotional level—it's hardwired into the body.

To really get it, we've got to zoom out. It's not just thoughts and feelings shaping your experience—it's biology. Enter one of the most fascinating fields of science: epigenetics.

If you've never heard of it, don't worry, you're not alone. Epigenetics is basically the study of how your genes and your life experiences have been having secret little conversations behind your back. Think of your genes as a movie script. Epigenetics? It's the director deciding which scenes get the dramatic close-up and which ones get quietly left on the cutting room floor.

And the wild part? Your environment, choices, and even your emotional state can affect which parts of that script are "switched on" or "switched off." The way you live, love, stress, rest, eat, move—it all plays a role in shaping both your mental and physical health.

But here's where it gets seriously fascinating (and a little spooky): trauma and chronic stress can leave epigenetic marks. Imagine someone scribbling notes in the margins of your genetic script. Those notes can alter how your genes behave. They can crank up your risk for things like anxiety, depression, or PTSD. And sometimes—plot twist—they can even be passed down to the next generation. That's what we call intergenerational trauma or ancestral trauma.

Think about it: your ancestors might have survived famine, war, or unthinkable hardships. Their bodies adapted to stay alive, and those survival strategies may have been handed down to you—not as stories, but as subtle little shifts in how your body reacts to stress. It's like you've inherited a quiet echo of their struggle. A living reminder of their resilience.

But (because life loves a twist) that inheritance can also come with baggage. Sometimes it makes us more sensitive to stress or trauma in our own lives, and we don't even know why.

Researchers have started to see this play out in real life. The children and grandchildren of Holocaust survivors and war veterans sometimes show biological signs of the trauma that came before them—like changes in how their bodies respond to stress. It's proof that the past doesn't always stay in the past.

But here's the empowering part: once we understand this, we can start to shift it. We don't have to carry the whole story forward.

I've felt this intergenerational imprint in my own life—not in birth, but just as deeply in my body. I'm the descendant of Holocaust survivors. I lost my grandparents when I was young, so I never got to hear much of their stories firsthand. But I've always carried this deep urge to understand what they went through. I read about the Holocaust as a child, and even more now as an adult. Not out of morbid curiosity, but because something inside me has always needed to know. That feeling never really left.

Years ago, during the COVID lockdowns in Australia, I felt a wave of unease that went way beyond frustration or inconvenience. It felt ancestral. Society started to divide. In many places, unvaccinated people were barred from everyday spaces—cafes, libraries, cinemas, universities, and events. Suddenly, you couldn't participate in normal life without showing proof of status. News, social media, even everyday conversations turned harsh. Unvaccinated people were painted as irresponsible, selfish, or dangerous. That shift—from disagreement to dehumanisation—was deeply unsettling.

There was also talk of government-run quarantine camps being built not far from where I lived. They were described as public health infrastructure, but something about it didn't sit right with me. It stirred a feeling I couldn't ignore, one that had nothing to do with the headlines and everything to do with something deeper in my bones. It felt familiar.

My nervous system went straight into high alert. It wasn't conscious fear. It was a body-level knowing. An echo. A visceral alarm that said, this has happened before.

I can't say for sure what was biology and what was memory—but something deep inside me reacted. Now I understand that what I felt wasn't just about the present moment. It was inherited trauma. The kind that bypasses logic and goes straight to the body.

And this is why I believe so strongly in the work of nervous system support in birth. Because what's in our body—ours or inherited—doesn't just vanish. It asks to be seen. And if we're not paying attention, it can show up right when we need the most safety.

The good news? We're not stuck with the stuff our ancestors—or our past selves—handed us. Epigenetics reminds us that our choices, environment, and actions can help rewrite the story. Healing is possible.

And one of the most powerful ways we can influence that healing is through how we care for both our thoughts and bodies.

That's where these practices come in. They don't just help you physically prep for birth; they retrain how your body responds to stress and fear. When your mind calms down and your body softens, birth gets the space it needs to do what it already knows how to do—with less tension and way more trust.

But here's another layer you might not have considered.

We don't just carry what's in our DNA. We carry the stories we've absorbed—TV dramas, family birth horror stories, cultural noise, even that random TikTok titled *"Why Birth Is Terrifying."* All of it sticks around, even if we don't realise it.

This connection between what we believe and how we feel in our bodies doesn't suddenly appear in pregnancy—it's been forming for years. And when the beliefs you've soaked up say birth is painful or terrifying, your body tends to brace for it. Muscles tense, fear rises, and labour feels harder than it needs to.

The good news is the opposite is true too. A calm, supported mind sends your body a signal of safety: *You've got this.* Tension melts, endorphins flow, and labour finds its rhythm. It's proof that your mindset matters.

And here's the thing: most of those beliefs? They're not conscious.

Your subconscious—the part shaped by years of subtle messaging—is often the one calling the shots. From childhood, we absorb everything: tone of voice, body language, unspoken fears. It all leaves an imprint. A song, a smell, a familiar room can pull you back to a moment you didn't even know you remembered. That's not just nostalgia. That's your nervous system speaking.

So of course, when something as big and primal as birth shows up, those old imprints come with it. Sometimes they support you. Sometimes they get in the way. That's why unpacking them before birth can be such a game-changer.

There's an exercise I love to use with my clients that helps uncover those deep-rooted beliefs and gently reshape the ones that aren't serving you. I encourage every mama-to-be to give it a go as part of her birth preparation. It helps you understand what you believe, where those ideas came from, and how you can start shifting them.

The best part? You'll create a personal mantra or affirmation to help rewrite the script. Repetition is the subconscious mind's favourite language. The more you repeat it, the more your subconscious accepts it as truth. Before long, it starts to feel like second nature.

BIRTHING WITH TRAUMA AND FEAR

EXPLORING THE CIRCLE OF LEARNED BELIEFS

Begin by reflecting on your thoughts about birth using the following steps. Write down your answers as you go:

1. **What Do You Truly Believe About Birth?**

    Think about your deepest beliefs about giving birth. Focus on how you felt before learning from childbirth education, books, documentaries, or anything else that has influenced you recently. What did you originally imagine birth would be like?

2. **Where Did These Beliefs Come From?**

    Ask yourself where these ideas originated. Were they shaped by family, friends, stories, social media, TV shows, or things you've read or heard or even from a previous birth experience?

3. **Is This Belief Serving You?**

    Consider if holding on to this belief has been beneficial. How has it positively influenced your thoughts or feelings about birth?

4. **Is This Belief Hurting You?**

    Reflect on whether this belief has had a negative impact on you. How might it be creating fear, doubt, or stress?

Take your time with each question, being as honest and thoughtful as possible. This exercise will help you better understand your mindset about birth and where it comes from.

TRANSFORMING YOUR BELIEFS FOR A POSITIVE BIRTH JOURNEY

Now that you've explored your beliefs, it's time to reframe them if needed. Follow these steps to make deep subconscious changes:

1. **Review and Reflect on Your Beliefs**

    Read over what you've written and take a moment to acknowledge your beliefs. Recognise that these beliefs, whether positive or negative, served a purpose in the past, often as a way to protect you or guide you.

2. **Honour Their Purpose**

    Understand that these beliefs have helped you get to where you are now. They've served their purpose, and it's okay to let them go if they no longer support your journey.

3. **Reframe Negative Beliefs**

    If some of your beliefs are holding you back, it's time to transform them into positive, empowering ones.

    - For example: If you believe, "Birth is hard and painful," reframe it to: *"I turn my pain into power."*
    - If you believe, "I won't be able to handle it," shift it to: *"My body is strong and capable of handling anything."*

4. **Choose New Beliefs**

    Write down 1–5 new belief statements that reflect how you want to feel about your birth journey. Make sure these statements align with your hopes and goals.

5. **Integrate Your New Beliefs**

   Place these new belief statements around your home where you'll see them often, on mirrors, doors, or your desk. Repeat them to yourself every day, especially when you feel doubt or fear creeping in.

6. **Reinforce Them Regularly**

   On tough days, when old beliefs resurface, lean into your new affirmations even more. The key is to consciously reinforce your new mindset to keep negativity and self-doubt from influencing your birthing experience.

By consistently practicing this inner work, you'll start to swap out those limiting beliefs for ones that actually lift you up. You'll build a strong, positive foundation for a beautiful birthing experience.

And this reflection isn't just for you. It can be just as powerful for anyone who'll be part of your support team—your partner, your mum, a family member, a friend. Everyone who steps into the birthing space brings their own emotions, stories, and beliefs with them (sometimes subtly, sometimes... not so subtly). Encouraging them to do a little inner work too can help keep the energy calm, grounded, and focused on supporting you, not bringing in any external fears or anxieties.

By doing this, you give yourself the chance to step into birth with a fresh perspective. You get to let go of old fears and assumptions and approach the journey with more openness, confidence, and trust in yourself. It sounds simple, but I've seen firsthand how powerful that shift can be.

When I was preparing for the birth of my second daughter, I approached things completely differently than I had the first time around. Yes, I still did some of the physical preparation, but what made the biggest difference was focusing on my mindset and emotional well-being. I started with the same mindset exercise I've shared with you here, working through what I believed about birth and reshaping the things that weren't helping me.

And I didn't stop there. I made mindset the foundation of everything. I worked on my thoughts, emotions, and inner strength just as much—if not more—than I prepared my body.

All the inner work I'd done showed up when it mattered most, and I was able to stay steady through the whole experience.

By the time I was preparing for my third daughter's birth, I already knew: mindset first, always. It gave me the tools to meet birth with a quiet confidence.

The work you do will be your own. What helped me might not fully resonate with you—and that's completely fine. But if any of it does, take it. Tweak it. Make it your own. Fold it into your self-care practice in a way that feels good to you.

And as you start exploring the list of practices at the end of this chapter, just remember, mindset work is one piece of the puzzle. Sometimes the biggest shifts happen when we go deeper—when we tend to old wounds, loosen fear's grip, and start unravelling the patterns and trauma that no longer serve us.

That's exactly what we'll explore next: the healing practices that can help you process, release, and rebuild from the inside out.

SIMPLE MIND-BODY TOOLS TO HELP YOU GET READY FOR BIRTH

Here are some of my favourite mind-body practices to support you through pregnancy and get you prepped for birth. I've used many of these myself over the years as part of my own healing and preparation, so I know how much they can help. None of these are "must-dos"—think of them as a menu to pick and choose from, depending on what feels right for you. I've also included where you can learn more or give them a go:

1. **Calm Breathing Exercises**

    Where to learn: Look for prenatal yoga studios, birth classes, or online platforms that teach breathwork for labour and relaxation.

2. **Meditation and Visualisation**

    Where to learn: Many doulas offer guided sessions or can point you to trusted resources. Look for meditation tracks or birth classes that include practices to support calm and focus.

3. **HypnoBirthing® Techniques**

    Where to learn: Certified HypnoBirthing® instructors or books—especially those by Marie Mongan, the method's founder—are excellent starting points.

    HypnoBirthing® is a registered trademark of the HypnoBirthing® Institute.

4. **Gentle or Prenatal Yoga**

    Where to learn: Check local yoga studios, online pregnancy yoga series, or apps with prenatal-specific classes.

5. **Progressive Muscle Relaxation (PMR)**

   Where to learn: Often taught in therapy or stress management programs. Also available through mental wellness apps and guided videos.

6. **Mantras and Affirmations**

   Where to learn: These are commonly included in HypnoBirthing®, birth prep courses, or doula sessions. You'll also find printable cards, apps, or playlists online.

7. **Guided Imagery**

   Where to learn: Often taught by HypnoBirthing® instructors or meditation teachers. Look for audio tracks or videos that walk you through calming, birth-focused visualisations.

8. **Acupressure**

   Where to learn: Some doulas, bodyworkers, or acupuncturists offer acupressure education. Trusted prenatal websites also have visual tutorials.

9. **Journaling**

   Where to learn: Some childbirth educators or therapists offer prompts and writing exercises. Pregnancy-focused journals and apps are also widely available.

10. **Sound Healing or Soothing Music**

    Where to learn: Try local sound healing classes or find curated playlists made for labour, meditation, or sleep. Look for those tailored to calming your nervous system.

11. **Positive Self-Talk Practice**

   Where to learn: Included in mindfulness-based birth courses, therapy sessions, or guided audio tools that support mental resilience during labour.

12. **Gentle Partner Massage and Self-Massage**

   Where to learn: Prenatal massage therapists, yoga instructors, or doulas may teach simple techniques. Books and trusted video tutorials are also helpful.

13. **Self-Help Books for Mind–Body Connection**

   Where to start: Check your local bookstore or library, or search online for summaries and audiobooks. Some impactful reads include:

   - *Feel the Fear and Do It Anyway* by Susan Jeffers
   - *A Mind of Your Own* by Dr. Kelly Brogan
   - *The Body Keeps the Score* by Bessel van der Kolk
   - *What Happened to You?* by Dr. Bruce Perry & Oprah Winfrey

   These books explore how mindset, past experiences, and emotions shape our health and healing.

14. **Tapping (EFT – Emotional Freedom Technique)**

   Where to learn: Look for certified EFT practitioners, online videos, or apps that offer guided sessions. Tapping involves using your fingers to gently tap acupressure points while repeating affirming statements. It's a great way to calm anxiety, release fear, and regulate emotions—especially during pregnancy and birth prep.

15. **Podcasts for Mind-Body Support**

   Where to learn: Many pregnancy and birth podcasts offer mindful tools, expert insights, and real stories from women. Listening to these can help you feel more grounded, less alone, and more connected to your body—whether you're walking, resting, or on the go.

MIND-BODY CONNECTION PRACTICE: BODY AWARENESS & GROUNDING

This practice helps you notice the physical signals your body gives you—before, during, and after stress. It's a simple way to check in, ground yourself, and build awareness of how your body responds.

1. **Body Scan & Awareness Journal**

    ☞ Sit comfortably or lie down. Slowly bring your attention to different parts of your body, from your head down to your feet.

    ☞ Notice and reflect:
    - Where do you feel any tightness, tension, or discomfort?
    - Where feels soft, open, or relaxed?
    - Are there areas where you feel warmth or coolness?
    - Are you holding your breath or breathing freely?
    - Are your hands clenched, your shoulders raised, your jaw tight?
    - Is your posture open or collapsed inward?
    - If focusing feels difficult, try a guided body scan meditation (many are available online or in mindfulness apps).

    ✎ Write down a few notes. You can list sensations, draw a simple body outline with marks, or describe the overall feeling of being in your body today.

2. 5 Senses Grounding Exercise

☞ When you feel overwhelmed or want to reconnect, pause and name:
- 5 things you can see
- 4 things you can feel
- 3 things you can hear
- 2 things you can smell
- 1 thing you can taste

✎ Notice which sense helps you feel most grounded. You can use this as a quick anchor during labour.

---

3. Daily Mind-Body Check-In Routine

☞ At three points during your day, pause for a moment:
- Morning: "What does my body need today?"
- Midday: "Where am I holding tension?"
- Evening: "What helped me feel grounded today?"

✎ Repeat for one week. Reflect on any patterns you notice in how your body responds to different situations.

Bringing It Together

Building this habit now makes it easier to notice, understand, and respond to what your body needs—not just in pregnancy, but in birth and beyond.

STEPH'S STORY

Steph's story gently opens the door to a conversation many of us carry quietly—how generational trauma can shape our experience of birth. The emotional weight passed down through our mothers and grandmothers doesn't just live in memory; it lives in the body. In sharing her journey, Steph reveals how this inherited pain impacted her first birth—and how healing, support, and reconnection helped her reclaim the joy and power that birth can hold.

> "The origins of my trauma can be traced back to the moment of my birth, as I was born during a war. This trauma flowed throughout my family and life; it was what I grew up hearing and knowing.
>
> I entered this world during the Yugoslavian war. My mother, carrying me within her, faced the constant threat of bombs and an uncertain future for us both. As her labour began, fear gripped her, not only for the process of giving birth but also for the daunting challenges of reaching a hospital and receiving necessary assistance. A curfew meant leaving the house was prohibited, leaving her in darkness without electricity or hot water.
>
> Despite these dire circumstances, my mother managed to contact emergency services, and an ambulance was dispatched. Upon arriving at the hospital, she found herself alone in a room with another expectant mother while the doctor casually strolled away with a cigarette in hand. Visitors were strictly prohibited, and she endured labour without any support. In the midst of her pain, she felt the urge to push. The

doctor returned and performed an unnecessary episiotomy without pain relief.

Due to complications and the need for a blood transfusion, I remained in the hospital for approximately two weeks. During this time, my father was unable to visit due to religious discrimination, further compounding the challenges my family faced.

Throughout my formative years, I was immersed in narratives of the harsh realities of the world I was born into, leaving me with a profound sense of trauma that persisted throughout my life. Moving to two different countries by the time I was seven and relearning three languages left me feeling as though I didn't belong anywhere. This sense of displacement, coupled with my family's experiences, shaped much of who I became.

The fear I felt surrounding childbirth was deeply rooted in the traumas I had endured. When I discovered I was pregnant, a wave of joy and fear washed over me simultaneously.

My journey through the birthing portal was long and difficult. My mother was with me, and I felt her anxieties and traumas resurface during this vulnerable time. After 28 hours of labour, an induction, and an epidural, I was told my son's heartbeat was dangerously high. The only way to avoid a potentially life-threatening c-section was to agree to an episiotomy and the use of forceps. In that moment, I felt as though I was reliving my mother's experience in a modern setting. This left me burdened with trauma and sadness that proved difficult to shake. I sobbed uncontrollably for months, even though I had never felt more in love than I did with my newborn son. The episiotomy scar served as a constant reminder of the disappointment I carried, symbolising the way I brought him into the world.

When preparing for my second birth, I made a conscious effort to avoid getting caught up in small details or overthinking things. I found solace in nature, regularly hiking in the mountains and visiting the ocean. There, I would meditate, swim, or simply enjoy the peace. Relaxing under the sun with my favourite book became a cherished ritual. Cooking with my son became a daily activity, as we prepared delicious meals, baked goods, and fresh bread together. We grew our own herbs and vegetables, and we cared for the animals we had.

Slowing down physically and mentally was essential.

I sought alignment through regular visits to a chiropractor and, later, to an acupuncturist. Self-care became a priority, and I embraced simple pleasures like reading, taking baths, and connecting with loved ones. I revisited hypnobirthing techniques I had learned during my first pregnancy, which helped me find calm and focus. I was fortunate to have two incredible midwives who provided unwavering support and confidence. They created a safe space for me to express my fears and concerns, allowing me to feel heard. My amazing husband and son were constant sources of love and encouragement, and my friends, fellow mothers, neighbours, and my own mother were part of my support system.

The morning of my birth, I went to see my midwives for a checkup. Although I was nearly two weeks past my due date, I wasn't worried. The midwives were nothing but supportive. All day, I felt small niggles, a sense that today might be the day.

Later that afternoon, I noticed what looked like a mucus plug, which my midwife confirmed. About an hour later, as I was stepping into a relaxing shower, my waters began to trickle.

Shortly after, I felt slight discomfort in my stomach. By 7 p.m., I decided to take a short stroll around the neighbourhood, but the surges quickly intensified, and I turned back home. The surges gradually became stronger, and by 10 p.m., they were coming closer together. My partner suggested calling the midwife, but I wanted to stay in bed a little longer. Soon after, I began vomiting and knew it was time. My partner called the midwife, who confirmed we should come in.

We arrived at the birthing centre at 12:46 a.m. The room was beautifully set up with fairy lights, and the birthing pool was ready. My midwife asked if I wanted to be checked, and I agreed. I was 6 cm dilated. I decided to use the shower, letting the water hit my lower back to ease the intense back pain as the surges started from my back and wrapped around.

As the surges came closer together, I felt doubt and fear creeping in. My partner held me and reassured me, reminding me how amazing I was and that everything was unfolding as it should. Suddenly, I felt my baby drop. In that moment, I saw and felt the presence of every strong and amazing woman in my life, their words, their strength, and their stories filled me with power. My grandmothers, my mum, the women who had been like mothers to me, my friends, even my neighbour who had given me encouragement on my walk the day before.

Their strength carried me through.

I realised I needed to surrender. I heard my midwife's voice from outside the shower, asking me what I was feeling. Moments later, I was in the birthing pool, sitting on my knees and feeling nothing but strength as I brought my son into the world. He was born at 1:58 a.m., just over an hour after we arrived.

Holding my son in my arms, I felt pure happiness and joy. I was overwhelmed with love, strength, achievement, and success. This birth healed immense trauma and forever changed my outlook on birth.

Trauma can have a profound impact on our lives, often holding us back and hindering our progress. Letting go of those experiences can be incredibly challenging. Yet, life moves forward, and our scars remain as reminders, not of pain, but of resilience. We need not forget or ignore them but embrace them as part of who we are. These experiences shape us, strengthening our resolve and defining our journey. For that, I am grateful."

EMILIE'S STORY

"I was a child with health problems that required seven surgeries between the ages of 6 and 18, spanning three different countries. These surgeries and hospital stays were traumatic experiences. I vividly remember the fear of sleeping alone in hospitals, I always had a parent sleeping on a chair nearby, even when it wasn't allowed. To this day, I can still recall the smell of the gas they used to put me to sleep with the mask when I was just six years old (I'm now 40).

Some hospital employees weren't kind, and I never felt truly cared for. I can still picture one instance clearly where the bandage removal process was so excruciating that, when I cried and complained, a nurse dismissed me as being difficult. That feeling of helplessness has stayed with me, shaping a deep fear of hospitals and a lingering distrust of medical professionals.

When it came time for my first birth in 2019, I was determined to avoid interventions and take back control of my experience. I prepared extensively, immersing myself in hypnobirthing, reading countless books on natural birth, watching documentaries, and even becoming a prenatal yoga instructor. I enrolled in a Midwifery Group Program at the local hospital. Despite all my preparation, what I truly wanted was a home birth. But at the time, I didn't know anyone who had birthed at home, and I wasn't aware of the many podcasts and resources available. I lacked the confidence to take that step, and my mum's strong opposition didn't help either.

The night I went to the hospital, my labour slowed down and eventually stopped altogether. Long story short, it ended in an emergency C-section, another surgery that left me feeling defeated.

For my second birth in 2023, I made the decision not to engage with the medical system at all. I hired a private homebirth midwife and kept my plans discreet, especially from my family. I did a lot of work to ensure my hospital trauma wouldn't play out again, even in the event of a transfer. I was determined not to face another emergency C-section.

I prepared meticulously. First, I made sure my midwife fully supported my choices, including birthing at home and opting out of routine scans and tests. I kept my plans quiet, especially from my parents and in-laws, to protect my energy and focus. During pregnancy, I underwent hypnotherapy and discovered that, deep down, I believed going to a hospital meant inevitable medical interventions. It was naive to think I could avoid them given my past experiences, and I had to forgive myself for that.

I also did past life regression sessions, where I identified the origins of my mistrust of hospitals. I uncovered a trauma embedded in my DNA, a lifetime where I brought a sick child to the hospital, and they didn't survive. This fear had replayed in different forms over lifetimes. Alongside this, I did energy work, tapping, affirmations, and listened to countless natural birth and homebirth podcasts to reinforce my belief in my body's ability to birth freely at home. I learned to fully surrender to the power of birth.

My support network was incredible. I had a village of friends, including three experienced homebirthers and freebirthers who shared wisdom and reassurance. A few weeks before my due date, they organised a beautiful Mother's Blessing Ceremony. I was intentional about protecting my energy, especially in the final months, and surrounded myself only with people and influences that felt supportive.

This pregnancy, I didn't focus on the technicalities of birth. I knew my mindset was the key to my preparation. I meditated daily, journaled, and shared my fears with my partner, working through them, often with hypnotherapy. We also discussed the rare scenarios where my midwife might recommend a hospital transfer, addressing any fears or feelings that arose.

The day of the birth felt magical. It was a stormy spring day, November 11th, my favourite kind of weather. Around 10 or 11 a.m., I lost my mucus plug and told my partner, "Today would be a really good day for this baby to arrive." I spent the morning painting on the deck with my daughter. Looking back, my only regret was waiting until surges were five minutes apart to start setting up the birth space and pool!

By mid-afternoon, my surges intensified. Around 5 p.m., I messaged my midwife and my daughter's support person to let them know things were progressing. While lying on the couch, I started timing contractions and realised labour was happening that night, not the next day as I'd thought. My partner and I set up the birth space, and I invited my daughter, who was at my mum's, to return if she wanted to witness the birth. Of course, she said yes.

As labour progressed, I embraced the surges, breathing deeply and finding relief in the shower. When the hot water ran out about 40 minutes later, I moved to the pool. My body was shaking, and I felt intense heat as my baby began her descent. My midwife arrived around 7:30 p.m. and discovered fresh meconium in the pool. She couldn't get a clear reading of the baby's heartbeat and recommended a hospital transfer, suspecting the baby was in distress.

For a moment, my mind raced. I envisioned giving up and resigning myself to another C-section. But then, I tuned into my intuition and felt my baby was fine. I explained this to my midwife, who offered to check me vaginally. She exclaimed, "Her head is here!" and confirmed there was no need to transfer.

Reinvigorated, I returned to the pool, meeting each surge with newfound strength. I talked to my baby, asking her to come gently and giving myself time to recover between surges. When I felt what I thought was her head, I asked my midwife to confirm. She realised it was her bum, my baby was breech but didn't tell me earlier to avoid alarming me. This didn't faze me; I trusted my midwife and her experience with breech births.

My baby's body emerged in the pool. Following my midwife's instructions, I stepped out of the pool, kneeled on the edge, and pushed with all my strength to deliver her head. After two massive pushes, she was born. At first, she wasn't breathing, but I wasn't worried. I knew babies born quickly sometimes take a moment to transition. Within seconds, she let out her first sounds. The Ambulance arrived but quickly left, as there was no need for intervention.

We moved onto the mattress to cuddle as a family. Time stood still as we basked in the magic of the moment. My friend fed me tea and banana cake while I cradled baby Maya and held my eldest daughter, Alaya. My partner had his arms around us, and it felt like the most powerful, loving moment of our lives. That night, we all went to bed high on love.

Maya was born at 8:20 p.m., the exact opposite time of day as her sister, Alaya, who was born at 8:20 a.m.

To other women, I say this: Don't ignore the grip trauma can have on you. Face it head-on, peel back the layers, and heal. You are capable of profound transformation and an empowered birth experience. Trust in your strength and the power within you."

CHAPTER 14

Therapeutic Healing - Finding Strength Through Healing Practices

"Healing doesn't mean the damage never existed.
It means the damage no longer controls your life."
—Author unknown

In Australia, many military veterans face ongoing challenges such as PTSD, depression, and anxiety after their service. Traditional treatments don't work for everyone, leading some to explore alternative paths to healing. In 2021, former professional surfer Rusty Moran founded the Veteran Surf Project (VSP), offering veterans the chance to reconnect with themselves and others through surfing.

The program provides a therapeutic experience grounded in mindfulness, movement, and time in nature. For many participants, riding waves offers more than just exercise — it becomes a way to quiet the mind, stay present, and form bonds with others who understand the weight of what they've been through.

The initiative highlights the power of nature-based, body-led approaches in supporting mental health and emotional recovery

— reminding us that healing can look very different for everyone, and that sometimes, the ocean itself becomes the medicine.

Finding my way to healing didn't happen all at once. It felt more like stumbling through a winding, unfamiliar path—filled with detours, slow progress, and moments where I had no idea if I was getting anywhere. But in between all that, there were quiet breakthroughs.

A few months after I had Bella, I started looking for a psychologist—someone who could really see what I was going through and help me climb out of it. But the truth? That search didn't start from a place of confidence. It started with a big, uncomfortable realisation:

I couldn't fix everything on my own.

The weight I was carrying was too much. I needed help. And as hard as that was to admit, somewhere deep down, I knew that asking for it wasn't weakness. It was strength. (Even if I'd been raised to believe the opposite.)

So, I booked an appointment with my GP. I finally opened up about the panic attacks that had turned into a constant undercurrent of anxiety. I told him how it had crept into every part of my life—how I was starting to fear leaving the house, how even everyday places could send my body into a spiral. It wasn't just mental. It was physical. I felt wired all the time, like my nervous system didn't have an "off" switch. I was exhausted—but I couldn't relax.

At the centre of it all was this burning question I couldn't shake:

Why can't I just snap out of it and move on?

That question—frustrating as it was—actually became a turning point. Because it was the moment **it hit me that** maybe I wasn't meant to do this alone.

And looking back, I can see why it took me so long to get there. I was raised to keep my struggles to myself. In my world, vulnerability wasn't safe—it was something to hide. I grew up hearing things like "Don't let them see you fall apart" and "Keep private things private." That stuck. I learned how to protect myself with strength—or at least the appearance of it—even when everything inside me was falling apart.

So when I became a mother to Bella, all of that conditioning came with me.

And back then postnatal anxiety and depression weren't really part of the public conversation. There was no Instagram. No reels about maternal mental health. No visible support circles like there are today. I felt completely alone in what I was going through.

My mental health put a strain on my relationship. My husband didn't know what was going on—and honestly, neither did I. I didn't have the words to explain it, let alone the tools to manage it. I felt like I was supposed to "just get on with it," and when I couldn't, I blamed myself. Apparently, the magical *just get on with it* switch was broken... and I couldn't find the manual.

And yet, I kept up the act. I showed up. Smiled when I had to. Went through the motions. But inside? I was quietly falling apart. Fear, anxiety, and shame had taken root, and postpartum only made it louder. I had this tiny human relying on me, and I was trying so hard to hold it all together. But the truth is—I was barely holding on.

Talking to my GP was the first crack in the wall I'd built around myself. When I finally opened up, he suggested medication. He believed I was experiencing postnatal depression. And maybe I was. But something in me resisted. The idea of changing my brain chemistry felt... off. What I really wanted was someone who could help me untangle the chaos in my mind and actually give me tools to cope.

I walked out of that appointment feeling defeated. He didn't offer much beyond the prescription—no referrals, no resources, just a vague pat on the back and "try the meds." I knew if I wanted to feel normal again—if I wanted to show up for Bella the way I wanted to—I'd have to take the next step myself.

That's when I started searching. Not just for *someone* to talk to, but for the *right* person. A psychologist who could give me practical support, not just platitudes. Someone who could offer a sliver of hope when every day was starting to feel like a battle.

I wasn't just looking to vent—I needed someone who could really meet me where I was. I wanted to feel heard, validated, and supported—not rushed into unpacking my past, but held in the thick of what I was going through *right now*. I needed practical tools to help me get through the day-to-day, to quiet the panic and steady the overwhelm. The deeper work could come later. First, I just needed someone to sit with me in the mess—and help me breathe.

Finding the right therapist wasn't easy. It took months of searching, trial and error, and more self-reflection than I was ready for. But when I finally found her, something clicked. She didn't try to fix me. She didn't rush. She just listened—with care, with patience. And in her presence, I started to feel something I hadn't felt in a long time: hope.

It wasn't just the practical stuff she gave me. It was how she made me feel—like I was still human. Not broken. Not weak. Just someone going through something hard, learning how to cope. That alone was healing.

Through that relationship, I began to understand that healing isn't linear. It's not a single lightbulb moment or a quick fix. It's a layered, messy, deeply personal process that needs both emotional support *and* practical strategies. And once I embraced that, I stopped waiting to feel "better" and started focusing on rebuilding—piece by piece, with compassion and patience.

Looking back, finding the right therapist was one of the most important investments I ever made for my own well-being. That process taught me that reaching out for help doesn't mean you're weak. It means you're ready to grow. It means you're ready to stop surviving and start healing.

Because here's the truth: healing isn't about fixing yourself. It's about understanding what hurt you, how it shaped you, and what you need to feel whole again. That journey looks different for everyone—and that's okay.

But even now, therapy still carries a bit of a stigma. For so long, it was seen as something only for people in crisis. Like you had to be at rock bottom to *deserve* that kind of support. Especially for women. Because nothing says "totally fine" like bottling it up and rage-cleaning the kitchen at midnight.

For a long time, the message was clear: keep it together. Don't show cracks. Don't ask for help. That mindset became a barrier for so many women who were struggling silently—women who could've benefited from real support but didn't feel like they were allowed to ask for it.

But times are changing. Our world moves fast. Life today is more connected than ever—and somehow, more disconnected too. There's more pressure, more noise, more demand. And mental health? Thankfully, it's finally getting the attention it deserves.

According to the World Health Organization, more than 280 million people around the world are living with depression. And it hits women harder—especially in pregnancy and early motherhood. More than 1 in 10 pregnant women and new mums experience it. That's not rare. That's real.

Anxiety is even more common. It's the most widespread mental health condition globally, affecting over 300 million people—and once again, more women than men. This isn't just about feeling nervous or overwhelmed now and then. For many, it's a constant state of tension, worry, and unease that can cloud what should be some of the most meaningful moments of life.

And here in Australia, the picture's clear: perinatal mental health struggles are common—far more common than most people realise. According to PANDA (Perinatal Anxiety & Depression Australia), up to 1 in 5 expecting or new mums experience anxiety or depression during pregnancy or after birth. That's around 20%—not just a few outliers, but tens of thousands of women every single year.

For some, it starts during pregnancy. For others, it hits after the baby arrives—sometimes gradually, sometimes all at once. And even though awareness is growing, many women still carry it quietly, unsure if what they're feeling is normal or if they're somehow failing.

But these aren't just numbers. Behind every percentage is a woman trying to keep it together. A mother smiling through the fog. Someone lying awake at night thinking, *Why can't I enjoy this? Why does everyone else seem to be coping but me?*

The more we talk about this, the more we break the silence that keeps women stuck. No one should have to suffer in isolation, wondering if they're broken—or failing. Because they're not. They're human. And they're not alone.

Still, a lot of women hesitate to reach out. I get it. There's that quiet fear—*Will they think I can't handle it? Will they see me differently?*

Social media doesn't help. All those polished posts and highlight reels make it seem like motherhood is meant to be glowing, effortless, natural. When your reality doesn't match, it's easy to start questioning yourself. *Is it just me? Why does this feel so hard?*

Thankfully, the conversation around mental health is starting to shift. More and more women are sharing their real stories—talking openly about anxiety, depression, and the messy, raw parts of postpartum that don't make the highlight reel. As we speak up, the stigma loses its grip. And slowly, it's becoming more normal to say, "I'm not okay right now," without shame.

Support looks different for everyone, and the beauty of healing is that there's no one right way to do it. For some, therapy with a psychologist or psychiatrist is exactly what they need. For others, healing might come through community, creativity, or movement. I started with a psychologist—but honestly, that was just one piece of the puzzle.

Healing, for me, has been personal, layered, and evolving. I've leaned on talk therapy, but I've also found grounding in things like mindfulness, yoga, support groups, and books that met me right where I was. One of the most powerful tools in my early recovery was Susan Jeffers' self help book *Feel the Fear and Do It Anyway*. That book was like a lifeline—it helped me feel like I wasn't stuck, like there was a way forward I could actually see. It gave me a sense of direction when everything else felt overwhelming.

That's the thing about healing: it has to feel right for *you*. It has to match your pace, your needs, your season of life. There's no checklist. No timeline. Just options—and the trust that your path gets to look however it needs to.

If you're just starting out, the first step might be the simplest one: reminding yourself that you're allowed to take care of your mental and emotional wellbeing. Not just when you're falling apart, but as a regular, everyday act of self-care. My mum once said something that stuck with me: "Think of it like a diabetic needing insulin. Without it, they can't stay healthy." That helped me reframe the way I saw my own mental health. It wasn't optional. It was essential—for me, for my daughter, for the kind of life I wanted to live.

The truth is, mental health often gets sidelined—treated like it's less urgent than physical health. But the two aren't separate. They're totally intertwined. And when we invest in things that bring us calm, connection, or clarity, we're not being indulgent—we're being wise.

And no, this doesn't have to look like big, dramatic change. Small steps matter. Taking a deep breath. Repeating a kind word to yourself. Letting go of the pressure to do it all. These things add up. And they're just as important as sleep, food, or water—because your emotional health deserves that kind of everyday care too.

There are so many different ways to support your wellbeing—some that worked for me, and others you might discover on your own. If you're wondering where to start or what might actually help, I've included a list of therapeutic options I explored—and a few more you might want to try.

1. **Cognitive Behavioural Therapy (CBT)**

    What it is: CBT is a structured, goal-oriented therapy that helps identify and reshape negative thought patterns and behaviours. It's particularly effective for anxiety, fear, and trauma-related responses.

    How it helps: CBT equips you with tools to challenge and reframe a fearful mindset and also help process fears around birth, the postnatal period or anything which you feel you need to work through. CBT aims to help replace anxious thoughts with positive, realistic perspectives. Working with a therapist trained in CBT can build confidence and reduce anxiety as you approach labour.

2. **Eye Movement Desensitisation and Reprocessing (EMDR)**

   What it is: EMDR is a trauma-focused therapy that uses guided eye movements to help process and release traumatic memories.

   How it helps: If past trauma is affecting your birth experience, EMDR can be a powerful way to process those memories in a safe, structured way, reducing their emotional impact and allowing for a more peaceful birth experience.

3. **Somatic Experiencing**

   What it is: Somatic Experiencing is a body-centred therapy that focuses on releasing trauma stored in the body.

   How it helps: Through gentle awareness of physical sensations and guided exercises, this method helps release tension related to trauma, easing fears and creating a stronger mind–body connection as you prepare for birth.

4. **Hypnotherapy and/or HypnoBirthing ®**

   What it is: Hypnotherapy uses relaxation and focus techniques to address deep-seated fears and anxieties, while HypnoBirthing® combines these with birth-specific visualisations and affirmations.

   How it helps: Hypnotherapy can help uncover and address subconscious fears, while

HypnoBirthing® builds confidence, teaching techniques to stay calm and focused during labour. This approach is particularly useful if fear is a primary barrier to feeling prepared for birth.

5. **Trauma-Informed Talk Therapy**

    What it is: This is traditional talk therapy with a trauma-informed approach, where therapists create a safe, non-judgemental space for exploring trauma and related emotions.

    How it helps: A trauma-informed therapist can guide you through any lingering fears or past experiences that may impact your birth, providing coping mechanisms and emotional support in a way that feels safe and respectful.

6. **Narrative Therapy**

    What it is: Narrative Therapy is a therapeutic approach that encourages you to reframe and re-author your life story.

    How it helps: By exploring your own life story or birth story or expectations for birth, this method allows you to focus on the strengths you bring to motherhood, while helping to reshape fearful narratives into more empowering ones.

7. **Art Therapy**

    What it is: Art Therapy uses creative expression as a way to explore and process emotions.

    How it helps: Creating art allows you to express complex feelings related to trauma, fears and birth without relying solely on words. It's especially helpful for processing fears or stress, offering a way to work through emotions in a non-verbal and often healing way.

8. **Acceptance and Commitment Therapy (ACT)**

   What it is: ACT is a therapeutic approach that emphasises accepting rather than avoiding difficult emotions, encouraging you to take mindful action in line with your values.

   How it helps: ACT can support you in accepting any lingering fears or anxieties about birth without letting them control your experience. It helps build mental flexibility, allowing you to approach birth with a calm, centred mindset.

9. **Group Therapy or Support Groups**

   What it is: Group therapy or support groups offer shared spaces where individuals with similar experiences come together to discuss their emotions and coping strategies.

   How it helps: In a support group, you can share fears and concerns with others who understand, learning from their experiences and feeling less isolated. Support groups specifically for pregnant women can provide a unique sense of community and understanding.

10. **Gestalt Therapy**

    What it is: Gestalt Therapy is an experiential approach that encourages you to explore your current feelings and experiences in real-time, often with a focus on body awareness.

How it helps: By bringing attention to what you're feeling in the present, Gestalt Therapy can help you become more aware of and address fears that come up about birth, building a sense of confidence and groundedness.

11. **Reiki or Energy Healing**

    What it is: Reiki and other forms of energy healing focus on restoring balance to the body's energy fields to promote relaxation and reduce stress.

    How it helps: Energy healing can help release stored tension and fear from past experiences, promoting a sense of calm as you prepare for birth.

12. **Kinesiology**

    What it is: Kinesiology is a holistic therapy that uses gentle muscle testing to identify and release emotional and physical stress stored in the body. Practitioners assess muscle responses to understand energy imbalances and areas of tension.

    How it helps: By uncovering subconscious fears or anxieties, kinesiology can help address emotional blocks, allowing you to enter your labour and birth with a more relaxed, confident mindset. Many women find it helpful for clearing old trauma or limiting beliefs, supporting a balanced and grounded approach to pregnancy and birth preparation.

13. **Emotional Freedom Techniques (EFT or Tapping)**

What it is: EFT, commonly known as tapping, combines elements of cognitive therapy with gentle tapping on specific acupoints along body's meridians to reduce stress and anxiety.

How it helps: Tapping can be especially helpful for releasing fears and calming anxiety related to pregnancy and birth. By tapping on key points while focusing on a specific fear, EFT can help rewire emotional responses, creating a sense of calm and control. It's a self-soothing tool that can also be used during labour to manage stress.

14. **Tension and Trauma Releasing Exercises (TRE)**

What it is: TRE is a series of exercises that activate the body's natural tremor response to release deep-rooted tension and trauma stored in muscles and the nervous system.

How it helps: TRE is especially beneficial for releasing trauma or fear stored in the body, allowing for a relaxed, more open approach to labour.

Each of these therapeutic approaches brings something different to the table—whether you're unpacking trauma, trying to calm anxiety, or just wanting to feel more steady and confident as you prepare for birth. The key is to take what resonates, leave what doesn't, and remind yourself that it's okay to shift direction as you go.

I can honestly say that many of the things I've shared here have been part of my own healing path. After Bella's birth, we moved a lot for my husband's work, which meant starting over with new therapists again and again. It was exhausting. Each time,

I had to open up all over again—and that kind of vulnerability, especially when you're already raw, is no small thing. Finding someone I could actually connect with and trust wasn't easy.

I still remember one session in particular. I'd just poured out my entire life—childhood, birth trauma, mental health struggles—laid it all bare. The therapist listened, paused, and then said: "I don't know how to help you; this is quite a complex case."

Exactly what every emotionally fragile new mum wants to hear, right?

I went home and cried to my husband. I told him, "If even a professional doesn't know what to do with me, maybe I really am a lost cause."

But I didn't let that moment stop me. I kept going. I stayed curious. I stayed open. Because healing isn't about finding the perfect person or the perfect method. It's about movement. It's about listening to your gut and trusting that the small steps matter. Every approach I tried gave me something—a new perspective, a sense of calm, or just the resilience to keep going.

And throughout it all, one thing stayed constant: I know I've said this before, but it's worth repeating—because even though my healing took years, I still chose not to lean into medication. Not because I'm against it—I have deep respect for the role it plays in so many women's journeys. But for me, it just didn't feel aligned. What I was going through was real, raw, and heavy. And still, something in me kept saying: try something else first.

There were moments I doubted that choice. But my husband was my anchor through it. He kept reminding me of my inner reserve. He encouraged me to focus on what I could change—my thoughts, habits, and beliefs. He didn't sugarcoat it. He told me it was going to take work. But he believed I could do it—and that belief became a lifeline.

One of the biggest mindset shifts came when I read *A Mind of Your Own* by Kelly Brogan. That book gave me a completely different lens *on* mental health and medication, and it helped me lean more into holistic healing. Around that same time, I started seeing a naturopath who supported my nervous system with herbal medicine. It was gentle, grounding, and honestly—really effective. My body, which had felt like it was permanently stuck in high alert, finally started to settle.

If you're considering alternatives, it's worth exploring support from a naturopath, herbalist, or Chinese medicine practitioner. Their approach can be a powerful complement to other healing paths. The most important thing is finding what works for *you*—because there's no one-size-fits-all when it comes to healing.

Something else that really changed things for me is movement. Exercise became one of my strongest anchors. Not just for my physical health, but for my mind. It gave me a sense of clarity, a release valve for stress. No, I wasn't running marathons—some days, walking to the mailbox in clean clothes was the win. But I moved with purpose. Enough to feel the shift. To get those sweet, sweet endorphins flowing. It wasn't about burning calories. It was about staying sane. I didn't need research to tell me it was helping—I could feel it.

So wherever you are in your own journey, I hope something in here makes you feel a little less alone. Growth doesn't always follow a straight line, but every step forward still counts. With the right support and grounding practices, change doesn't just happen—it reshapes you.

And one thing I've learned? You don't have to do it all on your own. Yes, this work is deeply personal—but it doesn't have to be solitary. Having someone by your side—a therapist, a partner, a friend, anyone who truly sees you—can lighten the load in ways you didn't even realise you needed.

And that's exactly where we're headed next: community. The people who walk with you. The ones who remind you that you're not alone, and you were never meant to carry all of this by yourself.

REFLECTION PRACTICE: FINDING THE RIGHT SUPPORT FOR YOUR HEALING

There's no single approach to healing. This practice will help you clarify what you need and what kind of support will work best for you.

1. **What feels most important to you right now?**

    ☞ Are you working through past trauma, building self-understanding, or seeking calm and stability?

2. **How does your body show stress or emotion?**

    ☞ Do you notice tension, headaches, shallow breathing, restlessness?
    ☞ Are you open to approaches that involve movement, breathwork, or body-based techniques?

3. **What kind of environment helps you open up?**

    ☞ Do you prefer talking one-on-one, being in a group, using creative expression, or working quietly on your own?

4. **What kinds of support do you naturally respond to?**

    ☞ Do you like to talk things through?
    ☞ Write or journal?

- Move your body?
- Be guided in meditation or visualisation?

5. How structured do you want your healing work to be?

- Do you prefer clear steps and goals, or do you feel more comfortable with open exploration?

6. Are you curious about exploring your past?

- Do you want to look at old patterns and memories, or focus mainly on present-moment tools and coping strategies?

7. What qualities help you feel safe with a therapist or guide?

- Think about the traits that matter most to you: gentleness, clarity, honesty, empathy, lived experience, or spiritual connection.

Exploring Options

If you're drawn to:
- Understanding patterns and thoughts → Cognitive Behavioural Therapy (CBT), Acceptance and Commitment Therapy (ACT)

- ☞ Calming the mind and body → Mindfulness, meditation, breathwork, hypnotherapy
- ☞ Creative expression → Art therapy, music therapy, therapeutic journaling

The clearer you are on what you need, the easier it is to choose the support that works for you.

AGATHE'S STORY

"I had a traumatic experience at the age of five but didn't remember it until my first pregnancy at 29 years old. I was sexually abused by a family member and lived with partial amnesia for years. I had a 'feeling,' and some doubts from time to time, but most of the time, I didn't remember anything. I can't say what I felt at the time as I was too young to process it.

Because of this, I struggled with very low self-esteem and little confidence. In my relationships, I often said yes to sexual encounters even when I didn't want to. I believed that once I agreed to an encounter, I had to accept everything the other person wanted.

During my first pregnancy, I began to remember everything, but I wasn't ready to talk about it. I doubted myself, thinking maybe I was wrong. After the birth, I managed to go back to my life as the feelings and memories faded again. The same thing happened during my second pregnancy.

It wasn't until my third pregnancy that I felt the urge to talk and finally face the reality of my past.

The most important step I took was to talk to my partner first and then to my therapist. That brought me a profound sense of liberation. It also made me aware of how my unresolved trauma had impacted my previous births. I realised that I had been unable to open up completely and let go during labour.

As a result, my first birth ended in a C-section, and my second was heavily medicalised. Finally, for my third child, I was able to have a home birth.

I worked with a therapist who practiced hypnosis and hypnobirthing, which became a major part of my preparation. I also practiced daily visualisation and meditation. I learned about vocalisation techniques during an online class (it was the pandemic at the time), and I had a doula for support.

Talking to my birth team about my trauma was incredibly helpful. It allowed them to take it into account during the birth. I know this isn't always possible, but having a birth team I trusted and felt safe with was a game changer for me.

When I went into labour with my third baby, I wasn't afraid at all. I felt ready and even excited. I was surrounded by my husband, my two children (aged six and four), and my birth team, which included one doula and two midwives.

I managed the waves of labour well, using vocalisation techniques and my hypnosis tools. Stimulating my clitoris during the surges was also incredibly helpful. I didn't feel any pain, there was intense pressure, but no pain. The process felt smooth and easy. I only needed my husband to be near me and very present; I even asked him to join me in the pool. At the same time, I craved privacy and asked the rest of the birth team to leave the room. I felt a strong need for intimacy in that moment.

For my fourth pregnancy, I followed the Mongan HypnoBirthing® method and further explored the use of my voice during birth. With immense preparation, I chose to freebirth this time."

CHAPTER 15

Community -
The Village That Lifts Us Up

*"It takes a village to raise a child, but it also
takes a village to support a mother."*
—*Unknown*

When a 7.1-magnitude earthquake hit Christchurch, New Zealand, in 2010, everything cracked open—buildings, streets, lives. The city was in chaos. Power lines were down, homes buried in sludge from liquefaction, and emergency services stretched far beyond their limits.

What happened next didn't come from a government agency or aid organisation. It started with one Facebook post.

A university student named Sam Johnson created a group and called for volunteers. Not because he had a plan—but because he couldn't sit still. Within hours, students showed up. Not a dozen. Thousands. With shovels, wheelbarrows, buckets, and bikes. No one was in charge. There were no titles. Just people showing up for people.

They dug out streets, driveways, and front yards—sometimes waist-deep in mud. But it wasn't just about the physical work. They brought hot meals, clean water, updates from the outside world, and—maybe most importantly—comfort to people who were shaken and scared.

They became known as the Student Volunteer Army. And without intending to, they built something far stronger than disaster response—they built a community out of crisis.

They didn't do it to go viral. They did it because sometimes the most natural thing in the world is to help. Because when systems break, community steps in.

And it's no different when you need community in pregnancy and postpartum.

Today, that same spirit of showing up—without being asked, without needing to be an expert—lives on in smaller, quieter ways. Meal trains. Group chats. A friend dropping off a lasagna and texting, "No need to reply." It doesn't have to be grand. Sometimes it's just someone folding your laundry while you nurse your baby. Or holding space while you fall apart a little.

These simple gestures? They matter. They nourish more than just your body—they feed your sense of being held.

That feeling—of being seen, of being supported—has always meant something to me.

Maybe because I didn't grow up with it. I've craved community for as long as I can remember. And when I finally experienced what it feels like to be held by others—not just physically, but emotionally—I understood just how much it matters.

It stayed with me. It's something I carried into motherhood—not just as a value, but as something I want my daughters to grow up knowing is normal. Watching them laugh with their friends, knowing they have people around them—that's the kind of belonging I always wished for. And while I'm grateful they have it, that craving for connection hasn't completely left me.

If anything, it got louder when I was pregnant with my second daughter, Portia. I'd done birth before, but this time felt different. I knew I didn't want to do it alone. I needed support. I needed women around me who got it.

I started small—just a few chats here and there with other mums. And slowly, something shifted. These weren't just casual conversations at the park. These women became my people. We didn't need to have the same stories—just the same intention: to hold each other through the messy, beautiful, unpredictable ride of motherhood.

One night, I went to a women's circle. I didn't know anyone there. I wasn't even sure what I was walking into. But something in me said, just go. Sit. Listen. Be open.

And I'm so glad I did. We shared stories—some soft, some raw. We laughed. We cried. And in that room full of strangers, something clicked. I felt seen. I felt safe. It was one of those moments that reminded me just how essential community really is—especially for women stepping into motherhood.

And that kind of connection doesn't always come from the people you expect. Sometimes it's a stranger, or a brand-new friend, who steps into your life at exactly the right time. Since having Bella, I've met women I probably never would've crossed paths with otherwise. Some stayed for a season, some for longer—but every one of them left a mark.

And it's not just in moments of crisis that community matters. It starts way earlier—during pregnancy, when everything feels uncertain and a little upside down. There's something powerful about being around other women who are walking the same path. Even if their stories are different, just knowing you're not alone makes all the difference.

Prenatal classes are often where those first connections start. I've seen it so many times—women walking in nervous, unsure, maybe even a bit guarded. But by week three, the room is buzzing. Someone cracks a joke about waddling or maternity pads, and suddenly everyone's swapping peri spray tips like they've known each other for years. It's not just about learning how to give birth. It's about feeling understood. Like you've found your people.

And community doesn't always come from formal spaces like classes. Sometimes it shows up in quieter, more random ways—a chat with a stranger at the park, a neighbour sharing her own birth story while you hang washing on the line. Tiny moments like that can make a big impact. Especially when you're carrying fear or healing from past trauma, those small moments of connection can be a lifeline. They can pull you back into the present—back to yourself—and for a little while, it doesn't feel so heavy. You're not overthinking, not carrying it all. You just get to *be*.

Belonging doesn't always come in big, obvious moments. Sometimes it begins with a smile, a shared story, or the quiet feeling of being understood.

And when pregnancy turns into motherhood, that need for belonging only deepens. The postpartum period can be beautiful—but it can also feel like you've been dropped into a whole new world with no map. Your body's healing, your hormones are all over the place, and everything feels raw and unfamiliar. That's when community really matters. Having people around you who *get it*—who've walked this path before—can change everything.

And this isn't new. Across cultures, community has always been part of the postpartum experience. In Mexico, there's *la cuarentena* —a 40-day period after birth where the mother rests while family and people in the community steps in to handle meals, tend to the older children, and take care of the house. In Nigeria, Africa there's *omugwo*—a tradition where, after childbirth, the new mother is cared for by her own mother or a close relative. They handle the cooking, cleaning, baby care—everything—so the mother can rest, recover, and be nurtured. It's support in the most practical, loving form. And in China, there's *zuo yuezi*—literally "sitting the month." It's a time for deep rest, where the new mother stays home for 30 days to recover while others step in to help. A *pui yuet*, or postpartum nanny, cooks nourishing meals to support healing and milk supply, offers massages and body wraps, and gently guides the mother through caring for her baby. It's not just physical support—it's care for the whole person. All of these traditions say the same thing: you're not meant to do this alone.

Honestly, how amazing would it be if every new mum had access to that kind of care? I'd sign up for *zuo yuezi* right now—massages, warm soup, someone handling the laundry? Yes, please.

***Around the world, women have always gathered to lift one another.
We don't need permission to do the same today.***

These days, with families living far apart and life moving fast, that built-in village can feel out of reach. A lot of mums are trying to do what used to take a group—on their own. It's like doing a group project solo while sleep-deprived, leaking milk, and forgetting what day it is.

That's why creating your own version of community—whatever that looks like—is more important than ever.

Prenatal classes, women's circles, online groups... they all offer ways to build your village. And let's be honest—digital spaces have become lifelines. Somewhere you can find advice, empathy, or just someone else who's awake at 2 a.m. Whether you're celebrating a win, venting about the day, or frantically Googling "is newborn poop meant to be that colour," there's comfort in knowing someone out there gets it.

Sometimes, that's all you need. Not a solution. Just someone who understands.

For so many women, those connections—online or in person—become essential. Because support doesn't have to come from family.

***The right people don't need to have known
your whole story to help you hold it.***

Building your village might be the most underrated form of self-care. Don't get me wrong—bubble baths are great. But try laughing with another mum about the time you left the house wearing breast pads... still in their wrappers. That kind of connection? It stays with you.

In all seriousness, having people around you—especially during pregnancy, birth, and the chaos that follows—helps you feel grounded. Held. Seen. It's about surrounding yourself with people who lift you up when you're too tired to lift yourself. These bonds—built on shared stories, side-eyes, and the kind of understanding that doesn't need words—create a kind of emotional safety that's hard to find anywhere else.

Because when everything around you says "be strong," community whispers, "lean on me."

We were never meant to do this alone. And we don't have to.

And with that mic drop... we're wrapping up this chapter. We've just explored one of the most important pieces of the Essential 10: community—the kind that shows up, holds space, and reminds you that you're part of something bigger (and no, it's not just your laundry pile).

Next, we shift gears and turn inward. We'll talk about your birth plan—but not just as a checklist or a form. Think of it as a way to put your voice on the page. This is where all the inner work starts to take shape in the real world.

REFLECTION PRACTICE: BUILDING YOUR SUPPORT CIRCLE

This practice helps you think about the relationships that support you and explore how to strengthen or expand your community.

1. **Who do you currently turn to for support?**

   ☞ List the people you trust or rely on and note what type of support they offer (emotional, practical, spiritual, or shared experience).

2. **Are there any gaps in your circle?**

   ☞ What kind of support do you find yourself craving most right now?
   ☞ Is it someone to check in with emotionally? A practical hand with the day-to-day? Or someone who just gets it without needing the full backstory?
   ☞ What kind of connection would actually feel nourishing—not just helpful?

3. **What qualities do you value in supportive relationships?**

   ☞ Consider traits like honesty, encouragement, empathy, shared experience, or simply someone who listens.

4. **What kind of support do you want to give and receive?**

   ☞ Is it emotional check-ins? Help with the little things? Someone to vent to, or laugh with, or just sit beside when you don't need advice—just presence.
   ☞ Think about the kind of support that feels good to offer—and the kind you'd love to receive without having to ask.

5. **What does community mean to you?**

   ☞ What makes you feel truly seen, safe, and supported?
   ☞ Is it deep chats with one trusted person? A group that makes you laugh when everything feels heavy?
   ☞ Forget what it's supposed to look like—what actually feels good to you?

6. **What small action could help you build or strengthen your connections?**

   ☞ Reach out to a friend, join a local group or online space, or plan a small gathering.

Circles of Connection

Draw three circles inside each other:

   ☞ Inner circle: people you are closest to
   ☞ Middle circle: regular connections or support

☞ Outer circle: people or groups you'd like to connect with in the future

Look at your map. Notice where you feel supported and where you may want to strengthen or expand your circle.

Pick one thing to try this week:

☞ Reconnect with a friend or family member
☞ Join a local group or online community
☞ Start a group chat or plan a casual meet-up
☞ Reach out to someone new who feels aligned

The clearer you are about what you want from your community, the easier it is to build one that supports you.

CHAPTER 16

Birth Plan - Your Vision, Your Voice, Your Birth

> *"If you don't know your options, you don't have any."*
> —Diana Korte

When the Duchess of Cambridge stepped out onto the steps of St Mary's Hospital just hours after giving birth—hair done, makeup flawless, baby in arms—the world watched in awe. It became an iconic image. But for many women, that moment stirred discomfort as much as admiration. Was this the gold standard of postpartum recovery? Was this birth—tidy, composed, public?

What we didn't see was what happened before or after. We didn't see her birth plan. We didn't hear her consent conversations. We don't know whether she had choices, or whether protocol dictated her experience.

And her story, like many others, reminds us that the most powerful parts of birth often happen behind the scenes—quiet, private, and deeply personal.

That's the thing about birth. From the outside, it can look one way. But from the inside, it's layered with emotion, decisions, power dynamics, and personal values.

In this chapter, we're not here to judge how someone's birth looked—we're here to ask: Did she feel included in the choices that shaped her birth? Because no matter where or how you give birth, what matters most is that you had a voice in the decisions, and a plan that reflected your values. A birth plan isn't about controlling the outcome—it's about making sure your part of every step.

And while birth planning might seem like a modern idea, it actually has deeper roots. Birth plans started gaining traction in the 1980s, when more women began asking for real agency in how their births were handled. They didn't want to just be told what to do—they wanted to be heard. They wanted their values, preferences, and needs to actually matter.

One of the key voices behind that shift was childbirth educator Penny Simkin. She started out as a physical therapist, but by the late 1960s she was deep into birth education and went on to become a huge advocate for personalised, respectful maternity care. Her work helped bring birth plans into the conversation—not as rigid checklists, but as tools for better, clearer communication between women and their care providers.

At its core, birth planning marked a real change. It moved things from routine, impersonal care to something more collaborative and mother-focused. A birth plan isn't about scripting every moment—it's about saying: *this matters to me. Please listen.*

It gives you a chance to reflect on what you want, how you want to feel, and what you need to feel safe and supported through labour. Whether it's your choices around pain relief, medical interventions, or comfort measures—it all counts. It all belongs on the table.

And more than anything, it opens up a conversation. When your care team understands what matters most to you, they can support you in a way that feels aligned and respectful. That kind of clarity helps everyone—especially when things are moving quickly or potentially don't go to plan.

But when those conversations are missing, and your voice isn't part of the process, that's when things can start to unravel.

As we've already seen, birth trauma is rarely just about the medical side of things—it's about how it felt in the moment. Studies show that what leaves the deepest marks isn't what was done, but how a woman was made to feel. Powerless. Dismissed. Shut out of decisions. It's not the procedures themselves that cause harm—it's being sidelined during a deeply personal experience.

That's why knowing your preferences—and making them known—matters. When your choices are understood, it's easier to stay grounded—even when things change. It's not about having control over everything. It's about protecting your autonomy, so that you're not just present—you're part of it.

A thoughtful birth plan can also help set boundaries that protect your emotional and physical safety. That might mean avoiding certain interventions—like routine vaginal exams or continuous monitoring—or setting the tone in the room with soft lighting, quiet voices, or calming music. It might include being clear about who you want in your space, or asking that care providers get consent before touching you or doing any procedures. Because even now, what should be standard... still isn't always guaranteed.

And while it's important to know what you want, it's just as important to stay open to how things unfold.

Birth has a way of doing its own thing, and even the most thoughtful plan might need to shift. What matters most is knowing your options, and leaving enough space emotionally so you don't fall apart if things don't go exactly to script.

I've seen it happen—when a plan is too rigid, and something changes, that's often when trauma can creep in. It's not the change that's traumatic—it's the feeling of having no room to adjust. That's why adaptability matters just as much as preparation.

And no, your plan doesn't need to be pages and pages long. You don't have to list out every single possibility. Just focus on what's essential—what helps you feel safe, supported, and protected. That's what your care team really needs to know. The rest? You'll figure it out in the moment, with the right support around you.

So, what does a birth plan actually include? Every plan looks a little different, but here are some areas you might want to think about:

Environment: What helps you feel centred and safe? You might ask for dim lighting, soothing music, essential oils, or personal items like a favourite blanket or photo. If water therapy or immersion relaxes you, consider requesting access to a birthing pool or warm shower.

Medical Interventions: Think about where your comfort lies. Would you prefer to not have vaginal examinations, or would you like this examination done only by your known care provider? Would you like to avoid continuous monitoring unless medically necessary? Are there certain procedures—that you want limited, explained beforehand, or skipped altogether unless essential? Your birth plan is a space to voice those preferences clearly.

Induction and Augmentation: If you're open to methods for starting or speeding up labour, your plan can note what you're comfortable with—like membrane sweeps, Syntocinon/Pitocin, or having your waters broken—and how you'd like those decisions to be approached if they come up. **And if you're not open to any of it? That's totally valid too. You don't have to consider these options at all if they don't feel right for you.**

Pain Management: What kind of support do you imagine needing? Some women prefer to lean into natural techniques like breathwork, active movement or HypnoBirthing®, while others plan to use gas, pethidine, or an epidural. There's no right answer—only what feels right for you.

Support People: Who do you want in your corner? Your partner, a doula, a sister or close friend? You can list who you'd like to have present and clarify their roles—whether it's physical support, emotional reassurance, or advocacy when you need it most.

Post-Birth Care: After baby arrives, what matters to you? This might include immediate skin-to-skin contact, delayed cord clamping, or having uninterrupted time to breastfeed and bond.

Of course, birth plans don't just live on paper—they live in real stories. For me, writing one became more than a document. It was part of how I healed.

For my second and third births, creating a birth plan was my way of taking back control after feeling completely out of control the first time around. During my first birth with Bella, I felt powerless. Like decisions were being made *for* me. Like birth was happening *to* me, not *with* me. I wasn't an active participant, and that left me feeling stripped of my power.

That's why, when I prepared for my next births, I knew things had to be different. The birth plan became my anchor. My way of reclaiming a sense of agency and making sure my needs were actually considered. For me it wasn't just a checklist of things like "dim lights" or "delayed cord clamping." It was about thinking through what really mattered to me—what would help me feel safe, calm, and in control.

But I also realised that a birth plan is only as strong as the team behind it. That's why involving my husband was one of the most important steps. He was going to be one of my main supports—the person standing beside me through it all. If he didn't fully understand what I needed—or why—then how could he really advocate for me?

We sat down together and walked through every part of the plan. It was kind of like prepping for a group project—except the deadline was unpredictable and the outcome involved bodily fluids. We talked about all the "what ifs": What if labour went differently than we imagined? What if interventions came into play? What would I need in those moments—physically, emotionally, mentally?

We explored all of it—plan A, B, and C—so that if I couldn't speak up during labour, he could. And not just speak *for* me, but speak *from* a place of truly understanding why each decision mattered, what I was hoping for, and what risks and benefits came with each option.

Having those conversations ahead of time didn't just prepare us logistically—it made us stronger. He wasn't just there as a bystander; he was part of it. Someone I could lean on. Someone who understood me deeply and had my back completely. Knowing that gave me so much peace. No matter how the birth unfolded, I knew I wouldn't have to go through it alone—or explain myself in the middle of it all.

And that's just my story. For other women—especially those carrying trauma or fear—having something in place that reflects their values and boundaries can hold even more weight. It's a way to name their fears, protect their space, and help their care team show up with the sensitivity and respect they need. It's about creating an environment where you feel emotionally safe, not just physically cared for. Because when you're part of the process, when your voice is central, the entire experience transforms—it becomes something you're doing *with* others, not something being done *to* you.

And I've watched women bring this to life in their own unique ways.

One mama I supported used her birth plan to ask for minimal talking during labour. Too much communication felt overwhelming, and she explained that quiet helped her focus on her breathing and stay calm. Her care team honoured that, creating a space that felt focused and safe.

Another woman, after a traumatic first birth, included a few key requests: that all procedures be clearly explained beforehand, and that she be given time to talk things through privately with her chosen support. Her care team took the time to walk her through each step with patience and care. She described her second birth as healing—a world apart from her first.

And then there was a mother who had experienced loss before welcoming her rainbow baby. She brought a small but meaningful item into the birth room: a blanket from her previous pregnancy. It wasn't written into her plan, but it helped her feel emotionally safe. What *was* written in her plan was a request to keep the CTG monitor loud enough to hear her baby's heartbeat throughout labour. That steady sound brought her calm and helped her stay connected. Her care team respected those wishes, and the birth became something more than clinical—it became sacred.

These stories show that a birth plan can be more than just a list of preferences. It can be a bridge—between fear and confidence, between where you've been and where you're going. For some women, it's the first time they've felt truly seen in a medical space. For others, it's simply the quiet reassurance that they have a say—and that their voice matters.

And when a woman feels that—when her autonomy is respected—it stays with her. Not just for the birth, but long after.

Because there's always that point in labour (you know the one) where everything feels stretched—physically, emotionally, sometimes even spiritually. That's when it's not the plan that holds you up—it's you. It's your resilience.

That's the final pillar.

The one that holds everything else together. Because no matter how things play out, your ability to adapt, to bend without breaking—that's what shapes your birth into something fully, powerfully yours.

REFLECT: OWNING YOUR BIRTH PLAN

A conscious birth plan isn't about controlling every detail. It's about understanding your options, making informed decisions, and ensuring your voice is part of every conversation. It's a tool for autonomy, not perfection.

Real Examples of Birth Plans in Action

One woman I supported came into our sessions unsure whether a birth plan was even worth doing. She assumed her midwife "knew what to do" and that making a plan would only set her up for disappointment if things didn't go according to it. But once she understood—through our time together—just how many different options, interventions, and pathways could arise within the hospital system, something clicked. She realised she wanted more control over what she was saying yes or no to.

Tuning into what truly mattered to her—like whether she wanted vaginal examinations on admission, whether she was comfortable discussing induction at 41 weeks, or if she preferred intermittent monitoring over continuous CTG—helped her see that a birth plan wasn't about scripting the perfect experience. It was about understanding her options, making informed choices, and making sure she was an active participant, not just along for the ride. She later said: "Putting it into words helped me see that I didn't want a birth that just happened around me. I wanted to be present in it. And my midwife was amazing—

she even made sure my husband understood the plan so he could advocate too."

Another client shared how her birth took an unexpected turn and ended in a Caesarean—but her birth plan still made a big difference.

"I'd included things like delayed cord clamping, no separation, and skin-to-skin—even in a surgical birth. Because we'd talked through it in advance, the team made it happen. They knew what I wanted and respected it. That helped me feel like I was still part of the process, not just a patient being wheeled through it."

These stories highlight what a birth plan is really about: not rigid control, but conscious participation. It's about making your needs visible and your values non-negotiable. Because birth autonomy is a right—not a request.

Your Birth Reflection & Planning Tool

Let this be a living document. A flexible, evolving reflection of what you want, what you're willing to consider, and where your boundaries are. Start here and return to it often.

Anchor Into What Matters Most

How do you want to feel during birth?
- Calm
- Supported
- Respected

- Safe
- In control
- Private
- Powerful
- Free
- Seen
- Sacred
- Heard

Which of these values resonate most strongly with you?

Choose the ones that feel most important, then write about how you'd like them to be honoured during birth. What do they look and feel like in real, practical terms?

For example: "Feeling respected might mean being spoken to with kindness and asked for consent before any hands-on care."

Outline Your Preferences

Environment
- Lighting, sound, people in the room
- Photography or filming
- Do you want people asking permission before entering the space

Monitoring
- Intermittent Doppler vs. CTG
- When are you comfortable switching if needed

Vaginal Examinations
- Do you consent on admission, or prefer to wait
- How will you indicate if/when you're open to one
- If you do consent to an examination, would you like to be told your dilation—or would you prefer not to know?

Induction Options
- Would you consent to or decline membrane sweeps or artificial rupture of membranes?
- How do you feel about induction after 41 weeks—routine, selective, or only if medically necessary?
- Are you open to medications like Syntocinon/Pitocin to start or strengthen contractions, or would you prefer to avoid them unless absolutely necessary?

Pain Relief
- What comfort measures or techniques would you like to use (ie; breathing, movement, water, TENS, massage)?
- Are there medical options (like gas, pethidine, or an epidural) that you're open to—or prefer to avoid?

Pushing
- Instinctive vs. directed pushing
- Positions you'd like to try or avoid

Perineal Support & Tearing
- If tearing is likely, would you prefer to tear naturally or discuss an episiotomy?
- Do you consent to hands-on techniques (ie; fingers on the perineum), or would you prefer a hands-off approach?
- Would you like a warm compress applied to the perineum during pushing to help reduce tearing?

Assisted Delivery
- How do you feel about interventions like forceps or vacuum if needed?
- Would you like time to discuss your options before any assisted delivery—with the understanding that your consent is always required, including in emergency situations?

Third Stage
- Physiological vs. managed
- Plans for placenta (lotus birth, delayed cord clamping, encapsulation)

Postpartum & Baby Care
- Immediate skin-to-skin, delaying weighing and newborn checks
- Vitamin K, newborn vaccinations, eye ointment, newborn bath—yes/no, or delayed

---

Define Your Deal Breakers

What are your firm boundaries—practices or procedures that would deeply compromise your sense of safety, autonomy, or trust?

Some examples might be:
- No vaginal checks without clear, informed consent
- No separation from baby unless medically necessary
- No directed pushing unless requested
- Clear explanations before any hands-on action

List your personal deal breakers here:
1.
2.
3.

This isn't about being difficult. It's about being clear—so you and your team know what matters most.

Plan for All Scenarios

Even with the best preparation, birth can unfold in unexpected ways. Planning ahead for different possibilities can help you stay grounded in your values, no matter what path your birth takes.

> If I have a spontaneous, physiological birth, I want...
>
> (ie: quiet space, no time pressure, dim lights, water immersion, minimal checks)
>
> If I require an induction, I want...
>
> (ie: informed consent at every step, time to try natural methods first, partner or doula present throughout)
>
> If I need a Caesarean, I want...
>
> (ie: delayed cord clamping, partner present, gentle Caesarean techniques, music of my choice, baby on my chest ASAP)

If You've Experienced Trauma

If you're coming into birth with a history of trauma—whether from a previous birth, medical experience, or another difficult chapter in your life—it's not just okay to include your emotional safety needs in your birth plan—it's essential.

These details might not show up in a standard template, but they can make a huge difference in how you feel throughout labour. You have every right to name what helps you feel safe, respected, and in control.

Here are a few examples to consider:
- "Even if I've consented, if I say 'stop' at any point, I need that to be respected right away."

- "Please don't stand over me—speak to me at eye level whenever possible."
- "Tell me before you touch me, even for something routine."

This is about more than preferences—it's about protecting your sense of safety in a vulnerable space. You don't need to explain your history in detail. You just need to be heard.

Prepare for Flexibility

Write a few grounding reminders for yourself in case things change:

I can pause.
I can ask questions.
I can make decisions moment to moment.
My voice matters—always.

Share It

Print a copy for your bag, and—if you can—email one to your care provider ahead of time.

Then talk it through. With your partner. Your doula. Your care provider. Don't just hand it over—have the conversation.

Because the real power of a birth plan isn't just in what's written down—it's in being heard.

This is your body. Your baby. Your birth.

ELIZABETH'S STORY

"It's 7.00pm: I'm feeding my 11-month-old baby girl her bedtime milkies while my 7-year-old packs our lunchboxes for tomorrow in the dim light of the kitchen. As she fusses around at my breast, I feel so grateful that I have the two most beautiful girls in the world. That I am still able to breastfeed little bub at nearly 1 year. That my big girl has survived the most difficult of starts in life, not due to any issues of her own, but due to my own mental health and my 'failure' as a mother. But although my life was drastically changed by both births, I know I am not a failure. What I went through pulled me apart and somehow, I was strong enough to work out how to put myself back together, a better version of me.

It's 4.00pm: I'm walking my dogs in the local park, heavily pregnant with my firstborn, Isla. It's my due date but I'm not feeling in any hurry. As I walk, I feel back pain intermittently, and it's annoying enough that I have to stop walking to get through it. It's been a pretty straightforward pregnancy, mild nausea, excitement, and working right up until the day before my due date. I'm completely naive and under-prepared. We reckon we will just 'go with the flow' and try for a natural birth, see how I go, I have a pretty good pain threshold, but I know what options are available to me due to the inadequate standard hospital antenatal classes. I figure that the back pain is just a normal part of carrying around a giant bowling ball in my tummy, don't mention anything to hubby and head to bed early.

It's 7.30 am the next morning: I'm convinced this isn't labour; cos it doesn't feel like anything is 'contracting'. What would I know? I've never been in labour before! Hubby isn't convinced. He starts timing the 'intermittent back pain' trying to find a pattern. We call the hospital, and they ask me to come in for a check. I refuse to let hubby bring in the suitcase as I am adamant that we will be sent home. However, the midwives hook me up to a monitor and confirm that I am in labour, 3cm dilated, experiencing 'moderate contractions' and can stay. I feel a surge of confidence, if this is 'moderate' it isn't that bad! I can do this! Hubby eventually returns, with the bags, but got lost getting out of the lift at the wrong floor. We walk the corridors and then get assigned to a room, I cope well with heat packs and use a bit of gas to get through transition. Then they take the gas off me as it's time to push. After an hour and a half of pushing and straining on my back in stirrups, she is born at 4.59pm. Not bad for a first birth, I am told.

I am shattered, exhausted and in shock. As I look down at this dark head of hair, I am astonished that such a big head could have come out of such a small hole! I don't feel any emotion, not love, not relief, not happiness. So far, it's a pretty good birth, but then the placenta doesn't want to come out. I have the syntocinon needle, the midwives hover and worry and fuss, then they talk about putting in a catheter because an empty bladder can apparently help. With everyone watching and the lights on, a bedpan is placed beneath me. I try to pee, but I can't remember how anything works down there, so the catheter is inserted. Then the doctor comes in and pulls on the cord so hard that it snaps. I have a retained placenta and am off to surgery.

It's 11.30 pm: I'm finally on my way to the maternity ward. The DNC (a surgical procedure to remove tissue from the uterus) was so traumatic. Firstly, the spinal injection missed my right side, and I had the most intense pain of my life. I had no support and was separated from my baby with little idea what was going on. The surgeon who pulled out the placenta laughed and joked and said I had given birth to a placenta and should call it Pete. And in recovery, I started to shake and vomit coming off the drugs. With no feeling in the lower half of my body, I couldn't cough it up and literally panicked as I thought I couldn't breathe.

It's 1.30 am: I am woken rudely by an abrupt midwife who shoves paperwork at me to sign, looks at my chart and exclaims that this baby hasn't been fed in 6 hours. The previously sleeping bundle is now a crying mess, I can't undo the button on my hospital gown to get to my boob, let alone work out how to latch her. I've had less than 2 hours sleep and am failing at this mum thing. The midwife collects colostrum in a little syringe as I awkwardly squeeze my nipple.

I went downhill very quickly. Eventually, three and a half months later I was hospitalised with postpartum psychosis which included hallucinations, delusions, mania and inability to sleep. You read this in a brochure and understand the words, but to experience it is out of this world. I was constantly on edge, talking a million miles an hour and rushing around doing all the chores. I forgot to eat and lost so much weight that my pre-pregnancy jeans were falling off me. I hated my baby; never felt any love for her at all, she looked ugly and wrinkled, she didn't sleep, she demanded boob all the time in the hot sweaty summer, and she turned me into this crazy person who wanted to drown her in the bath and had suicidal thoughts of my own. I couldn't tell anyone this though, I had to act as though I loved her, so I put on a brave face and smiled and went to the appointments and masked the hell out of everything, so no one ever knew.

It's something o'clock: I have no idea, is it morning or night? The lights in the psych ward are always on and I am always awake unless I'm drugged into sleep. I must keep a record of all the things in my notebook, so I'm writing constantly. The shift changes have a hidden meaning; the other patient's movements are clues to be deciphered; where they sit in the dining room has a significance that I must discover. Hubby and baby come to visit every day (although sometimes I refuse to see them), but I cannot breastfeed her due to the massive amounts of medications I am taking. So, I have to 'pump and dump' to avoid mastitis. I close my eyes and pour the milk down the drain as my heart breaks. I'm given a laughable brochure entitled "Your Rights as an Involuntary Patient". One day the psychiatrist (some guy in a suit I have never met – why should I trust him?) announces that the meds aren't working fast enough, and I am recommended to have ECT (electroconvulsive therapy). I refuse. The next morning, I am banging down the nurse's station demanding they take me to ECT immediately.

I recovered, slowly. It took 3 and a half weeks to get out of hospital, 2 years until I felt the warmth of love towards my daughter and 5 years to gradually wean off the antipsychotics. Hubby and I never planned to have an only child, but we couldn't go through that again.

Or could we?

Hubby says, 'Never again!' and I don't blame him. After a year of thinking, planning, researching and visiting a postpartum specialist, I have found out the stats of relapse (80% for me, with a previous episode of postpartum psychosis (PP) and a subsequent bipolar diagnosis.) and weaned off meds. I present hubby with a contract; here are all the things I will do differently. He reads it over, sits on it for about a month then agrees to try. We have an incredibly devastating miscarriage at 11 weeks' gestation when my big girl is 5. And when she is 7, I'm pregnant with our rainbow baby. I gather my supports around me to do everything in my power to make the second time around different and beat the stats. I cover all possible bases:

Medical

> engaging a private psychiatrist specialising in postpartum whom I will trust with all medication decisions regardless of my mental state, rather than a random public one whom I have just met.
>
> getting linked in with the Perinatal Mental Health Team at my chosen hospital.
>
> writing a 'worst case scenario' document called an Advanced Healthcare Directive stating my wishes if I am unable to consent for myself.

Emotional

> reconnecting with a peer support group for parents.
>
> hiring a doula to be with me throughout the process and on birthing day, who knows my story and can advocate for me.

Practical

> mobilising my friends and family around me, being honest and open with them.
>
> stocking the freezer with meals including those from White Cloud Foundation Meals for Mums.

Spiritual

> creating a prayer group of powerhouse women from church who support me and bub every step of the way.

In this new fresh space, I prepare to have a different birth experience and know that even if I do relapse, I have so much more knowledge and education than before. I am prepared and it will be ok.

It's 8.35 am, 29 March 2021: Tomorrow's my estimated due date and the Premier announces a snap Covid lockdown. My anxiety which is already through the roof continues to climb. I know this means that hospitals only allow one support person during labour, but I need my husband and my doula! I freak out, if this first part of the plan is denied then everything else falls apart. This isn't just a few hours of my life while I birth, it's my future mental health and bub's too! I continue to spiral. My doula, psychiatrist, psychologist and myself write emails and letters to various hospitals explaining my unique situation, begging for an exemption or a transfer and we are repeatedly denied. I shut down, my sleep is poor and, although my hospital bag lies packed at the foot of the bed, I tell myself I can't go into labour yet.

It's 3 pm on Thursday, 8 April: Over a week has passed and baby hasn't come. I awake from a diazepam nap to finally receive a phone call with good news! I'm allowed two support people at another local hospital; would I like to transfer? I can't believe it! I'm on the phone to my doula in happy tears, but immediately all my anxieties shift onto having an induction. It's going to be ok. I continue diffusing clary sage, gutter walking with my dogs and eating all the dates and curries.

It's 3.30 am on Saturday, 10 April: I wake to pee (not unusual) and can't go back to sleep (also not unusual). I listen to a fear release meditation again and realise that I have to let go of everything, all hopes and expectations, all fears and all physical tension. I pray and write a heartfelt email to my doula. Within minutes of hitting send, my contractions start. This time they feel like contractions, they come in waves and have lovely pauses in between. I move around quietly, throwing a few extra things into my bag, making sure my frozen colostrum is correctly labelled, and leaning on the wall during each surge. I feel a sense of peace.

It's sunrise: I'm still on my bed in my nighty, hubby has had a shower, and my doula has just arrived. She said I was sounding good, and we might head to the hospital soon, but my mum who is to watch our big daughter isn't here yet, and we have plenty of time. The curtains are drawn, I work through each contraction and introduce my doula to my big girl in the gaps.

My daughter is a champion, she has watched some birth videos and been prepped, so she is not phased. She gives me sips from a water bottle, rubs my back and fetches cool face washers. Then she pops out to have breakfast with her grandmother and returns again. We disclose the baby's name. It's moving fast, my waters break dramatically, and I feel a bit pushy. My doula says we won't have time to get to the hospital but will have the baby here. I don't care, the car trip was the thing I was least looking forward to. Hubby calls an ambulance, and I moan on knees leaning on the bedhead and scream through transition.

My baby was born at 7.10 am, crying strongly. There are six support people in my small bedroom – three masked paramedics, my doula, my husband and my daughter. After delayed cord clamping and the syntocinon injection, I worry about the placenta coming out. Crouching over my largest kitchen mixing bowl in the tiny toilet room, my doula tells me to thank my placenta for all its work and let it go. Feeling like a complete idiot, I say the words out loud and with a gentle tug, it plops into the bowl with a tiny amount of blood. My work is done.

I'm pleased to say that I avoided a relapse. After the birth, I travelled in the ambulance up to the hospital for an extended 5-day stay while my mental health was monitored as my hormones crashed and my breastmilk came in. My mind tried to go psychotic, and I had some strange thoughts, but this was managed by some low-dose medication and the wonderful night nurses feeding expressed colostrum to bub and looking after her overnight so I could get some sleep. Although hubby visited every day, my big girl wasn't permitted due to Covid restrictions, so it was very fortunate that she got to meet her sister at her birth. It wasn't easy, and there were many difficult moments, and time after time

I had to acknowledge that things were too hard for me, and I had to accept all the help. But I am so proud to say that I did it! I had a healing birth after trauma. And you can do it too."

TANYA'S STORY

Tanya was a strong and determined woman, a competitive powerlifter before motherhood, with a resilient mindset and a deeply ingrained belief in her strength. Her first birth was a quick (less than 5 hours) and uneventful experience in a small hospital outside of a military base, but it was her second birth that became a turning point in her life.

During her second birth, Tanya endured a deeply traumatic hospital experience. Despite entering labour confident in her strength and the decision to avoid interventions, she found herself overwhelmed by medical staff who dismissed her wishes. Her birth became chaotic, with a hastily administered epidural that left her unable to feel or push effectively, and a vacuum delivery without proper consent. Her husband, although supportive, felt powerless amidst the chaos and aggression of the hospital staff. The experience left Tanya feeling disconnected, disempowered, and stripped of her agency as a woman and mother.

The aftermath of this birth had a ripple effect on Tanya's sense of identity and confidence. She struggled emotionally and physically, even injuring herself when attempting to return to powerlifting postpartum. However, these challenges ignited a journey of healing and self-reclamation.

Tanya's journey to prepare for her third birth began with a strong decision to change the story of her past traumatic experience. She was determined to take back her power as a birthing mother. Tanya shifted from a hospital-focused approach to a more personal and intentional one, choosing a home birth with a midwife who respected her need for space and autonomy.

At six months pregnant, Tanya realised that hospital care wasn't meeting her needs. A conversation with a mother from a local gymbore group (later turned best friend), introduced her to the idea of home birth and hiring a doula. Curious and inspired, Tanya researched further and connected with a doula trained in hypnobirthing. This became a key part of her preparation. Hypnobirthing techniques like relaxation, visualisation, and affirmations helped her stay calm and work through her fears. By focusing on her nervous system, Tanya learned to trust her body and process past trauma.

Building a supportive birth team was also a priority. Tanya found a midwife who shared her vision for a quiet, hands-off birth. Their connection grew through open, trust-filled prenatal visits. This continuity of care, along with the emotional support of her doula, gave Tanya confidence and peace as she prepared for labour.

When her labour began with her membranes releasing, Tanya immediately knew her baby was on the way. Excitement replaced fear as she prepared for the intensity ahead. Her doula arrived first, offering calm reassurance, followed by her midwife and a student midwife, whose presence Tanya had agreed to. The atmosphere was peaceful and filled with quiet encouragement, honouring Tanya's autonomy.

As labour progressed, Tanya moved into the birthing pool, finding focus and comfort there. This birth was completely different from her past experience, there was no shouting or

pressure, just the freedom to labour at her own pace, guided by her instincts. Pushing took effort, but it was a moment of incredible empowerment for Tanya. She embraced the intensity of the process, knowing she was in control.

When Maximus was born, Tanya felt an overwhelming sense of triumph. Her daughter, Malayla, (along with oldest daughter Arianna) was there to witness the birth and later described Tanya as "roaring like a bear." This powerful image inspired Tanya to get a tattoo symbolising her strength and transformation. The birth not only healed her past trauma but deepened her connection to her family and herself.

Tanya emerged from this journey as a mother of three, now a doula herself and a fierce advocate for respectful, empowering birth experiences. Tanya went on to have another powerful and faith filled homebirth with her fourth baby, Ocean.

CHAPTER 17

Resilience – Bending Without Breaking

"I've had to learn to fight all my life—got to learn to keep smiling. If you smile, things will work out."
—Serena Williams

After giving birth via emergency Caesarean, Serena Williams knew something was wrong. She couldn't breathe properly and feared another pulmonary embolism—a condition she had faced before. She asked for a CT scan and blood thinners. At first, no one listened. Her concerns were brushed aside. But she kept asking. Kept insisting. Eventually, a scan confirmed blood clots in her lungs. She underwent multiple surgeries and spent weeks in bed, recovering while caring for her newborn. Less than a year later, she returned to elite competition. But her real victory wasn't on the court—it was in the hospital room, when she trusted herself and refused to be dismissed. That is resilience.

There comes a moment—often after the hardest seasons of our lives—when we stop and look back. Not to stay there, not to live in the ache, but to see just how far we've come. In birth, in motherhood, and in healing, that moment is everything.

For me, that moment came more than once.

In childhood, I had to get up every day and survive what I couldn't control—learning to hold it together before I even knew what safety felt like.

In the dark, in the mess, in the aftermath of a birth that cracked me open.

When I stood in the shower, unable to stop crying.

When I couldn't walk out my front door because my body was convinced the world outside wasn't safe. And when I held my baby in one arm and my brokenness in the other and kept going anyway. In the quiet hours, when I finally began to put words to my story.

And I know I'm not alone in that.

Before we talk about what carries us through, we have to acknowledge what it took to get here. Maybe it was getting up after a night of no sleep. Or walking into that hospital even though you were terrified. Maybe it was showing up for yourself when no one else did. That's resilience—not loud or grand, but steady and true.

For me, it was not stopping at one child. I was broken after my first. Defiant. Tired. Terrified to go through it again. But somewhere deep inside, I knew I wasn't done. Even after I experienced an early loss after having Bella, I held onto the truth in my heart—I wanted more children. And that desire became stronger than the fear. That's what resilience looked like for me: trusting that I could try again, even when I had every reason not to.

We don't just arrive at resilience—we earn it. Through the sleepless nights. Through the fear. Through the deeply personal storms no one else can see. The pain, the heartbreaks—none of it disqualifies us. In fact, it proves we were always meant to rise.

So let me ask you something:

Where did you first learn to keep going, even when it hurt?

Who taught you to stay soft in a world that wanted you hard?

What part of you refused to give up, even when you felt broken?

These aren't just rhetorical questions. These are the quiet check-ins we owe ourselves.

Because resilience isn't loud. It doesn't demand attention.

Sometimes, it's just letting go and moaning through the contractions.

Sometimes, it's speaking up when your voice shakes.

Sometimes, it's choosing yourself when you've been taught not to.

Resilience isn't about bouncing back. It's about becoming who we were always meant to be—despite everything that tried to shape us otherwise.

From the moment we entered this world, we've been absorbing messages about who we should be. Some of us were silenced early. Some were hurt. Some learned to survive before we ever learned to feel safe.

But even in the chaos—even in the absence of safety—something inside us kept us going. That quiet endurance didn't start in motherhood, but it's often where it shows itself most clearly.

Every woman who's made it to motherhood has already climbed mountains the world may never see. The path to birthing a baby is paved with every challenge we've faced, every story we've carried, every moment we were told we weren't enough and held our heads high anyway.

Resilience isn't a bonus trait. It's our backbone. Our birthright.

But it's often misunderstood. We confuse it with toughness, with stoicism, with pushing through at any cost.

Real resilience is choosing softness in a world that asks for toughness. It's staying open, choosing love over fear, and saying, "This stops with me," even when your voice shakes.

As women, we've faced generations of silencing, survival, and self-sacrifice. We carry the weight of lineage, culture, and systems. And yet, here we are. Birthing new life. Breaking cycles. Becoming the mothers we never had, or the ones we always needed to become.

Our grandmothers did what they could with what they had. Many of them weren't allowed to speak their truth, let alone process it. We are the generation breaking that silence. And with that freedom comes responsibility—to feel, to heal, to change the story for those who come next.

And to do that, we need more than tools—we need the inner foundation to actually *use* them.

The Essential 10 were never meant to stand alone. They are interconnected. But without resilience, they are tools without a foundation. Safety, intuition, oxytocin, continuity of care, doula support, mind–body connection, therapeutic healing, community, and birth planning—none of it matters if we don't believe we're worthy of care, of support, of being heard. That belief is born from resilience.

Resilience says: I am allowed to feel fear and still move forward. Resilience says: I can acknowledge my past and still claim my future. Resilience says: I will not be defined by what hurt me.

It means learning to live with our scars in a way that strengthens us. Our trauma isn't the whole story—just one chapter of it.

Sometimes we forget what it took to make it to this point. But I want you to know this: you didn't just arrive here. You fought to be here.

Whether you're preparing to birth your baby, holding your newborn in your arms, or bearing witness as a midwife, doula, or care provider—this moment is the result of strength, intention, and deep courage.

Birth doesn't just bring a baby into the world—it brings a new version of the woman too. One who knows more, feels deeper, and sees with clearer eyes. Whether you're becoming her, holding space for her, or remembering the moment you once did—it is sacred. And it matters.

And then there are the conversations—the ones that land and stay with you. The ones that shift something inside you. I recently did an interview with Billie Harrigan, a traditional birth companion—or as she lovingly refers to herself, the traditional neighbourly support, the kind of woman who, in our ancestral villages, simply knew how to support birth. We were talking about what women can do to prepare for birthing in the system, and how they can be ready for birth in all its unpredictability. She said one sentence that landed hard: "We need women to be resilient." I paused, and then asked her, "But how do we teach women to be resilient? Is there a play-by-play instructional manual?"

And of course, the answer is no. Not exactly.

Resilience can't be wrapped up in a neat checklist. It can't be handed down like a recipe. Some of it is built into us through our intergenerational inheritance—carried in our bones, our blood, our biology. And some of it is carved into us by the lives we've lived. That's why no two women will ever respond the same way to a situation. We all carry different histories, different wounds, different strengths.

But that doesn't mean we can't work on it. We can build resilience. Not like a fortress, but like a muscle.

Here are a few ways we begin:

Get curious about your story. Where have you been strong before? What have you survived that once felt impossible?

Build self-trust. Think about the hard things you've already faced. That strength is still inside you. And if life hasn't tested you yet, trust that when it does, you'll move through it. You've got what it takes.

Nourish your nervous system. Practices like breathwork, grounding, and rest aren't luxuries—they are foundational. And as Billie pointed out in our conversation, even your nutrition plays a role. Some nutrients actually support the brain and body in becoming more resilient. Nourishment isn't just emotional—it's cellular. Look at how you're fuelling yourself. It matters.

Surround yourself with safe people. Resilience grows in community, not isolation.

Reframe setbacks. Each time you felt like you were breaking, you were actually bending into something new.

And above all: know that resilience is not about perfection. It's about presence. It's about staying with yourself, especially when it's hard.

As you continue reading, my hope is that you don't just take away information. I hope you take away ownership. You own your story. You own your power. You own your rebirth.

Let this be the chapter where you finally see yourself as whole. Not because you were untouched by pain, but because you met it head-on and kept going.

What brought you to this book is courage. What carries you forward? That deep knowing inside you that you can handle whatever comes.

You are not broken. You are becoming. You are resilient.

It wasn't force that carried me forward—it was quiet faith in myself, rebuilt moment by moment. What came next wasn't just another birth—it was me, finally becoming the version of myself I'd been reaching for all along.

BIRTHING WITH TRAUMA AND FEAR

DONNA'S STORY

"For most of my life, I would have described my childhood as 'good,' because it was good in many ways. I excelled at school and dance and had strong support from my mother, siblings, and grandparents. It was this support that saved me from the not-so-good parts. My father was an alcoholic who never wanted children, so there was a lot of dysfunction and relationship struggles at play. Through the chaos, I learned to stay quiet and suppress my needs to avoid adding to the visible turmoil around me. These survival mechanisms shaped my relationships and sense of self-worth.

At the age of 14, I experienced sexual abuse by much older men while in the care of a relative I trusted. Quiet like a mouse, I kept my experiences hidden and didn't dare speak up. Honestly, I wouldn't have even known how. I lived in a time and place where boundaries and consent were not discussed with 14-year-old girls. I internalised the belief that my body was not for me, but for others to use. To survive, I disconnected from my instincts, the part of me designed to keep me safe.

By the time I was 19, I entered a relationship filled with physical, emotional, and sexual abuse. Like most people experiencing domestic violence, I didn't immediately see how bad it was. I justified and explained it away with what little self-worth I had. The violence escalated over five years, until one night, after yet another fight, I stood in front of my wardrobe and experienced a moment of clarity. I packed a bag, called a cab, and left. I knew in that moment that things would never be the same.

A short time later I started dating Mark, a work colleague. I wasn't attracted to him in the same way I had been to other men and wondered if it would work out. But when I checked in with my instincts, I realised that I felt safe with him. He was kind, thoughtful, and responsible. Taking a chance on him was one of the best decisions I ever made.

When I discovered that I was pregnant I saw that as an opportunity to rewrite what happens to my body. I educated myself on the injustices that occur in the modern medical model around birth. I wanted the safety of a hospital but without the patriarchal control that often comes with it. Thankfully, I was accepted into a birthing centre that aligned with my philosophy of birth.

I was really determined to approach birthing with intention and empowerment, and I set out to create a positive and deeply connected experience for myself, and my family. I dedicated myself to preparation – I have never had a better diet than when I was pregnant, and I embraced daily practices like yoga and body balancing. It wasn't just about ensuring my body was ready for labour, I was also mentally preparing myself too, because I knew from my past experiences that my resilience through stressful situations was determined mostly from my state of my mind. I created a vision board and pinned it up in my kitchen. I worked closely with my midwives and doula to build a supportive team that aligned with my values. I wanted them to know that "I've got this!" but also, what helps me feel so assured is the incredible support around me. I invited my support team to help me in the way that I wanted to be supported, because not all support is created equal.

I continued ongoing therapy to help me confront and work through past traumas, giving me the emotional clarity and strength I needed for birth. I also used mindfulness techniques, journaling, and affirmations to maintain a positive mindset, staying connected to my baby Banjo and my vision for the birth I wanted.

My actual birthing journey began with a mix of excitement and calm. When I reflect, I think well, it's easy to be calm when you have prepared mentally and physically for this moment. I didn't go into it wondering how it would play out or whether I would be capable, because for about 8 months I had been visualising and affirming just how this would go. Not that I was naive or arrogant enough to believe I had the power to control all aspects of my birth, but I had confidence in my ability to choose my response to whatever occurred and that's where the real power lies.

One morning, I went to the bathroom and noticed signs that labour was beginning. I was filled with a wave of joy and emotion, I walked out to tell Mark, "It's happening," I said, before bursting into tears of happiness.

We shared the moment together for a few minutes, letting it sink in, and then I excitedly told my mum who was there at my request as yet another member of my support team – she was equally overcome with tears of joy. Then I kind of wandered around the house for a little while waiting for the next escalation of labour.

From the start, I felt deeply in tune with my body and trusted my instincts. I remember telling Mark and mum, as though it was something that had to be announced. "Guys, I have a feeling this is going to be just a hard days work, we'll be done by five." I later reflected on how accurate that intuition was, as my little boy, Banjo, was born at 4:54 PM.

As my contractions began, I leaned into the practices I had prepared for during my pregnancy. Mark, also extremely excited, first thought he ought to mow the lawns, and quickly copped onto himself and we both had a laugh at the funny ways we responded to our desire to feel prepared. I redirected Mark to create the serene environment I had hoped for in our living room, complete with low lighting, calming music, and the loving presence of Mark and my mum. I relied on my support team without guilt or shame, I allowed myself to be held, and I discovered the true strength in my vulnerability. A very important part of my support team included my doula. I remember asking Mark to call and let her know that I was progressing, and my doula arrived as soon as she could to guide me through each stage of labour.

The intensity of labour grew, and I found myself fully immersed in the experience. I trusted my body, moving and listening to its signals and I absorbed myself into the prepared playlist that was running. Music has always helped me connect to myself and this was no exception.

Shortly after that I shifted to the bed, where my waters released, signalling a new phase of labour. At that point, my doula informed me that my waters were stained with meconium, and we decided it was time to head to the hospital. Only in reflection was I slightly disappointed with this news because it meant that according to hospital rules I could no longer birth in the birthing pool. However, I can also remember that in the moment there was not a hint of disappointment, only presence and acknowledgement, with an inner voice saying "okay, so it is." I had learned in meditation and my own personal line of work that there is no denying reality.

I laugh now whenever I tell this next story, because I have such a clear visual of my labouring in the car. I was originally set up to sit in the front seat of the car and with my doula's recommendation, we transitioned all the towels to the back seat. So here I kneeled, facing the back of the car, gripping onto the headrest and releasing the most primitive sounds I could make whilst maintaining eye contact with the driver of the car directly behind us. My contractions were strong, and I remember telling Mark that if there was a traffic jam, I was having this baby in the car. It felt strange to be out in broad daylight with people around me, and I craved the dark, private environment once more. Once at the hospital, although I was no longer allowed to birth in the birthing centre, the birthing suite was right next door, so it was a familiar space and honestly the only thing I think I cared about at that point was that it had water. I had an underlying urge since arriving at the birth suite to just get in the shower and have everyone else just step away and let me do what I needed to do to birth my baby.

I did have to adapt slightly to being monitored, due to the presence of meconium. I was fairly agreeable, as I saw it as a minor annoyance, so long as they hurried up so that I could get on with birthing my baby. I knew that there was some commotion happening around me about not being able to find my baby's heartbeat, or that it was at the least, intermittent on the monitor. Yet I felt none of the fear that was apparently leaching into the room between the midwives and my husband. I could feel Banjo moving, and I knew he was ready to come out because I had also agreed to a cervical check. I was curious about what I was feeling, and how it would be measured in medical terms. "Ahh so this is what 10 cm dilated feels like." I was so in tune with myself and my baby that I almost felt as though I was holding space for my midwife to allay her fears, so we could get this show on the road.

At some point during their attempts to get Banjo's heart rate through the ctg monitoring, my midwife told me that she was moments away from pressing the emergency button and that meant a team full of Dr's in white coats would be walking through the door. She then told my husband to press the emergency button and I'm so thankful to this day that my husband hesitated. Because in that moment of hesitation, the monitor once again picked up on my baby turning around in my tummy. When I asked him why he hesitated he said he doesn't remember sensing the same level of danger, yet he was conflicted because a person with authority was asking him to press one of many buttons on a wall full of equipment. I also wonder if he hesitated because he knew that we were very close to our birth going totally off track and knew this would lead to a cascade of interventions that I did not want. At this point I was annoyed enough by their fussing and insistence on hearing Banjo's heartbeat that I agreed to a Foetal Scalp Electrode so they could see there was nothing wrong and they could leave me alone to labour.

I asked next to move into the shower, and I positioned myself in the darkest corner with my back to everyone, this was an inner job, whilst knowing fully well that I had 3 people right behind me that I trusted, Mark, my doula and my Midwife. I used my hands and arms to support myself on the shower bars. I don't recall how long I was in active labour, towards the very end when I could feel my energy depleting, I knew I must be getting closer, and I won't lie the last few pushes took every last bit of energy that I had. Our doula took photos throughout the birth, and I'll always have those to look back on, especially the photo of Mark bringing Banjo earthside. He lifted Banjo to me between my legs, and I'll never forget the look of admiration and love that Mark shared with me in those moments.

One thing that surprised me about my labour was the lack of 'pain'. I've heard stories of awful pain, I'm not sure if I have a high pain tolerance or if I was so in flow that I simply wasn't registering it as a painful experience but rather a biological process. I genuinely experienced greater pain during the afterbirth than I did during labour, and that was short lived. Perhaps I simply held a belief about labour that it wasn't really going to be 'painful' as such, as both my mum and one of my sisters had confidently exclaimed that it's not painful when you're in the moment, and they each had 4 children. I guess I believed them, and I too had this experience. These shared experiences with me were also immensely supportive, they are strong women with positive experiences to share that allowed me to imagine a positive experience for myself.

I am so thankful my birth story turned out the way it did. I walked away feeling empowered and strong. It was deeply healing for me and in the following weeks I was overflowing with love and a sense of accomplishment."

CHAPTER 18

Birth After Trauma & Fear - My Rebirth in Birth

"Just when the caterpillar thought the world was over, it became a butterfly."
—*Proverb*

Time softens the sharpest edges of pain—but it doesn't erase the memories. Or the emotions that cling to them.

When you've been through something really hard, it can feel like a wall you'll never get past. But eventually, with time, tiny cracks appear. Light starts to seep through. And little by little, so does hope.

For me, the idea of having another baby after my first experience felt like one of those walls. It took three and a half years before I could even consider it. But when I finally did, I entered that second pregnancy with so much intention. I was clear on how I wanted to do things differently. And I was ready.

We conceived quickly, which felt like a blessing. But around 10 weeks, I started bleeding—and instantly, something in me just knew. I had a deep, instinctive feeling this pregnancy wasn't going to continue.

The sadness that followed wasn't just about losing the baby. It was also about losing the *possibility*. I had poured so much of myself into preparing for this baby—long before I even saw the two lines. Mentally, emotionally, spiritually—I was all in.

So, when it ended, it wasn't just grief I felt. It was devastation. Like something I'd worked so hard to rebuild had suddenly collapsed underneath me.

Coming home from the hospital after being told there was no heartbeat felt like everything had been stripped away. I sat with it—this raw, aching emptiness—and began questioning everything.

Was this a sign? Was the universe trying to tell me I wasn't meant to expand my family? Was this loss a warning to let go of the dream I'd held so tightly?

The doubts were relentless. Slowly, they chipped away at the fragile hope I'd only just started to trust again.

In my mind I'd always imagined having three children. It wasn't just a vague hope—it was something I truly, deeply wanted. So the idea that it might not happen? That maybe it wasn't meant for me? That was hard to sit with.

I gave myself time. Time to rest. Time to cry. Time to feel it all—not just the physical recovery, but the emotional weight of it too. I let myself grieve the baby I'd lost. I let myself acknowledge the dreams that wouldn't come true for now. And I reminded myself: this story isn't finished yet. Even if it felt uncertain, it wasn't over.

A few months later, we conceived again. And this time, I held hope gently. I was cautiously optimistic. Every small milestone felt huge. I clung to each one like a breadcrumb trail leading me forward. And slowly, as I moved into the second trimester, the heaviness began to lift. It didn't disappear—but in its place was something gentler: a quiet sense of peace.

It was around then that I reconnected with an old friend from Bella's daycare. As we caught up, she mentioned her friend's doula—someone who had played a huge part in making her birth experience a positive one. I was definitely intrigued. I knew one thing for sure: this time, I needed more support. More care. More presence.

Reaching out to that doula became one of the most transformative decisions of my entire journey.

This pregnancy with my second daughter Portia felt different in all the right ways—more grounded, more in tune with who I was. I wasn't the same woman who had walked into that first birth. I'd grown, I'd learned, and this time, I let those lessons lead the way.

I approached every step with care. With intention. I focused on the things you now know as the *Essential 10*—the pillars that helped me feel steady and strong as I moved through pregnancy, birth, and everything that came after.

The first thing I had to rethink was what *safety* even meant.

For a lot of women, safety means hospital. That's the default. It's what we're told is safest, so we don't question it. But for me, it wasn't that simple. My first birth happened in a hospital—and while it ticked the "safety" box on paper, the reality felt anything but safe. I left that experience feeling vulnerable, unseen, and unsupported.

Instead this time, I tried a different approach—even if it didn't *look* all that different from the outside. I chose a new obstetrician—someone known for being kind, compassionate, and the kind who actually listens. I figured, if I couldn't change the setting… maybe I could change the person. Maybe if the doctor felt different, I'd feel different too. Like I'd unlock some hidden sense of calm and confidence in aisle three of the maternity ward.

And at first, it kind of worked. He had this warm, respectful presence. His bedside manner was lovely—he listened, he reassured, he seemed genuinely kind. I felt more at ease than I expected. What I didn't know back then was that his intervention rates were actually quite high. But in those early weeks, I didn't dig that deep. I leaned into the good parts. I trusted my gut. I told myself: every small decision I make now is a step toward reclaiming confidence. Control. Trust in myself.

But one appointment in particular made me pause. It stirred something that had me quietly questioning what I'd felt until then.

He handed me a consent form for an epidural. Pretty standard, just in case I ended up needing one. Logically, it made sense. But something in me pushed back. I'd been preparing for a natural birth. I'd done the work. And this form—this quiet assumption that I'd need the epidural—didn't sit right with the vision I'd been building.

So I said, "I'm having a natural birth this time, and I choose not to sign this." He gave a small chuckle and said something like, "You know how women in labour are—if you sign it now, you won't have to worry about it later." But to me, it wasn't just a form. That moment felt huge. I was completely in sync with my body. With my baby. It wasn't about rejecting the epidural as a concept—it was about honouring my preparation. Saying: I know what I want. And I trust myself. That moment was a turning point. I walked out of that appointment with a new lens. I started asking myself: *Is this the right provider for me? Does this person actually reflect my version of safety?*

And the truth was… not really.

And that made something very clear: I needed support that didn't just sound good on paper—I needed support that truly aligned with what felt right *in my bones.*

That's when I realised: my doula was the support I needed in my corner.

My doula was a huge part of helping me get to a place of trust within myself. From the beginning, she was my anchor—steady, grounded, and deeply intentional in the way she showed up for me. She helped me reconnect with my body and reminded me that birth wasn't something to fear—it was something to meet with open arms.

But she wasn't the only one who helped me feel ready.

Therapy became another cornerstone. I'd already started working through some of my past before Portia's birth, but during that pregnancy, it felt even more essential. Those sessions helped me peel back the layers—fear, trauma, doubt—and gave me the tools to show up to this birth with more clarity. I saw my psychologist regularly and even arranged in-home visits postpartum to check in on my mental health. That kind of continuity meant everything. It gave me the steady reassurance that my mental health was being held, too

Alongside that care, books played a quiet but powerful role in preparing my mind and body. I returned to *Feel the Fear and Do It Anyway* by Susan Jeffers—a book that had helped me in the past. Reading it again gave me a new lens. I also leaned on *HypnoBirthing® – The Mongan Method* and *Birthing From Within* by Pam England. Both offered more than just techniques—they introduced me to rituals, tools, and ways of thinking that brought me back to myself.

Visualisation, especially, became my go-to. I'd close my eyes and picture the birth I wanted—how I'd move, how I'd breathe, how I'd feel. Replacing fear with calm. I could see it. I was doing it.

And then—community. For the first time, I felt like I truly had one. Friends wrapped around me like a warm hug. They showed up with love, with practical help, and with so much understanding. It made the pregnancy feel lighter. Happier. More joyful.

As my due date got closer, I sat down to write a birth plan that actually felt like me. A declaration of what mattered. Every detail I included came from a place of intention—what I needed to feel supported, and what I was ready to let go of. It wasn't about scripting the perfect birth. It was about feeling strong enough to make informed choices, whatever happened.

But maybe the most meaningful gift in this whole experience came in the form of someone I never imagined would be part of it: my mum.

She came to be with me for this birth and postpartum. And if you'd asked me a few years earlier if I'd ever imagined her in my birth space, I would've said no. There had been too much pain. Too much distance. Too much history.

But something started to soften when Bella was around two and a half. We both leaned in. Slowly. Gently. Honestly. And it wasn't easy—it took work. The kind of work that requires both people to show up fully. But over time, we found something solid. We began meeting each other with more compassion. More understanding.

By the time I was preparing to give birth again, our relationship felt different. It felt steady. Healed. I asked her to come and stay—not just to help, but because I *wanted* her there. Having her close wasn't just support. It was closure. It felt like something sacred had come full circle.

When labour began, my mum was there—holding space in the way only a mother can. But as things started to intensify, my sister gently took everyone out of my birthing space so that I could go inward. She knew what I needed, and she didn't hesitate. She had been with me in my first birth, but this time, she honoured my choice to do it differently. She gave me space, trusted my decision, and held the boundary for me. That's what it looks like when someone truly shows up—not by standing beside you, but by stepping back when that's what love requires.

Those final weeks before my daughter Portia's birth were soaked in something soft and powerful: love, laughter, and oxytocin. It was everywhere—in the way my husband quietly believed in me, in Bella's wide-eyed wonder about becoming a big sister, in my sister's quiet presence and gentle words. My mum's stories, our family meals, the belly laughs around the dinner table—it all created this warm, steady undercurrent of connection that settled me in the deepest way. I didn't just feel supported. I felt surrounded. Steeped in safety. Every shared moment was its own kind of medicine. And as the days counted down, I let that feeling carry me toward what was next.

Looking back now, I see it so clearly: the *Essential 10* weren't just birth tools—they were my turning point. They helped me write a new story. One that wasn't ruled by fear or past trauma. One rooted in strength, softness, and truth. What started out as birth prep turned into a life framework. Something that helped me meet this part of life with integrity and heart.

As I close this book, I leave you with Portia's birth story. The one where everything came together. A birth led by intuition, which for me, became the most profound of the *Essential 10*. It was the thread that wove all the others together. It helped me surrender, even when logic hesitated. It carried me through. And without it, that birth might have looked very different.

In sharing her story—and all the stories in this book—my hope is that you feel that same sense of possibility. That you see your own strength reflected here. Because no matter where you started, you get to choose your ending. And it can be powerful. It can be beautiful. It can be completely your own.

If you're on this path too, I want you to know this:

You're not defined by your fears.

You're not stuck in your past.

You're the author here.

And with the right support, the right preparation, and trust in yourself—you can shape a birth experience that not only brings your baby into the world...

but brings you back home to yourself.

PORTIA'S BIRTH

"When I was pregnant with Portia, we were living by the Gold Coast broadwater. There was something incredibly therapeutic about being close to the water during that time. Gazing out at the vast ocean had a calming effect that seemed to melt my worries away, reminding me how small we are in the grand scheme of things, like my worries could just float away with the tides. Taking walks along the water became a ritual for me, grounding me and connecting me to nature. It felt like this was exactly where I was supposed to be as I prepared to welcome Portia.

One day after my estimated due date, I woke up around 3 a.m. to a familiar feeling, mild waves of what felt like period cramps. But this time, something felt different from the practice contractions I'd been experiencing for weeks. These sensations felt deeper, and instead of bringing on a wave of fear like they had during Bella's birth, they filled me with excitement. I knew this was it; Portia's birth was beginning, and I was ready. I decided to rest a bit longer and fell back asleep, waking up the next morning with the contractions still gently rolling in and out. I told my husband that today might be the day. It was a cloudy morning, and while my mother took care of Bella, my husband and I decided to go for a walk by the broadwater. We stopped by a café for a croissant, and I remember breathing through the contractions as they came, calmly taking things one step at a time, fully in the present moment.

When we got home, I paced around the house, feeling grounded and focused. My mother kept asking if it was time to head to the hospital, and although she meant well, her concern was holding me back from fully letting go. I felt like I needed space to tune into my body. I called my sister and asked if she could pick up Bella and my mother to create a peaceful, distraction-free environment. Once they left, I noticed the contractions becoming stronger and more intense. I used a TENS machine, which helped tremendously, allowing me to manage each contraction with focus and confidence.

When my doula arrived, I was so relieved. Her presence was comforting, grounding me even more. We decided to go for another walk, but soon I felt the need to return home. I intuitively sensed that the birth was close. Around 2:30 p.m., my waters released, and I called out to my doula. She gently suggested that this might be a good time to head to the hospital, but in that moment, I felt a strong gut instinct. My intuition was speaking to me loud and clear. I realised that going to the hospital didn't feel right for me. The hospital had never felt like a place of safety and in that moment of vulnerability the sense of safety made itself abundantly clear and I knew deep down that I needed to be in a space where I felt completely secure.

In that instant, I made the decision to stay home. I asked my doula to fill the bathtub upstairs, knowing that I was meant to birth Portia right there, in the comfort of my own space. My husband, fully supportive and trusting my instincts, stood by my decision. My doula, who had experience with home births, filled the bath just as I asked. I remember removing the TENS machine and easing into the warm water, where the contractions immediately intensified, coming closer and closer together.

Right before Portia was born, I felt a rush of adrenaline and started to second-guess myself. I remember telling my doula that I wasn't sure if I'd made the right decision. I worried about Bella, thinking, "What if something happens to me? I have her to care for." My doula, understanding me so well, recognised this as my fight-or-flight moment. She looked me in the eyes and reassured me, saying, "You are safe." I trusted her completely, but more so, I trusted myself and with that I allowed myself to relax. At that moment, I felt the overwhelming urge to push, and with a few powerful, instinctual pushes, I brought Portia into my arms.

Thinking back on that moment, I still feel teary. "Epic" doesn't even begin to capture it. The room was humming with something sacred — a quiet intensity, a rush of Oxytocin, pure joy. My husband looked at me like he was seeing me for the first time, eyes wide, filled with pride and love.

Everything felt still and electric all at once. It was life-changing. That birth didn't just bring Portia into the world — it unlocked something I didn't know was there. It shifted how I saw myself, what I believed about birth, and what I believed about my own strength. I felt like I was being reborn too — stepping into a new version of myself. A more grounded powerful mother. A more whole woman. This was me!

AFTERWORD

If you've made it to this point, I want to thank you—genuinely and deeply. Whether you read every page or skipped to the parts that called to you, I'm grateful you chose to spend time with these stories, these reflections, and this important, often overlooked conversation.

Writing this book has been a raw and deeply personal process. It has asked me to be honest, to revisit painful places, to hold space for others in their grief, fear, power, and hope. And it's reminded me—time and again—that trauma and fear don't cancel out beauty or strength. They sit alongside it. They shape how we move, how we protect ourselves, and how we learn to trust again.

Birth is not just a physical experience. For so many of us, it's emotional, relational, spiritual, and sometimes even political. It can surface everything we've buried. It can be a portal into our deepest vulnerabilities and our fiercest power. It can bring us undone and put us back together in ways we never saw coming. And yet, so often, the deeper layers of birth go unspoken. That silence is part of what this book was written to break.

To the women who trusted me with their stories—you've given this book its heart. You've shown what it means to speak truth, to name pain, to take ownership of healing, and to remind others they are not alone. Thank you for your generosity, your honesty, and your strength. It's been an honour to hold your stories here.

To the reader: maybe you're still in the thick of it. Maybe you're preparing to birth, or reflecting on a past birth that left more questions than answers. Maybe you're supporting someone else through their experience. Whatever brought you to these pages, I want you to leave knowing this—your story matters. What you carry matters. What happened to you matters.

The Essential 10—safety, intuition, oxytocin, continuity of care, doula support, therapeutic healing, community, mind–body connection, birth planning and resilience—are not about doing things "right." They're not a formula. They are foundations that can help create space for agency, self-awareness, and support. They are tools. Anchors. Invitations. You can take what fits, leave what doesn't, and return to them at any point in your journey.

Birth may not always go the way we hoped. But that doesn't mean we don't get to own our story. It doesn't mean we stop asking for care that sees us fully. It doesn't mean we stop believing that healing is possible—even after everything.

If there's one thing I hope this book leaves you with, it's this: you are not broken. You're not too much. You don't need to rush your healing. And you absolutely deserve support that honours the whole of who you are—not just the parts that are easy to hold.

There is space for your story. For your truth. For your voice. Let that be the beginning.

With love and deep respect, Moran

RESOURCES FOR FURTHER SUPPORT & EXPLORATION

This section is here to support you beyond these pages. Whether you're preparing for birth, healing from trauma, or supporting someone else, the following books, organisations, and resources may offer the connection, tools, and reassurance you need.

Mental Health & Trauma Support

Blue Knot Foundation: Specialist support for adult survivors of childhood trauma (Australia)

www.blueknot.org.au

Birth Trauma Australia: An Australian-based organisation offering support, education, and advocacy for those affected by birth-related trauma. Their platform provides peer support, resources, and pathways to healing.

www.birthtrauma.org.au

PANDA (Perinatal Anxiety & Depression Australia): Helpline and resources for expectant and new parents

www.panda.org.au

Beyond Blue: Mental health support, including perinatal well-being

www.beyondblue.org.au

Postpartum Support International (PSI): Global support for postpartum depression, anxiety, and trauma

www.postpartum.net

Psychology Today: Use their directory to find a trauma-informed therapist in your area

www.psychologytoday.com

Birth Education & Advocacy

HypnoBirthing® International: Childbirth education focused on calm, connected birth

www.hypnobirthing.com

Birthing From Within: Holistic childbirth education integrating storytelling, creativity, mindfulness, and emotional preparation

birthingfromwithin.com

Evidence Based Birth®: Research-backed resources for informed birth choices www.evidencebasedbirth.com

Born at Home: A documentary offering powerful insight into women's home birth experiences, enriched by the wisdom of skilled birth workers

bornathomefilm.com

Maternity Choices Australia: Advocacy group for respectful and evidence-based maternity care

www.maternitychoices.org.au

Maternity Consumer Network: An Australian non-profit organisation focused on improving maternity services by amplifying consumer voices. They offer educational tools, birth rights information, and advocacy for systemic change.

www.maternityconsumernetwork.org.au

Lamaze International: A well-established childbirth education method rooted in evidence-based practices. Offers practical techniques for labour, partner support, and informed decision-making.

www.lamaze.org

Doula & Continuity of Care

Doula Network Australia: Doula Directory

www.doulanetwork.org

Homebirth Australia: Support and advocacy for families choosing to birth at home www.homebirthaustralia.org

DONA International: One of the most established and globally recognised doula training and certification organisations. Offers directories to find certified birth and postpartum doulas, as well as resources for parents and professionals.

www.dona.org

Books Worth Reading

> Birth with Confidence by Rhea Dempsey
>
> Why Birth Trauma Matters by Emma Svanberg
>
> The Body Keeps the Score by Bessel van der Kolk
>
> Reclaiming Childbirth as a Rite of Passage by Rachel Reed
>
> Newborn Mothers by Julia Jones
>
> The Fourth Trimester by Kimberly Ann Johnson
>
> A Mind of Your Own by Kelly Brogan
>
> Feel the Fear and Do It Anyway by Susan Jeffers
>
> Birthing From Within by Pam England
>
> The First Forty Days by Heng Ou
>
> How to Heal a Bad Birth by Melissa Bruijn & Debby Gould
>
> HypnoBirthing®: The Mongan Method by Marie Mongan
>
> What Happened to You? by Bruce D. Perry & Oprah Winfrey
>
> Gentle Birth, Gentle Mothering by Dr. Sarah Buckley
>
> Birthing Like a Feminist by Milli Hill

BIRTHING WITH TRAUMA AND FEAR

Podcasts That Inform and Empower

    Birthing Instincts Podcast

    Positive Birth Australia

    Orgasmic Birth

    The Great Birth Rebellion

    The Midwives' Cauldron

    Down to Birth Show

    Homebirth Stories Australia

    Pain Free Birth Podcast

    Boob to Food The Podcast

    The Renegade Mama

Documentaries to Watch

    Born at Home: A beautiful look into home birth stories and the emotional, physical, and spiritual aspects of birthing outside the system.

    Birth Time: The Documentary: An Australian film exploring the maternity system and the urgent need for reform.

    The Face of Birth: An empowering film sharing the stories of women navigating their birth choices in Australia.

    The Business of Being Born: A groundbreaking look at the medicalisation of birth in the U.S.

    Microbirth: Explores how the moment of birth affects lifelong health through the lens of microbiome science.

Orgasmic Birth: Challenges cultural taboos around birth, highlighting pleasure, connection, and empowerment in labour.

Why Not Home?: Features nurses, doctors, and midwives who choose to birth at home and why.

Dark Side of the Full Moon: Sheds light on the hidden struggles of perinatal mental health and the lack of systemic support.

REFERENCES & SOURCES

Australian Bureau of Statistics (2023). *Personal Safety Survey, Australia, 2021–22*. ABS cat. no. 4906.0. Canberra: ABS.

Beecher, H. K. (1955). The powerful placebo. Journal of the American Medical Association, 159(17), 1602–1606.

Bohren, M. A., Hofmeyr, G. J., Sakala, C., Fukuzawa, R. K., & Cuthbert, A. (2017). Continuous support for women during childbirth. Cochrane Database of Systematic Reviews, 7, CD003766.

Centers for Disease Control and Prevention. (2019). Preventing Adverse Childhood Experiences (ACEs): Leveraging the Best Available Evidence.

Cochrane Database of Systematic Reviews. Sandall, J., et al. (2016).

Copeland, W. E., Keeler, G., Angold, A., & Costello, E. J. (2007). Trauma exposure and posttraumatic stress in youth: A national survey. Journal of Traumatic Stress, 20(5), 833–844.

Dekker, R. (2023). The evidence for doulas. Evidence Based Birth.

Dick-Read, G. (1944). Childbirth Without Fear. Harper Perennial.

Hodnett, E. D., Gates, S., Hofmeyr, G. J., Sakala, C., & Weston, J. (2013). Continuous support for women during childbirth. Cochrane Database of Systematic Reviews, 7, CD003766.

Homer, C. S. E., Friberg, I. K., Dias, M. A. B., et al. (2018). Projected reductions in maternal and perinatal mortality with increased midwifery care. The Lancet Midwifery Series.

Klaus, M. H., Kennell, J. H., & Klaus, P. H. (2012). The Doula Book: How a Trained Labor Companion Can Help You Have a Shorter, Easier, and Healthier Birth. Da Capo Press.

Mongan, M. (2005). HypnoBirthing®: The Mongan Method. Health Communications.

National Sexual Violence Resource Center. Statistics In-Depth.

PANDA (Perinatal Anxiety & Depression Australia). Perinatal mental health statistics and support.

Reed, R., Sharman, R., & Inglis, C. (2017). Women's descriptions of childbirth trauma relating to care provider actions and interactions. BMC Pregnancy and Childbirth, 17, 21.

Rominski, S. D., et al. (2023). Prevalence of obstetric violence in high-income countries: A systematic review. Acta Obstetricia et Gynecologica Scandinavica.

van der Kolk, B. (2014). The Body Keeps the Score: Brain, Mind, and Body in the Healing of Trauma. Viking.

Western Sydney University. (2023). Study finds one-in-ten Australian women have experienced obstetric violence.

World Health Organization. Mental health: Strengthening our response.

Yehuda, R., Daskalakis, N. P., Desarnaud, F., et al. (2001). Intergenerational transmission of trauma effects: Putative role of epigenetic mechanisms. Journal of Clinical Endocrinology & Metabolism, 86(2), 295–301.

Australian Institute of Health and Welfare. (2023). Australia's mothers and babies (2021 data). Canberra: AIHW.

www.ingramcontent.com/pod-product-compliance
Lightning Source LLC
Chambersburg PA
CBHW040107100526
44584CB00029BA/3828